China's Economic Growth Prospects

China's Economic Growth Prospects

From Demographic Dividend to Reform Dividend

Cai Fang

Chinese Academy of Social Sciences, China

With editorial assistance from Ms. Virginia L. Conn

IN ASSOCIATION WITH THE SOCIAL SCIENCES
ACADEMIC PRESS

Edward Elgar
PUBLISHING

Cheltenham, UK • Northampton, MA, USA

Published by
Edward Elgar Publishing Limited
The Lypiatts
15 Lansdown Road
Cheltenham
Glos GL50 2JA
UK

Edward Elgar Publishing, Inc.
William Pratt House
9 Dewey Court
Northampton
Massachusetts 01060
USA

A catalogue record for this book
is available from the British Library

Library of Congress Control Number: 2015952664

This book is available electronically in the **Elgar**online
Economics subject collection
DOI 10.4337/9781781005859

ISBN 978 1 78100 584 2 (cased)
ISBN 978 1 78100 585 9 (eBook)

Typeset by Servis Filmsetting Ltd, Stockport, Cheshire

Printed and bound in Great Britain by
TJ International Ltd, Padstow, Cornwall

Contents

Introduction

With a view towards East Asia as one of the most dynamic regions in the world, the World Bank has published a thematic report series every four years that addresses the region's unique experiences with development and explores the problems and challenges of particular periods. A report from the 1993 series, entitled *The East Asian Miracle: Economic Growth and Public Policy*, introduced the most outstanding East Asian economies to the world for the first time. Those economies included Hong Kong, Indonesia, Japan, South Korea, Malaysia, Singapore, Taiwan, and Thailand.

While the World Bank report highly valued the economic performance of these East Asian economies, some scholars took issue with such praise. Based on a host of empirical studies, Paul Krugman, the famous economist and columnist, published an essay in the journal *Foreign Affairs* entitled "The Myth of Asia's Miracle," questioning the existence of such a miracle as well as the sustainability of economic growth in those East Asian economies.

The outbreak of the East Asian financial crisis in 1997, which seriously derailed most of the East Asian miracle's performers and exposed their systemic flaws, seemed to prove Krugman's criticisms true. Of those economies, Indonesia, South Korea, Malaysia, and Thailand suffered the most. Time ultimately seems to have favored the World Bank's judgment after all, however. After 1998, many of the economies in East Asia once again demonstrated strong economic growth. As of 2007, East Asia as a whole had not only recovered from its deep financial crisis, but also renewed its vigorous economic growth. In response, the World Bank published another thematic report on the region, entitled *The East Asian Renaissance: Ideas for Economic Growth*.

That the World Bank has cheered on the region's recovery from economic crisis reveals something significant, that is, the return of the region to historical importance. The World Bank demonstrably holds great expectations for the renaissance of an emerging East Asia. According to economic historian Angus Maddison, as late as 1820 the East Asia and Pacific region still produced 40 percent of the world's gross domestic product (GDP). The latest World Bank report indicates that East Asian economies are once again emerging as leading economic powers.

It's worth noting that, unlike the 1993 report, which did not focus exclusively on China, the 2007 report had an optimistic conclusion about the region that was almost entirely based on the successful economic growth of China and its contribution to the global economy. Therefore, when the report advanced the concept of the middle-income trap and warned of the challenges in avoiding such a trap, it is of prime relevance to China, specifically.

There are significant differences in the levels of economic development among Asian economies. The temporal sequence of those economies' development tells a complex story about economic growth and provides experiences and lessons from each individual economy. As an important component of the East Asian miracle, China can learn much from other economies' experiences and lessons as revealed by economics literature.

The rapid economic growth in China after reforms were initiated in the late 1970s can be characterized as a process that combines the development of a dual economy with system transition. That is, the massive labor migration from agriculture to urban sectors in the coastal areas mobilized by the gradual elimination of institutional barriers deterring labor mobility between rural and urban areas has translated to a comparative advantage for labor-intensive industries through China's participation in economic globalization.

American economist Lawrence Summers asserts that future historians who write the history of our time will consider China's rapid economic growth—which has increased living standards more than a hundredfold over the course of an individual's life span for the first time in human history—along with its significant impact on people across the rest of the world and the global economy to be among our era's most important events.

Such an assertion, however, is based on the assumption that China will continue to experience economic growth at an annual rate of 7 percent for more than 70 years (the life expectancy of the average Chinese citizen in the early 1980s). As a particular Chinese saying goes, however, a distance of 90 miles is only half of a 100-mile journey. Since this rapid economic growth has been sustained for less than 40 years (since 1978), there is still a long way to go if China is to make such history.

Dual economy development, characterized by an unlimited supply of labor, is considered by many to be an unalterable growth pattern in China. Though some observers have argued for years that a growth pattern characterized by the production and export of labor-intensive manufacturing goods cannot be shared by ordinary workers and low-income households, they still found it difficult to lend credence to the emergence of a labor shortage and the resultant increase in the wages of average workers in

China since 2004. These emerging phenomena, by definition of the inventor of the dual economy theory in development economics, Arthur Lewis, imply that enterprises can no longer hire from the workforce at a constant subsistence wage rate—in other words, the Lewis Turning Point has arrived in China.

Though there are conflicting opinions over whether China has arrived at its Lewis Turning Point or not, it is hardly deniable that the year 2004 represented a threshold, after which a shortage of migrant workers arose throughout the country, the wages of unskilled workers began to constantly increase, labor inputs in agriculture significantly decreased, and the substitution of capital for labor in all sectors began to become widespread. As a result, labor-intensive industries have begun to shift from coastal areas to inland areas in China, as well as to neighboring countries, and thus China's growth engine is bound to weaken. All those changes indicate a new phase of economic development.

Dual economy development is usually accompanied by a particular phase of demographic transition, at which the statistically large and increasing proportion of the working-age population forms an excessive supply of labor, which results in extremely low marginal productivity of labor in an agrarian economy. Accordingly, the Lewis Turning Point has a great deal to do with the changing phases of demographic transition. Therefore, with the arrival of the Lewis Turning Point, a country will eventually lose its demographic dividend, which is manifested in the shift from an increase to a decline in the working-age population and from a decline to an increase in the population dependence ratio.

Profound, rapid socioeconomic development and its unique population policies have helped China complete its demographic transition within a much shorter period of time than most other countries that have made the transition. This consequently gives China the unique characteristic of growing old before getting rich. In fact, the working-age population—ages 15 to 59—have already stopped growing and, in 2011, began decreasing. In the face of the disappearance of its demographic dividend and the slowdown of its potential GDP growth rate, the Chinese governments, both central and local, intend to make a concentrated effort to maintain an equivalent order of magnitude in terms of growth rate as over the past 30 years—namely, in a growth rate above the country's decreased potential capability, there would occur various distortions that would make Chinese economic growth far less balanced, coordinated, and sustainable. In the most extreme situation, there would be a risk of falling into stagnation, as happened in Japan after 1990. But in China's case the consequence would be what is called the middle-income trap.

China's possible fate of falling into the middle-income trap is also correlated with the characteristic of growing old before getting rich. Whether or not, and by how much, population factors negatively influence the future potential of economic growth depends profoundly on how China finds new sources of economic growth after its demographic dividend disappears. Any major policy failures will prevent China from finding such new engines for further growth.

With the help of a demographic dividend, China has accelerated its growth convergence over the past 30-plus years. The arrival of the Lewis Turning Point implies that the Chinese economy is nearing completion of the process of dual economy development. Many East Asian economies have experienced a similar transition, though Japan offers a lesson for how a country could stagnate at a high-income stage, while countries such as the Philippines, Malaysia, Indonesia, and some Latin American countries provide object lessons for being stuck in the middle-income trap. Will China continue its economic growth at a reasonable pace in order to become a high-income country, or will it stagnate for a long time at the middle-income stage?

Although the fate of China's economic growth is not predetermined, it can be predicted based on economic theories, lessons from other countries, and its own experiences. Most importantly, policy options matter a great deal in determining the direction of Chinese economic development over the coming decades. What we have learned so far suggests that continuing system reform that exploits the potential of the supply of production factors and productivity improvement is the only way to sustain the economic growth of China in order to place it among the world's recognized high-income countries.

Conflicting arguments exist as to whether or not China has passed through the Lewis Turning Point, how long China can enjoy its demographic dividend, what "growing old before getting rich" means to China's growth, and how the middle-income trap is relevant to China. Those questions cannot be fully answered based solely on knowledge of demography, development economics, or neoclassical growth theory.

Using the logic of economics theory and an objective assessment of China's reality, this book intends to combine all relevant arguments and current theories so as to form a consistent analytical framework. It also tries to draw lessons from international experiences that are relevant to China. In order to deepen the ongoing debates and reach a consensus (as much as is possible in this type of analysis), the book clarifies scholarly concepts through various means. The author does not, however, expect unanimous agreement across all issues; only if scholars and policy makers can recognize the urgent challenges confronting China in avoiding the middle-income trap will this book have attained its objective.

This book is also intended to be, however, an ambitious by-product of the applicability of economic theories born and developed in the west to China's unique experiences with economic development. During the second half of the twentieth century, various theories of development economics, for example Arthur Lewis's dual economy development theory, experienced both a rise and a fall insofar as they dominated the economic thinking of developing countries' economic catch-up. Their disappearance from the scene was due largely to the critics coming from neoclassical economics, although accepting the latter invites various unrealistic assumptions, for example that of a limited and constant supply of labor, that are not appropriate in explaining the realities that exist in developing countries.

China's successful economic growth since it initiated its reform and opening-up policies in the late 1970s cannot be fully explained by any single theory of economics. Different stages of economic development may follow different economic laws with possible variances. In this book, various economics theories are applied when they fit the practices and stages of China's economic development. The author tries to make the analysis consistent with economic theories while avoiding the rote application of western economics.

In what follows, the Chinese experiences with economic development are thoroughly discussed using a comprehensive analytical framework. Chapters are committed to proving the arrival of the Lewis Turning Point and the disappearance of the demographic dividend, and to depicting China's unique feature of growing old before getting rich, as well as its relevance to the country's risk of falling into the middle-income trap. Furthermore, the book aims to draw policy implications and suggest ways in which China can deepen reforms so as to sustain economic growth and social progress after exhausting the conventional sources of growth based on its demographic dividend.

Putting Chinese economic development—past, present, and future—in a wide framework that attempts to explain the global phenomenon of the great divergence and great convergence, Chapter 1 discusses why the dominant neoclassical economics failed in guiding, explaining, and predicting the practices in China and other developing countries, points out where the Chinese economy presently rests based on international experiences of economic slowdown, and raises a question about whether and how China can avoid the middle-income trap and realize its great renaissance.

Chapters 2, 3, and 4 explore the applicability of Lewisian theory to the transitional Chinese economy and narrate the process of dual economy development that has run parallel with the economic reform and opening-up in China since the late 1970s. Combining Chinese-style system reform, economic growth, and demographic transition, these chapters depict the phenomenal labor migration of the country, estimate the quantity and proportion of agricultural surplus laborers, and map their changes over the period from the late 1970s on. Based on the empirical examination of economic development and demographic transition, we conclude that the arrival of the Lewis Turning Point manifested itself as a labor shortage and wage increase and, consequently, the demographic dividend that the Chinese economy has enjoyed for so many years began to disappear.

In the following two chapters, Chapters 5 and 6, we reveal the unique characteristics concerning the relationship between economic development and demographic transition in China. For one thing, China has reached a higher phase of population aging with a relatively low per capita income. Such a property—commonly phrased as "growing old before getting rich"—poses particular challenges to the sustainability of China's economic growth and thus makes the phenomenon of the middle-income trap exceedingly relevant to China. Based on a review of economics literature and development experiences, Chapter 6 argues that not only does the so-called middle-income trap already exist in global economic history, but it is particularly applicable in comprehending the future of Chinese economic growth.

In Chapters 7 through 12, we attempt to debate issues of how China can avoid falling into the middle-income trap. Chapters 7, 8, and 9 discuss how to exploit new sources of economic growth primarily by focusing on enhancing the potential growth rate through tapping the potential of the labor supply, improving total factor productivity, and accumulating human capital, as China is facing diminishing traditional sources of growth. Drawing lessons from other countries and applying them to the situation facing China presently, we suggest ways of sustaining the growth rate from supply-side factors instead of demand-side factors, since the latter demands stimulation policies and therefore increases the risk for China of falling into the middle-income trap.

Whereas economic growth is increasingly reliant on the creative destruction mechanism as a necessary condition of total factor productivity growth—namely, those enterprises that have lost their comparative advantage, competitiveness, and therefore viability in the market will have to cease operations—workers ought to be protected no matter which sectors and enterprises they used to work in. Meanwhile, according to international experiences, narrowing the income gap is an unavoidable task for a country at a certain phase of development if it wants to avoid the middle-income trap. By respectively discussing problems such as significant income inequality, the imperfection of labor market institutions, and the lack of social protection, Chapters 10 and 11 suggest that the key to building labor market institutions and social protection mechanisms, which effectively protect workers without distorting incentives, lies in redefining the boundary of functions between the government and enterprises.

At the present stage of economic development, the transformation of growth sources from the demographic dividend to the reform dividend is vital if China is to manage the transition from middle-income country to high-income country. Chapter 12 elaborates on the logic that the economic reform has followed to this point and then summarizes the characteristics of the new round of economic reforms. By quantifying the reform dividends, the chapter tries to boost the confidence of the Chinese people and international observers in such reform and help decision makers to identify key areas in which immediate reform dividends can be gained. Echoing the issue put forward in Chapter 1, it concludes by asserting that reform is the only way to avoid falling into the middle-income trap and bring about an economic renaissance.

1. At the crossroads of long-term development

> It was the spring of hope, it was the winter of despair. (Charles Dickens)

For many years, economists, scholars across broadly diverse academic fields, and amateur observers have made various predictions on the Chinese economy, either praising or criticizing, which frequently draw the attention of the Chinese government and are the source of hot debates in the media and academia. Though some of these predictions are not based on rigorous, scientific analysis, they all serve as a wake-up call to warn of problems which pose challenges to Chinese economic growth and to suggest solutions.

This book, however, only cites predictions based on methodologically sound studies, while ignoring those "crying wolf" stories that are popular but not backed by sufficient evidence or economic rationale. Furthermore, predictions and forecasts on the macroeconomic cycles of China are not included within the scope of this discussion, because in the short run the macroeconomy fluctuates as external shocks come and go, the government changes direction on macroeconomic policy, and people alter their expectations. By reviewing existing predictions on the Chinese economy and other economies' slowdowns that are relevant to China, this chapter asserts that the Chinese economy is standing at a crossroad that divides its future prospects.

1.1 PROSPECTS OF THE CHINESE ECONOMY

Immediately after 2010, when China surpassed Japan to become the second-largest economy in the world, the question arose as to when China would surpass the United States to become the world's number one economy. As can be expected, a host of studies have emerged to predict China's next step. The most optimistic prediction made by the International Monetary Fund (IMF) asserts that, based on purchasing power parity (PPP), the total GDP of China will increase to 19 trillion US dollars in 2016, accounting for 18 percent of the world's GDP, whereas the total GDP of the United States will be only 18.9 trillion US dollars, accounting for 17.7 percent of the world's GDP (IMF, 2011). Similar studies by some other authorities have vindicated such a projection—that is, China will eventually surpass the United States and become the largest economy in the world.

Such a vision is not an imaginary story from *Arabian Nights*, but a natural extrapolation of the future based on previous trends. In 1990, China was only ranked as the world's tenth-largest economy. In 1995, its GDP volume surpassed that of Canada, Spain, and Brazil to be ranked as seventh in the world, and soon afterwards, in 2000, it further surpassed Italy to be sixth. In the first decade of the twenty-first century, China has successively outstripped France, the United Kingdom, Germany, and Japan to become the second-largest economy in the world.

An immediate reflection on this trend is that, as China has the world's largest population, accounting for a fifth of the world's total population, becoming the largest economy in the world is nothing to boast about. However, many researchers are quite optimistic about the per capita income of China in their predictions. For example, Robert Fogel, the Nobel Prize laureate in economics, estimates that, in 2040, China's GDP will total 123.7 trillion US dollars in PPP terms, accounting for 40 percent of the world economy. As its population will reach 1.46 billion at that time, the per capita GDP in China will be 85000 US dollars, which is 2.4 times the world average per capita GDP and 80 percent of the United States' per capita GDP (Fogel, 2007). As a matter of fact, according to a prediction by the United Nations, China's total population will peak at 1.44 billion in 2035 and then decline to 1.43 billion in 2040. Based on the population census conducted in 2010, the total population of China will peak at 1.38 billion in 2020 and decline to 1.3 billion in 2040. Divided by the newly predicted population, the per capita GDP of China will be much closer to that of the United States in 2040. Such prospects are hardly surprising if one looks closely at the Chinese economy's past 30-plus years of high growth rates.

After the eighteenth century, while western countries sped up their economic progress, Chinese economic growth greatly lagged behind. In the period from 1700 to 1820, the annual GDP growth rate was only 0.85 percent, and per capita GDP had no growth at all in China. For several decades before the People's Republic of China was established in 1949, the country had experienced domestic trouble and foreign invasion, economic stagnation, and extreme destitution. In the period 1820 to 1952, the annual growth rate of GDP was 0.22 percent and that of per capita GDP was −0.08 percent, compared to 1.71 percent and 1.03 percent, respectively, in Europe.

During the entire pre-reform period—namely, the period from 1950 to 1978—China failed to catch up with the world's developed and newly industrialized economies, struggling under the implementation of a central planning scheme characterized by a refusal of market mechanisms, excessive capital accumulation, and an imbalance in its industrial structure, along with frequent political movements that harmed overall economic growth. In fact, the gap in living standards between China and the rest of the world not only did not grow more narrow, but actually widened. In 1978, there were 250 million rural residents living below the absolute poverty line.

Since the late 1970s, China has undergone fundamental institutional changes, which include the abolition of the People's Commune system and introduction of the household responsibility system in rural areas, transformation of the resources allocation mechanism from a planning system to a market force-based system, and moving from a closed economy to participating in the global economy. As a result of such a process of reform and opening-up, market-based and effective economic institutions, such as incentive mechanisms, modern corporate governance, the public fiscal system, rival financial and banking systems, and a social security system, have all been established.

All these achievements are ultimately reflected in the strengthening of China's national power and the improvement of people's livelihood. In the period spanning 1978 to 2012, China achieved an annual GDP growth rate of 9.8 percent. Not only has the Chinese economy caught up with those of the world's economic powers in terms of size, but people's income has increased at a miraculous pace—the annual growth rate of GDP per capita in this period was 8.7 percent (Figure 1.1).

In what follows, we can compare the time span of China doubling its per capita GDP with that of more-developed forerunner countries at comparable stages of economic development. Historically, the doubling of per capita GDP took 58 years (1780–1838) in the United Kingdom, 47 years (1839–1886) in the United States, 34 years (1885–1919) in Japan, and 11 years (1966–1977) in South Korea. For China, however, the doubling of per capita GDP took only 9 years (1978–1987), 8 years (1987–1995), 9 years again (1995–2004), and 7 years (2004–2011).

In their book *The China Miracle*, the Chinese edition of which was first published in 1994, Justin Yifu Lin, Fang Cai, and Zhou Li (2003) forecast that, if the differential growth rates in China, Japan, and the United States remain unchanged as they were between 1980 and 1995, the size of the Chinese economy will surpass that of Japan and the United States in 2035, based on constant price and exchange rates, and that the surpassing will occur in 2015 if the forecast is based on purchasing power parity.

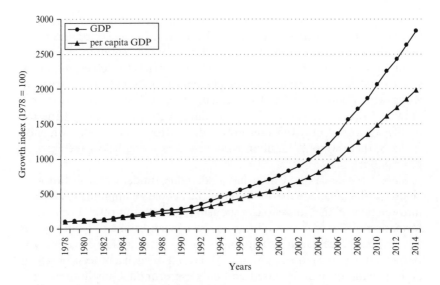

Source: National Bureau of Statistics (2014).

Figure 1.1   Economic growth rate in China's reform period

Lawrence Summers, the American economist, the Department of Foreign Affairs and Trade of Australia, Angus Maddison, the British economist and expert on quantitative macroeconomic history, and the World Bank all made similar predictions (Lin et al., 2003).

Since the beginning of the twenty-first century, most international organizations and economists, except for a small handful of what are called "China collapse fortunetellers," have held the belief that China will become the world's largest economy earlier than previously predicted. The debate on whether China can achieve this goal is now beyond just a matter of economic ranking, but is, rather, about whether China may become the only country in world history to have fallen from the zenith of human civilization into the trough and again climb to the apex.

1.2   FROM GREAT DIVERGENCE TO GREAT CONVERGENCE

In one of its reports, the World Bank expressed high expectations of the East Asian economies, which are called "the East Asia project" (Gill and Kharas, 2007). That is, the region is expected to grow 5.9 percent annually, much higher than the world average growth, and its share of GDP is expected to increase to account for 40 percent of the world total by 2025. In that case, East Asia will return to the historical glory held by the region in 1820. In view of the size of the Chinese economy and its contributive share in East Asia, China will play an overwhelmingly important role in the East Asia project.

In the field of world economic history, scholars have reached a consensus that the existing pattern of the world economy—namely, the absolute dominance of Europe and its western offshoots in economic development, technology, and per capita income—was not always so. The so-called California school of historical studies asserts that, around 1500, the world's wealth was mainly concentrated in the east, where China took the lion's share, and it was only as recently as 1750 that a great divergence occurred between the east and the west (Pomeranz, 2000; Goldstone, 2008).

Paralleling the course of this great divergence, the gaps in economic prosperity, scientific and technological progress, and standard of living between China and the west significantly widened as China became widely known as a poor and weak country. With intense debate on why the east lagged behind during the period following the industrial revolution, the "Needham Puzzle"—that is, why China had been in an advantageous position in scientific and technological developments compared to western countries in pre-modern times, yet lagged behind its western counterparts after the industrial revolution—became a sub-topic of a larger question, the "Puzzle of the Great Divergence."

China had been the country with the world's most advanced and prosperous science, technology, and economy for over 1000 years, until the industrial revolution swept the western world in the late eighteenth century and early nineteenth century. Historical studies find that China's agricultural productivity was among the world's highest from the ninth century through the thirteenth century, that its industry was the most developed in the world from the Han dynasty through the fourteenth century, and that its urbanization level—representing the development of commerce—was advanced compared to Europe's during the middle of the Song dynasty. Accordingly, various economic institutions relating to market development were well developed during those periods. Only after the sixteenth century did the economic development and technological advancement in China begin to lag behind that of European countries.[1]

Not only did domestic turmoil and foreign aggression impede China's economic development before 1949, when the People's Republic was established, but a series of political movements and failure of economic policy also delayed China's catch-up with more developed countries. According to one scholarly estimation, the Great Leap Forward and the Cultural

Revolution caused a 63 percent reduction of labor productivity (Kwan and Chow, 1996). Towards the end of the Cultural Revolution in the late 1970s, Chinese leaders realized that not only was the gap between China and western countries continuing to widen but China also lagged far behind other neighboring Asian economies, including its own territories such as Taiwan, Macau, and Hong Kong.

The mistakes made during the first three decades of the People's Republic of China led China to miss the opportunity for the great convergence, which allegedly started in 1950, according to Michael Spence, a Nobel laureate in economics (Spence, 2011). That is, the Chinese economy lost three decades' worth of economic growth. With economic reform initiated in the early 1980s, unprecedented fast growth has revived the Chinese economy and catapulted it to the world's second largest within three decades. Given the size of China's population and GDP, this dramatic reversal has led the world economy to another round of great convergence.

In his prominent works, Angus Maddison, the late economic historian, provides a widely citable, comparable dataset of total GDP and GDP per capita of major countries dated from an early point in human history. By updating Maddison's historical data, we now have a complete picture of China's share in the world's economy and its income level relative to the world average (Figure 1.2), which can, in a highly condensed manner, depict the fall and rise of the Chinese economy in history.

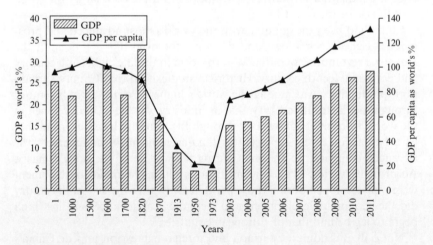

Source: Maddison (2007).

Figure 1.2   China's comparative economic size and income level in the world

Historically, in terms of China's standing in the world economy, its per capita income peaked in 1500, being 6 percent higher than the world average, and its GDP peaked in 1820, making up nearly one-third of the world's total. Figure 1.2 clearly shows that the share of the Chinese economy in the world has experienced a continuous increase since the early 1980s, after it had declined and bottomed out for more than one and a half centuries. That is, the data of this long history indicate a V-shaped change in the Chinese economy; the fall began in the nineteenth century, and the renaissance as the result of China's reform and opening-up.

1.3 FAILURE OF THE NEOCLASSICAL PREDICTION OF CONVERGENCE

An essential assumption about the neoclassical theory of growth is the law of diminishing return to capital. That is, given that the labor supply is limited, as physical capital is invested in the production process, its marginal return tends to decline. Therefore, less-developed countries may grow faster than more-developed countries. If such a differential in the growth rate between less- and more-developed countries lasts for a sufficiently long time, economic convergence among countries will occur. The implication of this theoretical prediction is that economically lagging countries potentially have the chance to catch up with their more advanced counterparts.

A host of observations and studies, however, do not confirm the hypothetical convergence between developing and developed economies. Instead, the facts show that, with a few exceptions in East Asian economies that have successfully caught up to their forerunners, the more advanced countries have in general grown faster than less-developed countries. The convergence has not happened and, what's more, the gap has instead widened.[2] On the other hand, the neoclassical theory of growth does not accurately predict or explain the distinct examples of economic catching-up, first in East Asia and, very recently, across a wider range of developing countries. There are three reasons for the failure of the neoclassical theory of growth.

First, a widely recognized fault of the neoclassical theory of growth lies in its treatment of technological progress as an exogenous factor, so that an important (virtually the only) source of long-term growth is excluded from its theoretical model. Growth theorists have tried to fill the gap by incorporating factors such as technological progress into their theoretical model. For example, the new theory of growth represented by Paul Romer, Robert Lucas, and others, which identifies the roles of human capital accumulation and technological innovation, has revitalized the theory of growth. Once human capital characterized by increasing returns and technological innovation and diffusion tending to generate monopolies are endogenized into the growth model, the assumption of perfect competition by neoclassical theory of growth has been broken.

Second, the neoclassical theory of growth simplifies economic growth as the result of the input of production factors and the enhancement of total factor productivity (TFP), and treats the latter as a statistical "residual," while simultaneously neglecting peculiar institutional features of countries at different stages of development. Empirically, scholars recognize a phenomenon of convergence clubs, which is that countries or regions with homogeneity—such as member states of the Organisation for Economic Co-operation and Development (OECD), states within the United States, or the counties of Japan—tend to converge in economic growth, whereas countries and regions with heterogeneity tend to diverge. These empirics, which partially confirm and partially reject the convergence assumption of the neoclassical theory of growth, have helped to form a new concept—the conditional convergence.

In fact, the neoclassical theory of growth implicitly suggests a conditional convergence. For example, it recognizes that the differences in population growth rate and in propensity to saving generate different long-term growth rates among countries. Only when those conditions are assumed to be constant can countries at a low starting point grow more quickly, which is necessary for convergence. Based on such a tradition of neoclassical theory of growth, Barro and Sala-i-Martin (1995) have put various variables in their empirical model of growth regression, having identified relevant conditions for convergence in trying to test the conditional convergence hypothesis.[3]

Both the new growth theory and the neoclassical theory of growth have their role in explaining the growth performances of countries. On the one hand, economists like Romer (1986) and Lucas (2009) point out how increasing returns can sustain the growth of developed countries, which also has implications for economies in the process of catching up. On the other hand, economists like Barro and Sala-i-Martin (1995) have found more than a hundred variables (factors) that have a significant impact on the growth performance of countries, positive or negative. These—including the level of savings and investment, infrastructure, institutions, government responsibility, human capital, and other demographic characteristics—are necessary conditions if lagging countries are to catch up.

Third, the neoclassical theory's assumption of labor scarcity and a diminishing return to capital is not appropriate for many developing countries. Based on empirical studies by certain economists in the early 1990s, Paul Krugman (1994), who won the Nobel Prize in Economics years later, criticized the East Asian model. Taking Singapore as an example, he asserted that the rapid growth in those economies could be solely attributed to the accumulation and input of production factors but not to the improvement of productivity. He therefore prophesied that such a growth pattern would not be sustained, much as had happened in the former Soviet Union.

The long-term growth performance of Singapore and other East Asian Tigers proves the failure of Krugman and his neoclassical colleagues' predictions, because they wrongly applied the neoclassical assumption to the growth patterns of the East Asian economies characterized by dual economy development coupled with an unlimited supply of labor, which not only broke the law of diminishing return to capital, but also created resources' reallocative efficiency through labor mobility from the low-productivity (agricultural) sector to the higher-productivity (non-agricultural) sectors.

In addition to the World Bank's publications, which are intended to generalize rather than modeling any specific East Asian experiences and lessons in economic development (e.g. World Bank, 1993), and inexorable criticism on the same experiences by neoclassical theorists of growth (for example Krugman, 1994), there has been a host of literature employing an analytical framework that is wholly unorthodox to the neoclassical approach of theorizing East Asian development.

For example, Kojima (2000) extends the early "flying geese paradigm" to a more thorough theoretical model in order to explain the catch-up process of the East Asian economies and the outward-oriented growth led by trade and foreign direct investment. As admitted by Kojima himself, however, such a model is yet incomplete in explaining economic growth in East Asia. More recent work trying to explain East Asian economies' catch-up can be seen in an example by Aoki (2012). By dividing economic development in this region into five successive phases and endogenizing institutional factors, he tries to explore the commonality of economic development patterns and the difference of institutional evolutionary paths among China, Japan, and South Korea. What he implies is that, given the path dependence of institutional evolution in different countries, imitating the western model does not guarantee any degree of success.

It is not hard to comprehend the China experience as long as one recognizes the limitation of conventional theories, grasps the commonalities and differences among developing countries, and knows the history of China's reform. The miraculous convergence of China with developed economies in the level of economic development and standard of living over the past three decades proves that, conditioned by the correct choice of development pattern in accordance with the unique features of the country, latecomer countries are bound to catch up with their more advanced counterparts after all. On the other hand, only if an economic theory is tested by practice can it be proven valid. The experiences shown in the successful reform, opening-up, and resulting rapid socioeconomic development of China, therefore, are much more meaningful than 2 million econometric regressions by growth theorists in testing a convergence hypothesis.[4]

1.4 WHEN AND WHY DOES FAST GROWTH SLOW DOWN?

The exciting predictions widely offered by many international institutions for the Chinese economy based on its past performance do not guarantee future sustainable growth. One cannot help comparing China with Japan when thinking about the sustainability of rapid economic growth. The Japanese economy was widely viewed to be bullish in long-run growth, manifested in the fact that it became the world's second-largest economy in the late 1980s. Japanese economic growth, however, has been stuck in "the lost two decades" or so since 1990, and Japan lost its position as the world's second-largest economy in 2010.

In a burst of appreciation and recognition for China's unprecedented economic achievements, some studies have appeared that aim to predict when, under what circumstances, and to what extent Chinese economic growth could slow down. On the basis of the statistical law of "regression to the mean," which asserts that any phenomenal economic growth will eventually return to the world average growth rate, Pritchett and Summers (2014) estimate that China's annual growth rate will be 5.01 percent in the period 2013–2023 and further drop to 3.28 percent in the years 2023–2033. Methodologically, a similar study was done by Eichengreen and his coauthors, which was intended to answer the questions of when rapidly growing economies—namely, at what level of per capita income—would slow down and what such experiences would imply for China (Eichengreen et al., 2011). Its findings are twofold. One, when fast-growing catch-up economies reach a per capita GDP of 17 000 US dollars measured by year 2005 international prices, they tend to slow down by 3.5 percentage points on average. Two, as China will soon reach this threshold, the probability is great that China will follow the same path sometime after 2015.

The slowdown in growth as revealed by studies of this kind is not necessarily a bad thing. Whether it is a natural trend or undesired outcome depends on the causes of each economy's slowdown. As Russian novelist Leo Tolstoy put it, happy families are all alike; each unhappy family is unhappy in its own way. While countries may share common causes, each individual country also has its own particular causes for suffering a slowdown of growth. For China, which has benefited from a demographic dividend throughout its entire reform period, the dramatic change in population trends is a critical force slowing growth. Such a characteristic outcome is generally expressed as "growing old before getting rich."

As a result of long being at a demographic transition phase with low fertility, China has witnessed a tremendous change in the age structure of its population. According to the 6th National Census, the population aged between 15 and 59 peaked in 2010 and has had negative growth since then. It is predicted that in the period from 2010 to 2020 the population within this age group will decrease by 29.3 million, which can be considered a significant decline in the labor supply. Primarily based on reversed population trends, the potential GDP growth rate is estimated to decline from 10.3 percent over the 1995–2010 period to 7.6 percent in the 2011–2015 period and 6.2 percent in the 2016–2020 period. That is, the year 2010 is the specific threshold for economic slowdown in China.

In terms of the year 2005 international dollar used by Eichengreen and others, in 2010 China's per capita GDP was 11 466 US dollars. It seems that there is little similarity between the China of the year 2010 and Japan of the year 1992 in terms of at what development stages they stand, because, although Japan encountered its slowdown threshold in that year, its comparable per capita GDP was 27 250 dollars, 1.38 times higher than China's in 2010. However, given that both China and Japan used to enjoy an opportunity window of population dividends and started slowing down in growth when demographic transition entered a new stage, at which point the working-age population began declining and the dependence ratio increasing, comparing China in 2010 to Japan in 1992 remains relevant for understanding the slowdown story.

Not coincidently, at the slowdown threshold, the dependence ratio—namely, the ratio of the population aged 14 and younger and 65 and older to the population aged 15–64 in Japan—began to increase dramatically. As shown in Figure 1.3, first, the Japanese economy has actually had two slowdowns, one being in the early 1970s and another in the early 1990s, along with the change in its demographic profile, and, second, the later slowdown was revealed as stagnation for quite a long period.

Three things should be emphasized about China's slowdown. First of all, although the reversal of population trends may be the key cause leading to slower growth, there are other factors that also matter. While researchers can name many such factors, the lessons from those economies—which experienced economic slowdown followed by falling into a middle-income trap—show that development strategies and social policies that are starkly

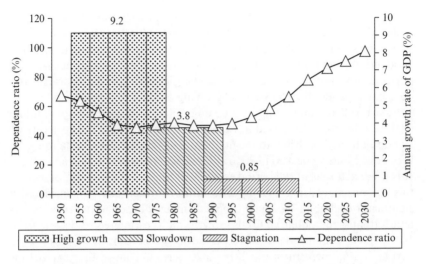

Source: Population data are from the UN, and GDP data are from the World Bank, and Hoshi and Kashyap (2011).

Figure 1.3   Japan's slowdown and stagnation along with its demographic transition

different from those previously employed must be chosen during a country's transition from the middle-income to the high-income phase.[5]

Secondly, if just following the average path of economic slowdown in the history of development—namely, if the growth rate drops by 3.5 percentage points, as is proposed by Eichengreen and others—China can still maintain its position as a rapidly developing economy. For example, even a slowed annual growth rate of 6.3 percent, compared to 9.8 percent during the period 1978–2012, is still reasonable. So, what matters to China is to avoid the economic stagnation that can be caused by misdealing in the face of such a slowdown.

Finally, while taking the place of Japan as the second-largest economy in the world in 2010, China just joined the upper-middle-income group, and the per capita GDP in China was only 42.1 percent of that in Japan in 1992. That is, unlike Japan's stagnation in the lost decades after its slow-down threshold, which can be viewed as a "high-income trap," if China falls into a rut it would become another example of the "middle-income trap" common among many developing economies, typically in Latin America and Southeast Asia.

In order to avoid such a worst-case scenario, China has to awaken from its past success and be prepared to meet the challenges it will face when its economic growth is bound to slow down. The issue is not *whether* the fast growth in China will slow down, but how China should live with a more moderate growth and prevent stagnation. Luckily, there have been a host of lessons from both successful and failed experiences in economic history.

1.5 CONCLUSION

International experiences show that the threshold for the slowdown in economic growth actually serves as a watershed dividing countries into three very different scenarios. In what follows, we simplify such scenarios, which can no doubt provide important implications for how China can strive for the best result and avoid the worst.

The United States and European countries are typical examples of the first scenario. Although these countries no longer grow as quickly as they previously did before reaching the threshold, they still remain pioneers on the scientific and technological frontier in order to sustain qualitative economic growth. For example, based on elements of the national economy that enable innovative activities, such as institutions, human capital and research, infrastructure, market and business sophistication, knowledge and technology outputs, and creative outputs, the top 20 economies in the ranking of the global innovation index in 2013 are all European and North American countries with the additions of Hong Kong (China), Singapore, South Korea, and Israel.[6]

This bright side indicates that although developing countries have the opportunity to take advantage of backwardness in their fast-growing stages of development—namely, they can borrow, purchase, and imitate applicable technologies from advanced countries—they eventually have to rely on independent innovation to sustain their long-run growth, which is particularly true following the slowdown threshold.

Even if there is a gradual slowdown due to the disappearance of its demographic dividend, if China can accomplish a transition from an input-driven growth pattern to a productivity-driven growth pattern its economy will continue to increase in quality and sustainability. While there is an urgent need for China to innovate more independently as it enters the new stage of development, the already-existing significant gap in sciences and technology between China and more advanced economies will still be able to furnish China with the advantage of backwardness—that is, China does not necessarily invent applied technologies in every area, but it can borrow them cheaply, which will enable China to grow more rapidly than its developed counterparts in the next decade or so.

Japan can serve as a perfect reference for the second scenario. Incorrectly coping with the inevitable changes in its development stages, Japan has turned its natural economic slowdown into an artificial stagnation since the early 1990s. Even though Japan still holds its place as the world's third-largest economy, with the highest income per capita in world rankings, its ability to innovate and influence the world economy has been diminishing over time. For instance, Japan's rank in the global innovation index in 2013 was downgraded to 22nd, not only after the most advanced North American and European countries, but also after its Asian neighbors—Hong Kong (China), Singapore, and South Korea.

The "lost two decades" story of Japan suggests that it is not the natural slowdown as a result of changes encountered during the development stages, but the policy choices in coping with such a slowdown that leads a country to different scenarios. In the face of a weakened potential growth rate, there is the temptation for China to make policy efforts to stimulate the economy through demand-side factors while failing to enhance its potential growth capability through supply-side factors, which may lead China to share the fate of Japan. Therefore, properly combining policy measures that cope with both short-term macroeconomic shock and long-term sustainability of growth is crucial for China at this crossroad.

Some Latin American and Southeast Asian countries represent the third scenario. Although many of them became middle-income countries long ago, they have never been able to catch up with the world's more developed countries in terms of per capita income. That is, they have been stuck in the middle-income trap. There are four sequences of their undesirable economic and social developments: (1) the failure of economic policies and institutions hinders economic growth, preventing a country's economic "pie" from enlarging; (2) the constant size of the pie cannot be equally shared among all groups within a population; (3) vested interest groups attempt to influence policy making to keep their bargaining power in determining income distribution; and (4) politicians only pay lip service to change instead of really altering their populist socioeconomic policies.

The middle-income trap scenario clearly shows that economic growth, income distribution patterns, and policies and institutions that influence income distribution are closely interdependent and interrelated with each other as both cause and effect. Up until now, China has witnessed shared growth in general. Even though there is growing concern regarding income inequality, it can still be tolerated as long as the economic pie is enlarging. Furthermore, as far as labor income is concerned, there has been a trend towards a reduction in inequality. Only if stagnated growth provided nothing to distribute among all groups while the most influential group received an even larger share of income would there be strong dissatisfaction towards the distributive pattern, which would inevitably lead to social unrest.

The Chinese leadership has been preparing for a slower, shared growth. In the 12th Five-Year Plan, the goal of the annual growth rate of China's GDP is set to be 7 percent, lower than that in the country's previous Five-Year Plans. Such a growth rate gives China more room to transform its economic growth pattern and to focus more on people's livelihoods. In what follows in this book, the theme of avoiding the middle-income trap is not about avoiding an economic slowdown entirely, but about keeping away from falling economic stagnation by tapping new sources of growth.

NOTES

1. About the concept of the Needham Puzzle and some comparative facts between early China and Europe, see, for example, Lin (2008).
2. Since the beginning of the twenty-first century, the growth performance of emerging markets has shown signs of reversal of the long-lasting divergence. However, whether such a trend can last requires further observation. The purpose of this book is to offer answers on why the convergence has happened and how it can continue by inquiring into the Chinese experience.
3. See, for example, Barro and Sala-i-Martin (1995).
4. Sala-i-Martin, a Spanish-born American professor, once used the title "I Just Ran Two Million Regressions" to describe his academic efforts in testing the convergence hypothesis of the neoclassical theory of growth. See Sala-i-Martin (1997).
5. See, for example, Gill and Kharas (2007).
6. http://globalinnovationindex.org/content.aspx?page=data-analysis.

REFERENCES

Aoki, Masahiko (2012), "The Five Phases of Economic Development and Institutional Evolution in China, Japan, and Korea," in Masahiko Aoki, Timur Kuran, and Gérard Roland (eds.), *Institutions and Comparative Economic Development*, Basingstoke: Palgrave Macmillan, pp. 13–47.

Barro, Robert, and Xavier Sala-i-Martin (1995), *Economic Growth*, New York: McGraw-Hill.

Eichengreen, Barry, Donghyun Park, and Kwanho Shin (2011), *When Fast Growing Economies Slow Down: International Evidence and Implications for China*, NBER Working Paper No. 16919, Cambridge, MA: National Bureau of Economic Research.

Fogel, Robert (2007), *Capitalism and Democracy in 2040: Forecasts and Speculations*, NBER Working Paper No. 13184, Cambridge, MA: National Bureau of Economic Research.

Gill, Indermit, and Homi Kharas (2007), *An East Asian Renaissance: Ideas for Economic Growth*, Washington, DC: World Bank.

Goldstone, Jack (2008), *Why Europe? The Rise of the West in World History, 1500–1850*, New York: McGraw-Hill.

Hoshi, Takeo, and Anil Kashyap (2011), "Why Did Japan Stop Growing?," report prepared for the National Institute for Research Advancement (NIRA), http://www.nira.or.jp/pdf/1002english_report.pdf.

IMF (International Monetary Fund) (2011), World Economic Outlook Database, April, https://www.imf.org/external/pubs/ft/weo/2011/01/weodata/index.aspx.

Kojima, Kiyoshi (2000), "The 'Flying Geese' Model of Asian Economic Development: Origin, Theoretical Extensions, and Regional Policy Implications," *Journal of Asian Economics*, 11, 375–401.

Krugman, Paul (1994), "The Myth of Asia's Miracle," *Foreign Affairs*, 73 (6), 62–78.

Kwan, Yum, and Gregory Chow (1996), "Estimating Economic Effects of Political Movements in China," *Journal of Comparative Economics*, 23, 192–208.

Lin, Justin Yifu (2008), "The Needham Puzzle, the Weber Question, and China's Miracle: Long-Term Performance since the Sung Dynasty," *China Economic Journal*, 1 (1), 63–95.

Lin, Justin Yifu, Fang Cai, and Zhou Li (2003), *The China Miracle: Development Strategy and Economic Reform*, rev. edn., Hong Kong: Chinese University Press of Hong Kong.

Lucas, Robert (2009), "Ideas and Growth," *Economica*, 76 (301), 1–19.

Maddison, Angus (2007), *Contours of the World Economy, 1–2030 AD: Essays in Macro-economic History*, Oxford: Oxford University Press.

National Bureau of Statistics (2014), *China Statistical Yearbook 2014*, Beijing: China Statistical Press.

Pomeranz, Kenneth (2000), *The Great Divergence: Europe, China, and the Making of the Modern World Economy*, Princeton, NJ: Princeton University Press.

Pritchett, Lant, and Lawrence H. Summers (2014), *Asiaphoria Meets Regression to the Mean*, NBER Working Paper No. 20573, Cambridge, MA: National Bureau of Economic Research.

Romer, Paul M. (1986), "Increasing Returns and Long-Run Growth," *Journal of Political Economy*, 94 (5), 1002–1037.

Sala-i-Martin, Xavier (1997), "I Just Ran Two Million Regressions," *American Economic Review*, 87 (2), 178–183.

Spence, Michael (2011), *The Next Convergence: The Future of Economic Growth in a Multispeed World*, New York: Farrar, Straus and Giroux.

World Bank (1993), *The East Asian Miracle: Economic Growth and Public Policy*, World Bank Policy Research Report, Oxford: Oxford University Press.

2. The development of a dual economy

[U]nto a land flowing with milk and honey. (Old Testament, Exodus)

The possible slowdown facing China has to do with changes in the stages of economic development undergone by the country. In order to understand such developmental changes, we must first enumerate the unique characteristics that have distinguished economic growth in China since the 1980s, when economic reform was initiated. The Chinese story, however, cannot be told within the framework of the mainstream theory of growth, which considers economic growth to be a unitary, homogeneous process in which wealth slowly—but linearly—expands. The homogeneity assumption might be applied to countries in the early stages of industrialization, perhaps, but it does not hold explanatory power over existing developing economies.

Until the dual economy development theory (coined by Arthur Lewis, a Nobel laureate in economics) came to prevail, conventional wisdom concerning the neoclassical theory of growth had failed to capture the characteristics distinguishing developing countries from developed countries and thus to identify the factors that prevent developing countries from catching up with their developed counterparts. The Lewisian theory has made at least two important contributions to development economics. One, it has built a bridge between two well-recognized phases of economic development, that is, the Malthusian poverty trap and neoclassical growth (Hansen and Prescott, 2002). Two, it provides a tool for understanding a unique phase of development—dual economy development—which many early industrialized economies have gone through and through which currently developing countries are still going.

The Lewisian theory helps observers understand a host of uniquely Chinese phenomena, such as surplus labor in agriculture, rural-to-urban migration, and the dual labor market, all of which characterize the economic growth of the past over the three decades since China initiated its economic reform. Most importantly, it helps theorists and policy makers identify the Lewis Turning Point, a point in time that distinguishes the Chinese economy from its previous stage of development. Correspondingly, the characteristics of China's growth have added to and developed the Lewis model, contributing thus to the progress of development economics.

17

This chapter employs a theoretical framework regarding the development of a dual economy in order to analyze the unique characteristics and major phenomena of the Chinese economy during the reform period.

2.1 APPLICABILITY OF THE LEWIS MODEL TO CHINA

In his prominent 1954 paper, Arthur Lewis abandoned the neoclassical assumption—that is, that a supply of labor is limited—and instead both applied a classical economics framework to developing countries and divided a typical developing economy into two sectors: the agricultural and modern sectors. Because a labor force is superfluous relative to capital and land in agriculture, its marginal productivity in the agricultural sector is very low, even as low as zero or below. As Lewis points out, the characteristics of the "agricultural sector" are also applied to other traditional sectors, and the key to understanding the "modern sector" is that the wage rate is determined by workers' marginal product.

According to the dual economy theory, in the traditional sector the numbers of the labor force are excessive relative to capital and land, which keeps marginal productivity of labor (and thus the opportunity cost of labor migration) very low. As the expanding modern sector is able to obtain an unlimited supply of labor from the agricultural sector by offering a constant, subsistence wage rate, the critical constraint for economic growth in a dual economy is therefore the accumulation of capital. As the early development economists put it, the core of economic development is to accomplish a critical minimum savings rate (Rostow, 1991).

Traditional agriculture and modern industry coexist in most developing economies. Correspondingly, dual economy development is characterized by a shrinkage of the traditional sector (releasing surplus labor) and an expansion of the modern sector (absorbing surplus labor at a constant, low wage rate). Only when underemployed labor is drained from the traditional sector will the agricultural and industrial sectors be integrated and dual economy development shift to homogeneous economic growth. As a result, the period at which surplus labor is exhausted is a critical turning point.

According to development economic theories, dual economy development is divided into three sequenced phases on the basis of labor movement. In Figure 2.1, the relationship between the outflow of surplus labor and agricultural output at each of those phases, as well as the order in which they occur, is depicted. The vertical axis denotes agricultural output, the horizontal axis denotes labor engaged in agriculture, OCST represents

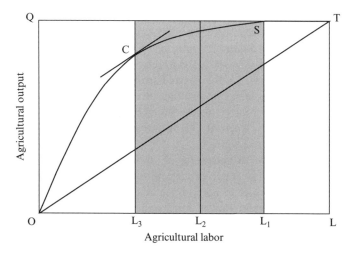

Source: Ranis and Fei (1961).

Figure 2.1 Phases and turning points of dual economy development

the curve of agricultural output, and its convex shape represents the feature of diminishing marginal output resulting from a labor surplus in agriculture.

The first phase shows typical dual economy development, during which time, owing to a surplus of labor, the marginal product of labor in agriculture is very low and wages in the modern sector remain constantly at the subsistence level. According to Lewis's assumption, in the entire range of LL_1 of labor reallocation, the marginal product of agricultural labor remains zero and the wage rate of laborers is not determined by the marginal productivity of labor but is defined by sharing an average output (OQ/OL).

This phase of dual economy development is characterized by continued labor mobility from the agricultural to the non-agricultural sectors. Until the labor force has moved from L to L_1 (corresponding to S of the output curve), as both the marginal product of agriculture and the opportunity costs of labor mobility are zero, the reduction of labor input in agriculture will not result in a decline in agricultural output, and wages in the non-agricultural sectors will not significantly increase.

A second phase corresponds with the arrival of the Lewis Turning Point, the point at which the demand for labor at constant wages exceeds the actual supply of labor. When such a turning point is reached, even though wage rates in the modern sector begin to rise, since wages in agriculture

are not yet determined by the marginal product of labor, the marginal productivities of labor remain different between the agricultural and modern
sectors. As is shown in Figure 2.1, this new phase ranges from S to C of the
output curve and from L_1 to L_3 of the labor movement out of agriculture.
Therefore, by definition, S is the Lewis Turning Point. Until the outflow of
labor moves to L_3 the marginal product of labor will still be smaller than
the average product—that is, at any point between S and C, the slope is
always smaller than the slope of OT until the exact point C is reached and
meets with L_3 of labor allocation.

There are thus two implications of arriving at this phase. First, as
long as the marginal product of agricultural labor is still smaller than
both the average product in agriculture and the marginal product in the
modern sector, there remains a continued need to move surplus labor
out of agriculture. Second, since the marginal product of labor in agriculture increases positively with the arrival of the Lewis Turning Point,
further labor mobility from the agricultural to the non-agricultural sectors
requires synchronous enhancement of labor productivity in agriculture,
say through utilizing machinery to substitute for manual labor.

A third phase is arrived at when wages in both the agricultural and the
non-agricultural sectors are determined by the marginal products of labor
and thus become identical, as the national economy as a whole is no longer
dualist but homogeneous. As shown in Figure 2.1, when agricultural labor
moves to L_3, the corresponding point of agricultural output C has an
identical slope to OT. That is, surplus laborers have been exhausted, so the
marginal product of labor in agriculture equals the marginal product in
the modern sector, wage rates in both sectors are determined by their marginal products, and the economy concerned has reached its second turning
point—the commercial turning point.[1]

In fact, the point is not about how to define the turning point or to
which turning points more attention should be paid, but about which of
the turning points leads to more significant change and therefore poses
more of a policy challenge to a given economy at a certain stage. As will be
indicated later in this chapter, the arrival of the Lewis Turning Point challenges the growth pattern and alters the path of the Chinese economy over
the long term, and it is therefore important to investigate whether and, if
so, when the Lewis Turning Point has arrived in China.

For a long time, the Chinese economy could be characterized by a
large surplus of agricultural labor, institutionalized segmentation between
the rural and urban labor markets, the massive migration of labor from
rural to urban areas, and the stagnation of migrant workers' wages. In
addition to those phenomena typical of a dual economy, however, the
institutional backgrounds which specifically characterize the growth of the

Chinese economy make China a unique example of the development of a dual economy.

Prior to the economic reform initiated in the early 1980s, this dual economy development was accompanied by the implementation of economic planning. During this planning period, the institutional troika—namely, state-monopolistic distribution of agricultural products, People's Communes, and the household registration (or *hukou*) system—prevented underemployed laborers from migrating to urban non-agricultural sectors, leading to inefficiency in two ways. One, the lack of farmers' rights to exit from the Commune harmed existing incentive mechanisms and produced technical inefficiency in agriculture. Two, labor immobility between the agricultural and non-agricultural sectors generated inefficiencies in resource allocation. Together with similar inefficiency in non-agricultural sectors, the contribution of productivity enhancement to economic growth was negligible across the entire period of economic planning, typically defined as the period from the late 1950s through the early 1980s.

In the reform period, dual economy development was typically accompanied by the gradual abolition of those institutional barriers deterring labor mobility, along with other measures of institutional transition. As a result of more than 30 years of massive labor migration, China's large surplus labor force in agriculture was on the verge of exhaustion, and labor shortages and wage inflation took China to its Lewis Turning Point in 2004 (Cai, 2008).

Most scholars disagree with the assertion that the Lewis Turning Point of the Chinese economy has arrived. However, time is in favor of the argument that such a turning point has, indeed, come to pass, and now the evidence of the turning point's arrival has been used to support further propositions regarding China's collapse. For example, Nobel laureate Paul Krugman uses the Lewis Turning Point argument to predict that China will soon hit a wall after many years of rapid economic growth. However, neither ignoring the facts nor proposing misleading arguments properly explains the challenges facing China today and in the future. In the rest of this chapter, we will discuss the arrival of the Lewis Turning Point, its resulting changes, and their policy implications.

2.2   SURPLUS LABORERS IN AGRICULTURE

The dual economy development theory has witnessed three distinct phases of acceptance since it was first coined by Arthur Lewis. First, its theoretical assumption of a labor surplus in the traditional sector was critically questioned by neoclassical economists. For example, Theodore

Schultz, who shared the Nobel Prize in economics with Lewis in 1979, empirically rejected both the existence of surplus labor and the hypothesis of zero marginal product of labor in agriculture based on studies of poor economies. Following the first stage of outright rejection, it was ignored and forgotten for many years as the neoclassical theories dominated the economic mainstream (Ranis, 2004). Assuming perfect production factor markets and commodity markets, the neoclassical theory is reluctant to accept the notion that the labor market cannot effectively resolve the huge gap in wages between the two sectors and that, therefore, surplus labor persists. Finally, China's unique institutions, such as the *hukou* system, which serve to deter labor mobility and to maintain institutional wages, provide a useful and novel case for understanding how Lewisian theory works in assuming a labor surplus and zero marginal product of labor.

Throughout the entire reform period since the early 1980s, Chinese economic development has progressed with the fading-out of its dual economic structure, including the reduction of surplus laborers and, as such, has arrived at the Lewis Turning Point. Therefore, if one can learn from China's experiences regarding the reasoning behind the introduction of the *hukou* system in the late 1950s, the resultant institutional arrangements it induced afterwards, and how those institutions segmented labor markets between rural and urban areas and between formal and informal sectors in urban areas in planned and reform periods, accepting Lewis's assumption of surplus labor, and relinquishing the neoclassical assumption of homogeneous growth, is effortless.

There are numerous examples, in fact, of staunch defenders of the neoclassical model of growth coming to accept the Lewisian model of economics after evaluating China's unique institutional transition. For example, unlike many mainstream economists who fail to grasp the critical role an unlimited supply of labor plays in understanding dual economy development, D. Gale Johnson, a professor considered to be a "Chicago School" economist, eventually accepted the existence of surplus labor. In one of his papers, he admitted that there were abundant surplus agricultural laborers and that their productivity was significantly lower than the productivity exhibited by laborers in the urban sectors (Johnson, 2002).

A labor surplus or underemployment prevails in almost all developing countries, which can thus be defined as a dual economy with an unlimited supply of labor. China has been a typical case where there exists a huge pool of surplus laborers making up a significant proportion of the total labor force in agriculture, which is the root cause of various situations such as the low productivity of agriculture, an unequal relationship between the rural and urban sectors, and urban-biased policy.

Under the People's Commune system during China's period of a planned economy, collective team work prevailed in farming; work points were recorded based on work days but not on the work quality of the laborers. At the end of each year, the products of the production team were allotted to team members according to their work points earned in the previous year. Because the connection between work points earned by a laborer and the actual contribution made by the same laborer was extremely weak, this system severely dampened labor incentives. Thus a reluctance to contribute while others reaped the rewards led to very low productivity of labor, and, while other production factors (capital and land) were increasing, before rural reform, any agricultural labor surplus can be considered practically invisible.

The overall introduction of the household responsibility system (HRS) in the early 1980s returned the land originally under the collective unified management of the production team to peasant households according to their headcount and working strength; after having finalized their agricultural tax and procurement obligations and paying any remaining deductions to the collective, the household would then keep the remaining product, that is, have claim to any surplus remaining after what they themselves had contributed. This operational mode, while not legally changing the collective nature of land ownership, greatly stimulated labor incentives, and production was immediately greatly enhanced. According to an estimate by economist Justin Lin, about 46.9 percent of agricultural output between 1978 and 1984 can be attributed to the national inception of the HRS (Lin, 1992). With this manifold increase of work effort, there was a significant decline in the labor time needed for agriculture, and a labor surplus subsequently emerged.

In the mid-1980s, when the impact of rural reform on labor incentives was revealed, most scholars and policy researchers believed that, because massive numbers of laborers were released from agricultural positions, the size of the surplus labor force ranged from somewhere between 100 million and 150 million workers, accounting for 30–40 percent of the total labor force in rural China (Taylor, 1993). Carter and others estimated that, in 1990, even with years of the rapid expansion of township and village enterprises (TVEs) that served to absorb the massive labor force, there were still 172 million surplus laborers, making up 31.5 percent of total rural labor (Carter et al., 1996). Liu offers a more exaggerated figure, suggesting that, in 2000, there were 170 million surplus laborers, accounting for 46.6 percent of the total rural labor force (Liu, 2002). The puzzle is why, after many years of massive migration, the number and proportion of surplus laborers became no smaller, to say nothing of the inconsistency between data suggested by different studies.

2.3　MEASURING THE LABOR SURPLUS

There is no consensus as to how the number of surplus laborers should be estimated among economists. Whether the wage level is higher than the marginal product of labor is naturally suggested in accordance with the theoretical definition of a labor surplus. In reality, however, in many cases the availability and consistency of data make any estimation based on such a definition practically infeasible. As a matter of fact, since our purpose is to judge the alteration of those development stages divided by the arrival of the Lewis Turning Point and characterized by the emergence of a labor shortage at an existing constant wage rate rather than discussing a commercial point signaled by the equalization of the marginal productivity of labor between the agricultural and non-agricultural sectors, it is more meaningful to look at whether surplus labor is moving towards its decline than to compare those wages with marginal product with accuracy.

In order to avoid conflicting debates on the methods of estimation and to obtain comparable results in measuring changes to the labor surplus over time, we have adopted an approach that duplicates the calculations made by Carter et al. (1996) cited above. In this way, the magnitude of surplus laborers in 1990 and 2005 can be compared in a consistent way.

The idea underlying this assessment is to single out those laborers who are neither necessarily needed in agriculture nor engaged in non-agricultural work by deducting migrant workers, the self-employed, and employees of the non-agricultural sectors in rural areas, and the required agricultural laborers at their current productivity of labor (Cai and Wang, 2008).

According to officially published figures, there were 485 million rural employed persons in China in 2005. This statistic is categorized in accordance with the residence of laborers aged 16 years and older, regardless of whether they actually work as farmers in agriculture, as TVE employees, as owners or employees in private non-agricultural businesses in rural areas, or as migrant workers in urban areas. In rural areas, the HRS guarantees that everybody has his or her own share of land, so it is a reasonable assumption that overt rural unemployment based on the definition laid out by the International Labour Organization[2] is almost negligible, because these laborers work either in the non-agricultural sectors or in agriculture. Therefore, this category of "rural employed persons" can also be viewed as equivalent to the stock of rural laborers.

In 2005, 232 million laborers, accounting for 47.9 percent of the total rural labor force, had already shifted to the non-agricultural sectors in either rural or urban areas, while agriculture required 190 million laborers, or 39.2 percent of the rural labor force, to be fully engaged in the sector. As a result, the estimated number of surplus laborers in rural areas was 63 million, accounting for 12.9 percent of rural laborers. This finding shows that the number of surplus laborers in rural areas shrank substantially in the years between 1990 and 2005.

The inconsistency of official statistics on laborers engaged in agriculture has puzzled many observers and researchers on China, particularly those running regression statistics based on official bodies of data. According to official data, the share of agricultural labor in the total Chinese labor force dropped from 70.5 percent in 1978 to 33.6 percent in 2012, a decline of 2.2 percent per annum.

Though this pace of decline is relatively rapid in comparison to the pre-reform period between 1953 and 1978, in which the share of agricultural labor only declined by 0.6 percent annually, it does not seem to be accurate for at least two reasons. First, the mobility of labor from the agricultural to the non-agricultural sectors has been unprecedented and condensed within the three decades of China's economic reform, and is recognized as the largest-ever migration in human history in peacetime (Roberts et al., 2004). Secondly, the annual rate of decline in the agricultural labor share in China over the past 34 years is only less than half that seen in Japan and South Korea over a comparable time span. For example, the agricultural labor share in Japan declined by 4.5 percent annually between 1953 and 1987, and that in South Korea by 5.1 percent annually between 1963 and 1997.

It is an "iron law" of development economics that the agricultural share of both production and the labor force shrinks as the economy grows. After more than 20 years of delay during the period of planning, the unprecedented economic growth and industrial structure change during the reform period witnessed a substantial drop in agricultural shares, leading to a logical reconciliation between supply and demand for labor. If the official statistical data collected cannot reflect this rapidly changing reality, any conclusions or observation and analysis based on false data can be unintentionally misleading. For example, a variety of studies with advanced econometric methods and improper use of statistical data con-clude that surplus labor is still abundant and the marginal productivity of labor still low in agriculture, and that the Chinese economy is therefore far from the Lewis Turning Point.[3]

According to economists at the World Bank, the Chinese economy changes rapidly enough for traditional statistical systems to be unable to capture its changing features (Chen and Ravallion, 1999). The perceived overestimation of agricultural labor, to a large extent, stems from the ina-bility of the current statistical model to accurately distinguish between the number of laborers and the time they have worked in agriculture. A more accurate definition of agricultural laborers that is in accordance with their actual engagement in farming work will therefore help in obtaining more definitive data on the actual share of agricultural labor.

Based on rural household survey data, one study redefines the actual distribution of the rural labor force among different activities on the basis of monthly work and concludes that the total number of agricultural laborers rests at around 187 million, instead of the officially released number of 289 million (Du and Wang, 2010). According to this study, the officially published figure of agricultural labor share is overstated by 13.4 percentage points—that is, the share of agricultural labor is only 24.7 percent, not the 38.1 percent officially announced in 2009.[4]

Now, having laid out some basic assumptions, we can build a new series on the estimated number of agricultural laborers and their proportion of total Chinese employment, which can not only provide a better reflection on the actually occurring structural changes, but also shed light on the related reallocation of the labor force and certain policy implications (Figure 2.2).

First, we extended the estimated result of 2009 to a time series of data spanning from 1984 to 2012. To update the data for the latest years, taking 2009 as benchmark, we assumed that the estimated numbers of agricultural laborers were all 64.7 percent of the official numbers for 2010–2012. We further took 1984 as the starting year, in which the difference between

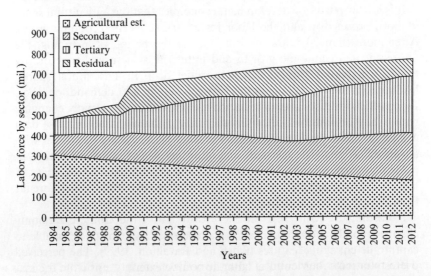

Source: National Bureau of Statistics (various years); Du and Wang (2010).

Figure 2.2   Actual distribution of the labor force among sectors

official numbers and estimated numbers began to accumulate at a constant growth rate, since the significant movement of laborers from the agricultural to the non-agricultural sectors started in that year as a result of the nationwide introduction of HRS.

Secondly, we treated the difference between the official and estimated numbers of agricultural laborers as a "residual," owing to the fact that we cannot know how the extra laborers shifted from agriculture were allocated between the secondary and tertiary sectors. In reality, such "residual" laborers can either enlarge the labor pool in the secondary and tertiary sectors in a certain proportion, as a general pattern, or return to agricultural production only in particular and specific years. For example, the latter situation occurred in the late 1980s and early 1990s, when the Chinese government implemented a macroeconomic rectification policy and dismissed tens of thousands of laborers who worked in TVEs or urban sectors, and again in the global financial crisis of 2008 and 2009, when coastal manufacturing factories were hit and a number of migrant workers were laid off temporarily.

An important implication of this residual labor force, however, is that, given present agricultural productivity, as long as the previously surplus laborers are released from the agricultural sector they are no longer in demand for farming production. Securing their employment in the non-agricultural sectors and accommodating them in urban society is therefore essential for maintaining a stable supply of labor and, as a result, sustained economic growth.

2.4   LABOR MIGRATION

The significant reduction of surplus laborers in China is the result of massive labor migration from the agricultural sectors with low productivity to the non-agricultural sectors with higher productivity, and from the underemployed rural area to urban areas of expanding employment. While most observers have highly praised the HRS for improving the effectiveness of work incentives, following the increase in production efficiency, this system had a more important effect on the peasants' reallocation of labor: namely, by engaging their enthusiasm and granting them autonomy in arranging the time, method, and content of their work. The peasant workforce's labor was thus liberated. Therefore, the introduction of the HRS reform can be viewed as both the point of departure and the basis for the current reform of worker migration policy.

Following improvements in agricultural productivity, the capacity of either cultivation or "expanded agriculture" (including forestry, animal husbandry, and/or fisheries) to absorb labor was ultimately limited. However, in the early 1980s, the government did not actively encourage labor to leave the countryside. Noting the necessity of transferring agricultural labor and the developmental potential for small rural industries in the countryside, the government promoted a mode of agricultural labor transfer known as "leaving the land but not the hometown," that is, encouraging peasants to shift out of agricultural production to employment in TVEs.

With the nationwide spread of HRS, the People's Commune system was abolished. Communes became townships (乡, *xiang*), constituting the first tier of government. Production brigades became villages (村, *cun*), constituting the basic level of autonomous peasant organization. The concept of TVEs (乡镇企业, *xiangzhen qiye*) generally refers to collectively owned enterprises at either of these levels.

In 1978, the labor force employed in commune and brigade enterprises (then analogous to TVEs) numbered 28.3 million, rising sharply to 69.8 million in 1985. In 1987, Deng Xiaoping—the architect of China's reforms—said in praise of the TVEs that he himself had never anticipated this result. In 1985, however, the 69.8 million rural people who had transferred to jobs in TVEs accounted for only 18.8 percent of a total of 370 million rural laborers, with an additional 300 million workers remaining in agriculture.

Faced with the surplus labor force seeking jobs, the government expanded the "leaving the land but not the hometown" policy in order to encourage farmers to shift to small towns. While small towns reaped the rewards of the policy, owing to their lack of jobs these same towns were ultimately unable to accommodate around 100 million surplus rural workers. Moreover, the TVEs' rapid development, given that reform in the cities and in particular in the state-owned enterprises (SOEs) had yet to get underway, was due to the pressing demand for consumer goods brought about by an increase in income levels, and the two-track system in the markets for products and production materials.

With the acceleration of urban reforms in the mid-1980s, the development of TVEs began to falter. Peasants thus began to transfer to large, medium, and small cities (as opposed to small towns) in search of non-agricultural jobs. The gradual removal of various institutional barriers was crucial to the trans-regional flow of workers. Since the 1980s, the government has gradually lifted the policy restricting the mobility of rural labor.

For example, in 1983, with the channels for transfer *in situ* of the rural labor force becoming narrower, the government began to allow peasants to engage in the long-distance transportation and sale of agricultural products, for the first time legitimizing businesses outside local residences for peasants. Controls on labor mobility were further relaxed in 1984, and workers were even encouraged to take jobs in nearby small towns. By 1988, the central government had set a precedent when it allowed peasants, prior to the abolition of the grain coupon system, to bring food supplies into the cities, to take jobs, and to set up businesses.

In the early 1990s, the Chinese leadership officially adopted the socialist market economy as its ultimate reform objective. Since then, and especially after China's entrée to the World Trade Organization (WTO), the development of labor-intensive industry in coastal areas and the expansion of urban sectors with diverse forms of ownership have generated an increasingly robust demand for laborers. Consequently, the increasing scale and scope of labor migration from rural to urban sectors and from inland to coastal areas have expanded, resulting in the now world-famous migration tide.

Along with this trend of labor market development and integration, the central government and local governments have taken a series of measures to address the increase in migration, suitably relaxing policies restricting movement (implying a gradual reform in the *hukou* system). For example, in 1992–1993, the food rationing system in urban areas was abolished, which removed the institutional barriers deterring labor mobility between rural and urban areas and among cities, and began the process of increased acceptance of rural migrant workers into cities.

Another arena for labor market development lies in the reform of urban employment policy and the labor system of SOEs. Since the mid-1990s, SOEs have gained autonomy in hiring their own employees; while enterprises are facing increasing pressure to compete, employment has become more and more market-oriented, with the gradual abolishment of the "iron rice bowl" (铁饭碗, *tie fan wan*) system of secured labor. In coping with the massive lay-off of SOEs' workers—caused by the economic downturn and rapid structural change in industry that accompanied the East Asian financial crisis of the late 1990s—the Chinese government initiated proactive employment policies, which not only promoted the reemployment of laid-off workers, but also provided impetus for labor market development. By the time the urban employment situation recovered in the early 2000s, the institutional environment of labor migration had seen a great improvement.

As a result of these institutional changes and policy adjustments, the scale of rural labor mobility has grown, developing into a "tide of migrant workers" that has caught the attention of the world. There has been no consistent official figure regarding the migration of rural workers, and scholars often roughly estimate on the basis of partial surveys. Using previous estimations, a broad account can be drawn from numerical changes

Table 2.1   Migrant workers beyond and within townships

	Migrant workers		Locally employed	
	Numbers (millions)	Growth rate (%)	Numbers (millions)	Growth rate (%)
2000	78.5	–	–	–
2001	84.0	7.0	–	–
2002	104.7	24.7	–	–
2003	113.9	8.8	–	–
2004	118.2	3.8	–	–
2005	125.8	6.4	–	–
2006	132.1	5.0	–	–
2007	137.0	3.7	–	–
2008	140.4	2.5	85.0	–
2009	145.3	3.5	84.5	-0.7
2010	153.0	5.3	88.9	5.2
2011	158.6	3.7	94.2	5.9
2012	163.4	3.0	99.3	5.4
2013	166.1	1.7	102.8	3.6
2014	168.2	1.3	105.7	2.8

Source: Rural Socio-economic Survey Team, National Bureau of Statistics of China (various years).

in inter-township labor mobility beyond township boundaries prior to 2000. In 1983, there were only 2 million migrant workers, a figure which had increased to 30 million by 1989, and 62 million by 1993, and reached 75.5 million in 2000 (Cai, 2010).

Since 2000, the National Bureau of Statistics' (NBS) annual survey has provided official numbers of migrant workers (defined as those leaving their home townships for six months or longer on an annual basis). In 2014, the total number of migrant workers amounted to 168 million. Since 2008, the NBS has also published the number of rural laborers who have non-agricultural jobs within their home townships (Table 2.1).

2.5   CONCLUSION

While the Chinese economic growth pattern demonstrates unique features, it nevertheless conveys the basic characteristics of dual economy development as conceptualized by Arthur Lewis. In the entire period since the late 1970s (when China adopted economic reform and opening-up policies), the country's rapid economic growth has been accompanied by massive labor migration from rural to urban areas, which is widely viewed as the most significant phenomenon of the present era. This is especially apparent following China's admission to the WTO. Taking advantage of its abundant labor force, China has gained an obvious comparative advantage in labor-intensive manufacturing in world trade and has accomplished successful dual economy development. The Chinese economic experience is able to function both as perfect proof of and augmentation to Lewisian theory, while the theory per se can itself extrapolate upon what China has experienced, what's currently happening vis-à-vis Chinese economic growth, and what challenges China will likely face in the future.

Across the great sweep of economic history, dual economy development is only one of the stages of development that typical countries usually undergo. As surplus labor is exhausted, this stage will be replaced by a new one—that is, neoclassical growth. Whether a country can complete the transition from dual economy development to neoclassical growth poses great challenges, some of which are universal to any country, while others are unique to China. Before turning to discussions of those challenges over the course of the next chapters, we must first examine two trends challenging labor mobility in China today.

First, although the total number of migrant workers continues to grow, the growth rate itself has tended to decrease. The annual growth rate of the number of migrant workers was 5.5 percent in 2002–2007, whereas it slowed down to an annual rate of 3.6 percent in 2007–2012, and to 1.7 percent and 1.3 percent in 2013 and 2014, respectively. There are two factors impacting the growing number of migrant workers, one positive and the other negative. While the improved institutional environment in favor of migration promotes the outflow of rural laborers, diminishing growth before 2011 and the negative growth afterwards of the working-age population restrain the potential magnitude of migrant workers.

Secondly, the overwhelming majority of migrant workers do not have an urban residence identity. By excluding migrant workers from possessing secure jobs and thereby getting equal access to social security programs, the *hukou* system still serves as an institutional obstacle deterring labor migration. That is, when admitting the diminishing amount of labor in agriculture, one has to take into account the existence of institutional factors, which tends to make premature the turning point at which any further outflow of a surplus labor force must be encouraged by wage inflation.

As labor migration slows, a dearth of migrant workers becomes apparent, first in coastal China, followed by an overall labor shortage nationwide. At the same time, the wage rates of unskilled workers will begin to increase, substantially and continuously. These phenomena mark an important turning point in China's economic development. Now that such a turning point appears as a transition phase of Lewisian dual economy development, we call it the Lewis Turning Point. The following chapters argue for the arrival of the Lewis Turning Point and its implications for China's future social and economic development.

NOTES

1. Lewis approved the categorization of two turning points and defined their properties and qualities in his later work. For convenience of discussion and for consistence between Lewis's original intention and the Fei–Ranis modified and extended model, the Lewis Turning Point is hereafter referred to as the turning point where the labor shortage and wages increase of ordinary workers occur and the commercial point as the point where the marginal products of the agricultural and modern sectors become identical. See Lewis (1972) and Ranis and Fei (1961).
2. Those who had no paid work in the week preceding the date the survey was conducted and are willing and available to take a job are defined as unemployed.
3. For a typical example of such studies, see Minami and Ma (2009).
4. By using survey data collected by the Ministry of Agriculture, Brandt and Zhu also use alternative numbers of agricultural laborers. They find that the share of agricultural labor is 26.2 percent in 2007, which is quite close to the estimate in this text. See Brandt and Zhu (2010).

REFERENCES

Brandt, Loren, and Xiaodong Zhu (2010), "Accounting for China's Growth," Working Paper No. 395, Department of Economics, University of Toronto.

Cai, Fang (2008), *Approaching a Triumphal Span: How Far Is China towards its Lewisian Turning Point?*, UNU-WIDER Research Paper No. 2008/09, Helsinki: UNU-WIDER.

Cai, Fang (2010), "The Formation and Evolution of China's Migrant Labor Policy," in Xiaobo Zhang, Shenggen Fan, and Arjan de Haan (eds.), *Narratives of Chinese Economic Reforms: How Does China Cross the River?*, Hackensack, NJ: World Scientific, pp. 71–90.

Cai, Fang, and Meiyan Wang (2008), "A Counterfactual Analysis on Unlimited Surplus Labor in Rural China," *China and World Economy*, 16 (1), 51–65.

Carter, Colin, Funing Zhong, and Fang Cai (1996), *China's Ongoing Reform of Agriculture*, San Francisco: 1990 Institute.

Chen, Shaohua, and Martin Ravallion (1999), "When Economic Reform Is Faster than Statistical Reform: Measuring and Explaining Income Inequality in Rural China," *Oxford Bulletin of Economics and Statistics*, 61 (1), 33–56.

Du, Yang, and Meiyan Wang (2010), "New Estimates of Surplus Rural Labor Force and Its Implications," *Journal of Guangzhou University*, social science edn., 9 (4), 17–24.

Hansen, Gary, and Edward Prescott (2002), "Malthus to Solow," *American Economic Review*, 92 (4), 1205–1217.

Johnson, D. Gale (2002), "Can Agricultural Labor Adjustment Occur Primarily through Creation of Rural Non-Farm Jobs in China?," *Urban Studies*, 39 (12), 2163–2174.

Lewis, Arthur (1954), "Economic Development with Unlimited Supply of Labor," *Manchester School*, 22 (2), 139–191.

Lewis, Arthur (1972), "Reflections on Unlimited Labour," in Luis Eugenio Di Marco (ed.), *International Economics and Development*, New York: Academic Press, pp. 75–96.

Lin, Justin Yifu (1992), "Rural Reforms and Agricultural Growth in China," *American Economic Review*, 82 (1), 34–51.

Liu, Jianjin (2002), "Basic Situation of Rural Employment in China," in Fang Cai (ed.), *Problems and Solutions of Employment in Urban and Rural China*, Reports on China's Population and Labor No. 3, Beijing: Social Sciences Academic Press, pp. 48–76.

Minami, Ryoshi, and Xinxin Ma (2009), "The Turning Point of Chinese Economy: Compared with Japanese Experience," *Asian Economics*, 50 (12), 2–20.

National Bureau of Statistics (various years), *China Statistical Yearbook [year]*, Beijing: China Statistics Press.

Ranis, Gustav (2004), "Arthur Lewis' Contribution to Development Thinking and Policy," Yale University Economic Growth Center Discussion Paper No. 891.

Ranis, Gustav, and John C.H. Fei (1961), "A Theory of Economic Development," *American Economic Review*, 51 (4), 533–565.

Roberts, Kenneth, Rachel Connelly, Zhenming Xie, and Zhenzhen Zheng (2004), "Patterns of Temporary Labor Migration of Rural Women from Anhui and Sichuan," *China Journal*, 52, 49–70.

Rostow, Walt (1991), *The Stages of Economic Growth: A Non-Communist Manifesto*, New York: Cambridge University Press.

Rural Socio-economic Survey Team, National Bureau of Statistics of China (various years), *China Yearbook of Rural Household Survey*, Beijing: China Statistics Press.

Taylor, Jeffrey (1993), "Rural Employment Trends and the Legacy of Surplus Labor, 1978–1989," in Yak-yeow Kueh and Robert Ash (eds.), *Economic Trends in Chinese Agriculture: The Impact of Post-Mao Reforms*, New York: Oxford University Press, pp. 273–310.

3.   The Lewis Turning Point

> [T]he thought is always prior to the fact; all the facts of history preexist in the mind as laws. Each law in turn is made by circumstances predominant, and the limits of nature give power to but one at a time. (Emerson, "History")

While the very first indication of the change in China's stage of economic development is the arrival of the Lewis Turning Point,[1] the debate over whether or not it has arrived in China at all remains unsettled. With time, however, public and academic opinion is increasingly swinging in favor of a positive affirmation, but, even though China's labor shortage and the wage inflation of ordinary workers have proven to be both undeniable and irreversible, scholars and policy researchers still disagree on the implications of such a change in the development stage.[2]

Some economists additionally reject the Lewisian theory of dual economy development in general, and further question its applicability to the Chinese economy in particular. For example, some scholars suggest that, in studying the transition of the Chinese economy, an alternative approach—that is, the neoclassical theory of economic development—should be used instead. Such studies not only criticize the Lewisian hypothesis of "zero marginal product of labor," but also deny the existence of surplus labor in the Chinese economy (Ge and Yang, 2011). The previous chapter has already responded to these issues. Any observers who admit that economic development in China can be adequately characterized by the Lewis-type dual economy will agree that it is important to identify a specific, critical period of time as the Lewis Turning Point, during which certain fundamental changes occur as recognizable phases of dual economy development.

In China, the arrival of the Lewis Turning Point is related to and intertwined with the following facts (Cai, 2010). First, the demographic transition has reached that phase at which—as a result of a constant decline in fertility—the working-age population between 15 and 59 peaked in 2010 and started to shrink afterwards, which resulted in a labor shortage throughout the country. Second, rapid economic growth has created tens of thousands of jobs, absorbing rural surplus laborers and reemploying laid-off urban workers. Such economic growth and employment expansion continue to generate strong demand for a large labor force. Third, as a result of the growth in demand for labor exceeding the growth of the labor supply, the labor market profile has changed fundamentally—that is, the marginal productivity of agricultural labor is no longer zero, and marginal productivities of labor and the wage rates of workers between the agricultural and the non-agricultural sectors have tended to converge. In short, the Chinese economy can no longer be characterized by an unlimited supply of labor.

Leaving the population-related issues to later chapters, this chapter argues for the arrival of the Lewis Turning Point and its resulting challenges by indicating a series of new phenomena, for example the alteration of the relationship between the supply of and demand for labor, trends in the substitution of capital for labor in agriculture, a strong demand for migrant workers in urban sectors, an increase in wages across all sectors, and the convergence of wages between sectors and groups of workers.

3.1 LABOR SHORTAGE

As early as 2004, an apparent labor shortage was noted in the Pearl River Delta region, where outward-oriented, labor-intensive enterprises and migrant workers are concentrated. Employers were surprised to find at this time that they were running into real trouble as a result of the difficulty in recruiting unskilled workers compared to previously. At first, limited by the conventional wisdom that there was an inexhaustible pool of surplus labor in agriculture, most observers hardly believed that such a phenomenon could last long, just as some scholars argued that the labor shortage would be a temporary phenomenon, suggesting that the *hukou* system impeded the full mobility of migrant workers without going so far as to imply that the pool of surplus labor was in any way shrinking. Instead of disappearing, however, the labor shortage spread successively to the Yangtze River Delta region, then regions traditionally known for providing surplus labor, and eventually the whole country.

Since 2004, the media, investment economists, and even local government officials have paid close attention to the labor shortage, indicating that those concerned with a changing labor market and its inevitable consequence—an increase in labor costs—are much more impressible than many macroeconomists. While within scholarly circles the simple question of whether or not there is a persistent labor shortage is still being debated, it is widely known among managers and even among local officials that recruiting workers has become more difficult than attracting investment. If one considers how painful it is for government officials tasked with attracting a certain investment quota in the first place, it's not difficult to imagine the gravity of such a statement.

In business, the phenomenon of this widespread labor shortage has translated into underproduction by enterprises, operational difficulties caused by an increase in labor costs, and the industrial relocation of labor-intensive manufacturing from coastal China to central and western regions, or even neighboring countries. Even during 2008–2009, when the global financial crisis hit the Chinese economy, the labor shortage was only temporarily eased and quickly reemerged as soon as the economy recovered.

In the first half of 2008, despite the consecutive appreciation of the renminbi, soaring prices of raw materials, and an increase in labor costs that caused operational difficulties in enterprises engaged in exportation along the coastal areas of China, the focus of China's macroeconomic policy was to prevent inflation and economic overheating prior to August of that year. In the first nine months of 2008, 15 000 small and medium-sized enterprises—mainly producers of labor-intensive goods such as garments, textiles, electronic components, and plastic products—shut down in Guangdong province. At the time, eastern coastal China, of which Guangdong makes up the overwhelming bulk, contained 60 percent of China's total GDP, 91 percent of its exports, and one-third of all migrant workers. The situation there, therefore, could well represent the severity of the macroeconomy of the country as a whole.

The negative impacts of the global financial crisis on the Chinese economy became clearly visible in August 2008, when migrant workers suffered a severe employment shock. The orientation of the macroeconomic policy began to turn towards "maintaining growth and curbing inflation." In the second half of 2008 and first half of 2009, however, the impacts of the financial crisis spread throughout China, hiking up the unemployment rate. Although the rate of urban-registered unemployment was 4.2 percent in 2008 and 4.3 percent in 2009 (only 0.2 percentage points and 0.3 percentage points, respectively, higher than those of 2007), those figures were still the highest since 2003. More strikingly, around the period of Chinese New Year, a massive flood of migrant workers returned to their home villages. According to a survey conducted by the National Bureau of Statistics, 70 million migrants returned home before the 2009 Spring Festival. Among those returning migrants, 12 million returned because of factors related to the financial crisis, such as the shuttering of enterprises, layoffs, not being able to find jobs, and low incomes, making up 17 percent of the total.

Not long after the Chinese New Year (in early 2009), however, another official survey showed that 95 percent of these migrants had returned to the cities, and, surprisingly, 97 percent of the migrant workers who returned to the cities had found jobs. Furthermore, the authorities announced that the total number of migrant workers in urban areas had increased from 140 million in 2008 to 150 million in September 2009, the biggest jump in six years. As early as mid-2009, the concerns over the labor market had once again shifted to a migrant labor shortage.

Incorporating a unique Chinese institution—namely, the *hukou* system—into our analysis, we can gain a better understanding of the labor market phenomenon during the financial crisis. The easiest explanation is that the financial crisis caused the slowdown of the Chinese economy, in turn giving rise to cyclical unemployment. What's unique is that migrant workers, almost alone, bore the consequence of the shock to the labor market, since the cost of firing migrant workers was relatively low (as most of them had neither a local *hukou* nor a work contract). While *hukou* regulation is no longer able to restrict migrants from residing and working in cities, the lack of access to social security and locally provided employment assistance made it difficult for the laid-off migrants to stay in cities seeking another job. As the Chinese New Year season arrived, it was natural for them to return to their home villages.

Although the *hukou* system served as the institutional root cause for the vulnerability of migrant workers in the labor market, the long-term trends controlling labor's supply and demand eventually stabilized after the short-term impact of the financial crisis was over. When the Chinese economy recovered in the second half of 2009, the phenomenon of a shortage of migrant workers quickly reemerged, and a general labor shortage has never disappeared entirely from the country since then. It can be expected that, while the labor shortage will persist for a certain period of time, migrant workers' suffering from cyclical unemployment and shortages of migrant workers will alternately occur as the macroeconomy experiences ongoing boom-and-bust cycles.

3.2 THE CHANGING PATTERN OF LABOR DEMANDS

Let us further discuss the relationship between long-term trends in the labor market and short-term employment shock. Migrant workers, literally called "farmers-turned-workers" in Chinese, originate from surplus labor in rural areas. In other words, they are not wanted in agricultural production and other rural sectors in the first place. In addition, the changed labor market makes it impossible for migrant workers to return to rural jobs. What follows will illustrate these changes and consequences in detail.

The pattern of agricultural production has changed in response to China's massive and unremitting outflow of laborers. In considering what determines the pattern and direction of technological changes in agriculture, economists have theorized about induced technological change, given that the relative prices of production factors reflect their relative scarcity (Hayami and Ruttan, 1980). This theory asserts that technological change in agriculture tends to be of the land-saving type if arable land is scarcer than labor, but the labor-saving type if labor is scarcer than land. Therefore, under conditions of an unlimited supply of labor, the existence of surplus laborers in agriculture is not conducive to the advancement of labor-saving technology, and vice versa. These Chinese experiences serve as proof of theoretical predictions such as the pattern of technological change in agriculture having shifted from biological technology aiming to enhance the productivity of land to mechanization that aims to increase the productivity of labor.

In response to labor shortages in rural areas and an increase in agricultural labor costs caused by massive, unremitting labor migration, labor inputs have decreased and physical capital inputs have, conversely, significantly increased in agricultural production. For example, in the period from 2003 to 2009, the ratio of physical capital input to labor input went up by 64.4 percent in rice production, 41.2 percent in corn production, and 72.9 percent in wheat production, all as a result of the substitution of capital for labor.

This mass outflow and the corresponding increase in labor costs have accelerated agricultural mechanization and pushed a transformation of agricultural technological change from the labor-use type to the labor-saving type, exemplified by the changes taking place in agricultural mechanization. During the three decades of economic reform in China, the total power of agricultural machinery has strengthened, and its growth has shown no sign of decline in recent years. More notable is the changed composition of different-sized agricultural tractors and tractor-towing machinery. Although there is no clear-cut distinction between the utilization of machinery for the purposes of conserving the labor force and for improving the quality of cultivation, large and medium-sized tractors and towing machinery can roughly be viewed as labor-saving technology, while small-sized tractors and towing machinery may be considered land-saving technology. The shift in the relative proportion of different sizes of machinery to the overall number of tractors and related machines visibly demonstrates the new trends in agricultural technological change that have been introduced by China's labor shortage.

In the period between 1978 and 1998, when there was a surplus of labor in agriculture, the annual growth in the use of large and medium-sized tractors was 2 percent, while that of small-sized tractors was 11.3 percent. In the period 1998–2010, as the labor force shifted from the agricultural to the non-agricultural sectors and a stronger demand for labor-saving technology emerged, the use of large and medium-sized tractors increased by 13.0 percent annually, while that of small-sized tractors fell to 4.6 percent. The changes in the growth rates of different sizes of tractor-towing machinery indicate a similar trend, with the annual growth rate of large and medium-sized tractor-towing machinery increasing from zero in the period 1978–1998 to 14.5 percent in 1998–2010, whereas the annual growth rate of small tractor-towing machinery declined from 12.1 percent to only 6.2 percent in the same period.

It is increasingly difficult for younger generations of migrants (who make up an increasing percentage of the migratory workforce) to go back to agricultural jobs. In China, migrant workers who were born after 1980 are considered the "new generation" of migrant workers. In 2012, this new generation made up 61.6 percent of 163 million migrant workers, and thus represented a major percentage of the migrant group as a whole. According to a 2010 survey (abbreviated as CULS) conducted by the Institute of Population and Labor Economics, Chinese Academy of Social Sciences in Shanghai, Wuhan, Shenyang, Fuzhou, and Xi'an, 32.8 percent of rural-to-urban migrant workers aged between 16 and 30 lived in cities and towns before they turned 16 years old, and 38.4 percent went to primary school in cities and towns (Table 3.1). Having grown up and been educated in cities and towns, they cannot and do not intend to farm, resulting in an irreversible rural-to-urban labor migration.

Table 3.1   Features of the new generation of migrant workers

	Age		
	16–30	31–40	41–50
Where the migrant workers lived before age 16:			
Municipality	2.9	1.0	0.5
County seat	17.4	12.6	11.9
Town	12.5	11.3	12.9
Rural areas	67.2	75.1	74.7
Total	100	100	100
Where the migrant workers went to primary school:			
Municipality	4.2	1.2	0.5
County seat	17.3	12.4	12.3
Town	16.9	15.4	14.4
Rural areas	61.6	71.0	72.8
Total	100	100	100

Source: Calculated based on CULS data.

For a long time, researchers took for granted that agriculture was a reservoir of surplus laborers, a viewpoint supported by theoretical assumptions and empirical studies in development economics. In practice, every time the non-agricultural sectors took a hit—followed by the subsequent return of migrant workers—it was agriculture that served as a reservoir of returned laborers and, therefore, a social stabilizer. As China passes through the Lewis Turning Point, however, agriculture will no longer provide a pool of surplus labor, labor migration will no longer exhibit a come-and-go pattern, and so theories must be updated and policy revised.

Michael Todaro is widely known for his profound research on internal migration within developing countries, with his most influential theory being the so-called "Todaro paradox" (Todaro, 1969; Harris and Todaro, 1970). He argues that it is the differential of expected wages between the rural and urban sectors that encourages rural workers to migrate. By his definition, the expected urban wage is the nominal urban wage adjusted by the unemployment rate. Thus, the paradox is this: efforts made by the government to reduce the unemployment rate may actually increase the difference in expected wages between the rural and urban sectors and thus motivate additional migration, which in turn gives rise to more unemployment. A further implication is that any efforts made towards improving the status of migrants working in urban areas may encourage more migration, thereby decreasing the potential for migrants to find employment and residency in urban areas.

The theoretical "Todaro paradox" has accordingly been translated into a "Todaro dogma," which views labor migration as a pattern of "come-and-go" rather than as a process of permanent settlement, and thus policies aiming to control and even restrict the process of rural-to-urban migration are regularly implemented.[3]

The Todaro paradox rests on the assumption that there is no unemployment in the agricultural sector—namely, that agriculture is a pool for collecting the surplus labor force. Correspondingly, the Todaro dogma tends to mitigate the social risks potentially raised by labor migration, through balancing the push-and-pull forces between the rural and urban sectors, especially by strengthening the role of rural areas in the absorption of surplus workers. From the viewpoint of economic development, such an assumption is insufficient to conducting a dynamic analysis, because it fails to take into account the fact that the agricultural share of employment declines over time in the development of a dual economy and, as a result, such an economy will reach its Lewis Turning Point sooner or later.

Based on a survey conducted in the early 1990s, researchers found that, whenever urban unemployment increases and job growth slows down, migrant workers choose to return to agricultural production so as to withstand the employment shock and to make up for any reduction in income (Zhang et al., 2001). Linking the employment cycles in urban areas and policy preferences of municipal governments with migrant workers, however, another study finds that migrants are forced to return, as opposed to returning voluntarily. That is, when urban employment slumps, municipal governments are apt to implement policies restricting migrants' abilities to reside and work in cities, resulting in the involuntary return of migrants to rural areas (Cai et al., 2001).

If, before the turning point arrived and with agriculture still the reservoir of surplus labor, conventional policy efforts were made to keep the balance of the pushing-and-pulling forces that affect migration between rural and urban areas so that rural jobs—particularly those engaged with agricultural production—could play a role in resolving social risks, when agriculture no longer serves as the reservoir of surplus labor and labor migration no longer functions as part of a "come-and-go" pattern, such a dogma would lose its basis for existence. That is, the conventional policies controlling labor migration based on the "Todaro dogma" can be seen to be outdated.

Urban demand for migrant workers has become increasingly unrelenting. As the result of China's demographic transition, during which the age structure of urban populations has changed faster than that of rural areas, economic growth in urban sectors depends heavily on labor supply through migration. And yet, while the total number of migrant workers from rural to urban areas who remain in place for six months or longer continues to grow, the growth rate itself decreases over time. In the meantime, the total number of urban employed continues to increase at a constant rate of growth, thanks to the influx of migrants. In 2012, over one-third of urban employees were rural migrants and, in fact, the dominant group in certain sectors such as construction, were migrant workers. In any event, urban sectors can no longer afford to lose such a large proportion of their workforce. Migrant workers are, therefore, no longer a reserve labor force, but rather the pillar of the urban labor market.

Many researchers and observers have the impression that the expansion of employment has not kept pace with economic growth—or "growth without employment"—in China, mainly because they are confused by the employment statistics, which are typically both incomplete and inconsistent. Such an impression comes from omissions (and thus underreporting) of several important employment groups by the official statistical sources.

First, employees who migrate from rural to urban areas—namely, what we call migrant workers—are not fully included in urban employment statistics. The current official statistics of urban employment come from two sources. The first source is the reporting system, which requires all economic units to report their employees. Since most migrant workers work as casual workers or agent workers, in most cases, they are not considered by their employers to be formal employees and are therefore not officially reported. As for those who are employed by small private businesses or self-employed, it is even more difficult for them to be officially included in the statistical system. The second source for official statistics is the household-based labor sampling survey conducted in urban areas. As migrants do not have urban *hukou* and live without a fixed abode, they are typically not selected as representative samples in this type of survey.

In 2012, there were 163 million migrant workers, with 95 percent living and working in cities—a figure calculated as part of a separate survey aimed at monitoring migrant workers. As this statistical information has no connection to or consistency with urban employment statistical systems, even such a sizable migrant group is missing from employment statistics and forgotten by observers.

Second, a large portion of new entrants and reemployed workers have primarily taken informal jobs since the late 1990s, and they, like migrant workers, are likely to be missed by the urban employment reporting system. By comparing the household-based survey with reported statistics, we can estimate the number of those missing workers—that is, they are the difference between the disparate numbers claimed by the two statistical systems. Since we cannot break them down by region or by sector, any efforts toward aggregate analysis tend to omit this group of employees, who accounted for one-fourth of total urban resident employees in 2012.

Third, those who take non-agricultural jobs within their home townships are often out of sight of researchers and observers. Although this group has not grown in recent years, given their absolute size—roughly 100 million in 2012—such a significant portion of the workforce should not be overlooked. In addition, the present statistics on migrant workers are mostly based on migration across townships for durations of six months or longer; thus, those who work outside their home townships for fewer than six months a year are also absent from the official statistics.

Merging various statistical sources, we try to compose a complete dataset reflecting the supply of and demand for labor in urban areas by taking the annual increase in the number of people between ages 15 and 59 on the supply side and the annual increase in the number of urban workers on the demand side. Since the number of agricultural workers has fallen, while that of non-agricultural workers in rural areas is not expected to expand, we may treat the increase in the number of urban workers (migrant workers included) as representative of the magnitude of the overall labor demand in the Chinese economy.

According to estimates made on the basis of micro data from the 2009 official survey on urban labor, only 42 million (or 12.5 percent) of the 333 million urban employees recorded by the National Bureau of Statistics (NBS) were migrant workers. This can be used to estimate the total number of urban employees—namely, the sum of resident workers with local *hukou* and migrant workers without urban *hukou*—while eliminating an overlap in figures between the two groups. As mass rural–urban migration has only become a notable phenomenon since the beginning of the twenty-first century, we can assume that the inclusion of migrants in urban statistics—namely, the 12.5 percent in 2009—has gradually accumulated since 2000, and that the proportion of migrant workers recorded in urban employment statistics increased to 30.8 percent in 2014. Based on the above knowledge, we are in the position now to build two datasets of complete urban employment without any overlap by eliminating migrants from urban employment statistics to get purely residential employment and, by eliminating rural-to-rural migration to get pure migrant employment in the urban labor market, to compare them with the working-age population aged 15 to 59, which we take as representative of the labor supply (Table 3.2).

As shown in Table 3.2, urban employment (labor demand) grew faster than the working-age population (labor supply) from 2001 to 2014. Data-based trends also indicate that the ratio of the labor supply to demand for labor increased over time. Given factors which tend to reduce labor force participation rates (that is, the ratio of the economically active population to the overall working-age population)—such as the relative constancy of the unemployment rate, the expansion of higher education, and the official retirement age for females being 50 to 55 years—labor shortages serve as a factor that significantly increases labor force participation and largely offsets opposing unemployment or non-participation.

3.3   WAGE INCREASES AND WAGE CONVERGENCE

Based on the Japanese experience, Minami (2010)—known for recognizing the Lewis Turning Point in Japan—suggests five characteristics of wage-related change as criteria to test the Lewis Turning Point. That is, if the Lewis Turning Point arrives, one can empirically observe that (1) wages in the subsistence sector equal the marginal product of labor, (2) wages in the subsistence sector become determined by the marginal product of labor, (3) wages in the subsistence sector indicate a change from a constant (or slowly increasing) trend to a rapidly increasing trend, (4) wage differentials between unskilled and skilled workers tend to close,

Table 3.2   Increases in demand for and supply of labor in urban China

	Urban resident workers		Urban migrant workers		Working-age population	
	Numbers (millions)	Growth rate %	Numbers (millions)	Growth rate %	Numbers (millions)	Growth rate %
2001	232	2.9	81	7.0	844	−0.1
2002	239	2.9	101	24.7	859	1.8
2003	246	2.7	109	8.8	872	1.6
2004	251	2.4	114	3.8	886	1.5
2005	257	2.1	121	6.4	900	1.6
2006	275	7.0	127	5.0	907	0.8
2007	283	2.8	131	3.7	912	0.6
2008	288	1.8	135	2.5	917	0.5
2009	292	1.4	140	3.5	920	0.3
2010	295	1.2	147	5.3	939	2.1
2011	295	−0.1	152	3.7	939	−0.1
2012	291	−1.2	157	3.0	936	−0.3
2013	284	−2.5	159	1.7	932	−0.4
2014	272	−4.2	161	1.3	928	−0.5

Source: Employment data come from the author's own calculation based on National Bureau of Statistics (various years), Rural Socio-economic Survey Team, National Bureau of Statistics of China (various years), and Division of Population and Employment Statistics, National Bureau of Statistics (various years); data on the working-age population come from China Development Research Foundation (2012).

and (5) there is a trend that the elasticity of the labor supply shifts from being indefinite to being between zero and infinity.

It is obvious that Minami set those criteria to test the commercial turning point rather than the Lewis Turning Point. He himself agrees that the first criterion is too strict to directly test and that empirical works should be devoted to the other criteria instead. Since we intend to define the Lewis Turning Point in a different way, this chapter focuses on discussing the third and fourth criteria—namely, the increase in ordinary workers' wages and the wage convergence between unskilled and skilled workers.

In a dual economy characterized by an unlimited supply of labor, the wage rate of ordinary workers typically remains constant at a subsistence level above the marginal productivity of labor in agriculture.[4] The reallocation of the agricultural surplus of labor to the non-agricultural sectors in China began with the introduction of the household responsibility system in the farming sector, and has made extraordinary progress as the institutional barriers deterring labor mobility were eliminated in the urban labor market. In the entire 35 years of the reform period, rural surplus labor has shifted from the agricultural to the rural non-agricultural sectors, and a mass migration ensued from rural to urban sectors and from central and western regions to coastal regions.

Since labor policies have become more tolerant toward labor mobility across regions and sectors, migrant workers have become a significant component of employees and residents in urban areas, which significantly mitigates the extent of the labor surplus in the agricultural sector. Meanwhile, China's demographic transition has reached the point at which the increase in the working-age population became negative. Given the continuously increasing demand for labor, the growth of labor demand exceeds the growth of labor supply.

As a result, labor shortages, especially shortages of migrant workers, initiated in the coastal areas in 2004, subsequently became widespread throughout the country. As can theoretically be expected, the wages of migrant workers have substantially increased since then. The changing relationship between supply of and demand for labor is bound to change the nature of the Chinese economy. That is, as the marginal product of labor in agriculture starts to increase, the wage rate is no longer determined by the subsistence level but is instead determined by the labor market situation. The property of an unlimited supply of labor, by which Lewis characterizes dual economy development in his works, cannot perfectly characterize the Chinese economy anymore.

To illustrate the new trend governing unskilled workers' wages, this section explores three selected categories of wage data. Instead of using aggregate data on the urban sector as normally presented in statistical yearbooks, we have utilized data on wages in those sectors employing mainly unskilled and semi-skilled workers, the wages of migrant workers, and the wages of agricultural workers (Figure 3.1). The reason is twofold: first, urban employees, particularly in the state sector, are more or less protected in terms of wage determination, with an over-aggregation of data on wages in these formal sectors; thus the wage movement in these sectors is less representative than that available for unskilled workers. Secondly, regular statistics on wages often omit the wages of informal urban workers and migrant workers, so there is a need to seek out the wages of migrant workers as a proxy for the wages of unskilled workers. In what follows, we explain their sources and depict their changing trends.

First, the change in migrants' wages must be investigated, statistics for which come from the NBS survey monitoring migrants. Although regular systematic data on migrants' wages only became available after 2001, different sources provided evidence that the wage rates of migrant workers had been stagnant for many years before surging in 2004. In the period between 2004 and 2014, the real wages of migrant workers grew at an

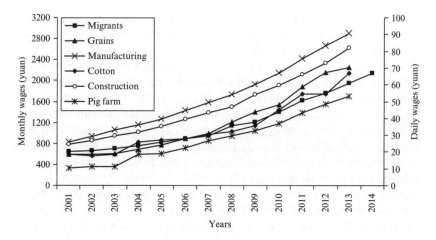

Note: All wages are based on a 1998 constant price.

Source: Daily wages in grains, cotton, and pig farms with over 50 pigs are from National Development and Reform Commission (various years); monthly wages in manufacturing and construction are from National Bureau of Statistics and Ministry of Human Resources and Social Security (various years); monthly wages of migrant workers are from Rural Socio-economic Survey Team, National Bureau of Statistics of China (various years).

Figure 3.1   Wage trends in selected sectors

annual rate of 11 percent. Wages did not stop growing even during the financial crisis period from 2008 to 2009, because the Chinese economy had recovered rapidly as a result of the government instigating a massive stimulus package. Apart from the NBS source shown in Figure 3.1, there are other surveys and reports asserting even higher and faster levels of growth of migrants' wages. According to a survey conducted by the People's Bank of China, for example, the average wage of migrant workers increased by 17.8 percent in real terms in 2009 (Department of Survey and Statistics, People's Bank of China, 2010), with the biggest surge in migrants' wages—21.2 percent of real growth—occurring in 2011.

Secondly, we must examine the wage trends in selected non-agricultural sectors. Data regarding wages by sector come from the reporting system of enterprises, which reflects both the level and the dynamism of employees' wages in the formal sectors. In Figure 3.1, we selected manufacturing and construction, in which a relatively larger number of unskilled and semi-skilled workers are employed, to show wage changes. From 2004 to 2011, real annual growth rates in these two sectors were 11.2 and 11.0 percent respectively, indicating that the increase in wages of ordinary urban workers kept pace with that of migrant workers.

Finally, we can observe trends in the wages of paid workers in the major agricultural sectors. The same causes that have triggered a sharp increase in the wages of unskilled workers in the non-agricultural sectors and a reduction of surplus laborers in rural areas have resulted in a labor shortage in key agricultural sectors, and have in turn caused a dramatic increase in the daily wage rates of paid agricultural workers since 2004. While waged employment has just become widespread in the agricultural sectors as a result of labor shortages in recent years, the National Development and Restructuring Commission has long collected data concerning the wages of paid workers in agriculture, allowing us to distinguish labor income from the gross earnings of farms. From 2004 to 2011, the annual growth rate of real daily wages was 15.5 percent in grain production, 11.3 percent in cotton production, and 12.8 percent in pig farms (those with a size of 50 or more pigs).

The wages of ordinary workers are, in essence, determined differently in pre- and post-Lewis Turning Point periods. In a typical dual economy characterized by an unlimited labor supply, the wage rate for migrant workers moving from agricultural to non-agricultural sectors in urban areas is not determined by the marginal product of labor. When passing through the Lewis Turning Point, however, the changing conditions governing labor supply and demand begin to affect the wages for various groups, that is, a relatively unchanged scarcity of skilled workers yet an increasing scarcity of unskilled workers. The determinant for the wage rate of migrants begins to shift from subsistence wages to the marginal productivity of labor. Hence, wage convergence is expected to take place during such a transitional period.

Struggling with the contradiction between China's actual observed labor shortage and the conventional wisdom regarding the unlimited labor supply of such a populous country as China, many researchers must alter their preexisting hypotheses—that is, instead of admitting a labor shortage, they maintain that there is a shortage of skills. The fact is, however, that the new phenomenon in the labor market is due to nothing but a shortage of unskilled workers and, after controlling for differences in human capital, can be evidenced by the trends of wage convergence between skilled and unskilled workers.

In what follows, we take the changing trend in the wages of migrant workers as an example showing wage convergence, as there are significant differentials both in human capital among migrant workers and between the wages of migrant workers and urban resident workers.

Although migrant workers as a whole represent unskilled workers, variations exist among migrant workers in terms of human capital. For example, among the 163 million migrant workers making up the workforce

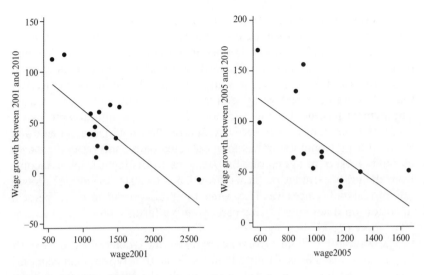

Source: Cai and Du (2011).

Figure 3.2   Unskilled workers have faster wage growth

in 2012, 11.5 percent were primary schooled or illiterate, 62 percent had finished junior high school, 12.8 percent had finished senior high school, and 13.7 percent had graduated from a technical secondary school or above (Household Survey Office, National Bureau of Statistics, 2013). In other words, three-fourths of migrant workers are unskilled workers with a junior high school diploma or below.

Migrants would be unable to catch up with local workers' wage rates unless those unskilled workers were to experience faster wage growth. Migrants' wage growth by educational group is observed in Figure 3.2, where each dot represents real wage growth for a given group of workers with the same educational attainment; the horizontal axis is the wage level in the base year (2001 and 2005 respectively), and the vertical axis is the wage growth from the base year to 2010. Although workers with higher educational attainments earn higher wages across all three years—namely, 2001, 2005, and 2010, when the surveys (CULS) were conducted—the figures clearly display the unusual circumstance in which workers with less education and lower wages in the base years nevertheless reported faster wage growth during the subsequent period. As a result, an analysis based on the same data indicates that the Gini coefficient for migrant workers alone has decreased, from 0.396 in 2001 to 0.334 in 2005 and 0.319 in 2010.

Compared to urban resident workers, migrant workers have lower levels of education and less work experience. For example, CULS data show that, in 2010, migrant workers had received 1.56 fewer years of schooling than urban resident workers, and 5.6 years fewer of working experience. Given these statistics, the fact that the wages of migrant workers grew more rapidly than did those of their urban counterparts indicates a convergence of wages between skilled and unskilled workers.

What's more, many scholars have further observed that the wage rate of migrant workers has grown faster than that of college graduates in the urban labor market, another convergence of wages between skilled and unskilled workers that is consistent with the arrival of the Lewis Turning Point. However, this phenomenon is complicated and deserves further discussion in later chapters.

3.4 CONCLUSION

Whether China has, in fact, passed through the Lewis Turning Point remains a point of debate. For a while, I myself only vaguely foresaw an approaching turning point (Cai, 2008). As evidence accumulates, however, I—along with an increasing number of economists, entrepreneurs, and government officials—have become more confident that the Lewis Turning Point has arrived for the Chinese economy. Opposing views remain, however, ranging from those based on a demonstration of the existence of surplus laborers and denying any increase in migrants' wages to questioning the applicability of the Lewis theory to China in general. Apart from a lack of direct observation and personal experience with Chinese economic reality or an in-depth comprehension of China's statistics, that which Galbraith labeled "conventional wisdom" prevents many people from recognizing the newly emergent phenomena of the Chinese economy, which are vital to formulating economic policies.

As has been repeatedly demonstrated by economic development and the history of economics overall, healthy and serious confrontational questioning is a necessary force driving the intense developmental study currently and historically taking place on the issue of economic turning points. The discussions in this chapter are intended to convince fellow economists and lay observers that, given the definition promoted by Lewis and his adherents and provided that a labor shortage and resultant wage inflation can be observed, it is ultimately impossible to deny the arrival of the Lewis Turning Point.

As for the question of when, if pressed to indicate a single year as the turning point, 2004 is the most likely point. In addition to the extant facts in the labor market at that time defining the turning point, the logic of political economy also supports such a supposition. In my 2003 paper (Cai, 2003)—based on a political economy that suggests that, once the political cost of maintaining a certain public policy becomes larger than the political cost of changing the policy, policy change tends to occur as a matter of course—I predicted that, when the income gap between rural and urban areas grew to the level of the year when economic reform was initiated in rural areas, a critical point of institutional change would have been reached. In 2004, the ratio of urban household income to rural household income increased to 2.4, exactly the same level as in 1979 (adjusted by constant price). The reasoning for this logic can be approached from the following three aspects.

First, a noticeable shortage of migrant workers first appeared in coastal areas in 2004, and quickly spread throughout China. Meanwhile, 2004 became the dividing point between stagnation and the rise of ordinary workers' wages, which, by definition, is the indication of the Lewis Turning Point.

Secondly, since the turning point is not only a phenomenon of the labor market but also linked to patterns of economic development, a host of changes may be observed in the economy. Thus 2004 served as a turning point that witnessed the critical alteration of certain socioeconomic indicators. For example, as a result of labor shortages and wage inflation, the capital–labor ratio increased dramatically, the adoption in agricultural production of technological advances began to significantly affect labor, and the income gaps among regions and population groups began to grow increasingly narrow.

Finally, government policies in regard to income distribution and redistribution, the social security system, minimum wage policies, and the enforcement of labor laws increasingly grew to favor ordinary workers and low-income households. Many important policy changes, including several dramatic events, took place in 2004 as part of both the country's central and local governments' response to trends in social and economic developments.

While debating the Lewis Turning Point, some scholars suggest using the phrase "Lewis Turning Period" instead of "Lewis Turning Point," so that the features defining China's regional heterogeneity and characteristics in long-term economic development can be captured. Whereas the following chapter is intended to depict such a turning period, it will change nothing in understanding Chinese economic development and its change in stages.

NOTES

1. For the scholarly definition, see Ranis and Fei (1961) and Lewis (1972).
2. Two English-language journals have published special issues that include articles from both sides of the Lewis Turning Point debate in China, in which readers can find representative papers regarding the issues. See *China Economic Journal* (2010), 3 (4) and *China Economic Review* (2011), 22 (4).
3. For an explanation of the Todaro dogma and the policy implications of the Todaro paradox, see Todaro (1985, chap. 9).
4. Wage constancy is only an abstract expression in theory. Because the subsistence standard changes over time, the subsistence wage rate changes as well, which has no nexus, however, with the marginal productivity of labor.

REFERENCES

Cai, Fang (2003), "The Rural–Urban Income Gap and Critical Point of Institutional Change," *Social Sciences in China*, 5, 16–25.

Cai, Fang (2008), *Approaching a Triumphal Span: How Far Is China towards its Lewisian Turning Point?*, UNU-WIDER Research Paper No. 2008/09, Helsinki: UNU-WIDER.

Cai, Fang (2010), "Demographic Transition, Demographic Dividend, and the Lewis Turning Point in China," *China Economic Journal*, 3 (2), 107–119.

Cai, Fang, and Yang Du (2011), "Wages Increase, Wages Convergence, and Lewis Turning Point in China," *China Economic Review*, 22 (4), 601–610.

Cai, Fang, Yang Du, and Meiyan Wang (2001), "Household Registration System and Labor Market Protection," *Economic Research Journal*, 12, 41–49.

China Development Research Foundation (2012), *China Development Report, 2012*, Beijing: China Development Publishing House.

Department of Survey and Statistics, People's Bank of China (2010), "The 5th Monitoring Report on Migrant Workers," in Fang Cai (ed.), *Labor Market Challenges in the Post-Crisis Era*, Reports on China's Population and Labor No. 11, Beijing: Social Sciences Academic Press, pp. 35–47.

Division of Population and Employment Statistics, National Bureau of Statistics (various years), *China Population Yearbook [year]*, Beijing: China Statistics Press.

Ge, Suqin, and Dennis Tao Yang (2011), "Labor Market Developments in China: A Neoclassical View," *China Economic Review*, 22 (4), 611–625.

Harris, John, and Michael Todaro (1970), "Migration, Unemployment and Development: A Two Sector Analysis," *American Economic Review*, 40, 126–142.

Hayami, Yujiro, and Vernon Ruttan (1980), *Agricultural Development: An International Perspective*, Baltimore, MD: Johns Hopkins University Press.

Household Survey Office, National Bureau of Statistics (2013), "Monitoring Survey Report on Migrant Workers in 2012," in Fang Cai (ed.), *From Demographic Dividend to Institutional Dividend*, Reports on China's Population and Labor No. 14, Beijing: Social Sciences Academic Press, pp. 1–15.

Lewis, Arthur (1972), "Reflections on Unlimited Labour," in L. Di Marco (ed.), *International Economics and Development*, New York: Academic Press, pp. 75–96.

Minami, Ryoshin (2010), "Turning Point in the Japanese Economy," presented at the Workshop in the Project of the Institute of Asian Cultures, Toyo University's "The Discussion on the Changes in East Asia Labor Market Based on Lewisian Turning Point Theory," Tokyo, July 18–19.

National Bureau of Statistics (various years), *China Statistical Yearbook [year]*, Beijing: China Statistics Press.

National Bureau of Statistics and Ministry of Human Resources and Social Security (various years), *China Labor Statistical Yearbook [year]*, Beijing: China Statistics Press.

National Development and Reform Commission (various years), *Compilation of National Farm Product Cost–Benefit Data [year]*, Beijing: China Statistics Press.

Ranis, Gustav, and John Fei (1961), "A Theory of Economic Development," *American Economic Review*, 51 (4), 533–565.

Rural Socio-economic Survey Team, National Bureau of Statistics of China (various years), *China Yearbook of Rural Household Survey*, Beijing: China Statistics Press.

Todaro, Michael (1969), "A Model of Labor Migration and Urban Unemployment in Less Developed Countries," *American Economic Review*, 59 (1), 138–148.

Todaro, Michael (1985), *Economic Development in the Third World*, New York: Longman.

Zhang, Linxiu, Scott Rozelle, and Jikun Huang (2001), "Off-Farm Jobs and On-Farm Work in Periods of Boom and Bust in Rural China," *Journal of Comparative Economics*, 29 (3), 505–526.

4. The demographic dividend

> Let the producers be many and the consumers few. Let there be activity in the production, and economy in the expenditure. Then the wealth will always be sufficient. (*The Book of Rites* [*The Li Ki*])

Since the formation of a dual economy is closely related to one specific phase of demographic transition—that is, a phase characterized by high birth rates, a low death rate, and consequently a high growth rate—the phase of population development that is characterized by low birth rates, a low death rate, and a low growth rate has inevitably drawn China out of the dual economy. The crux of the debate regarding at which stage the development of the Chinese economy lies is in the lack of unanimous judgment on China's demographic transition and different understandings of the impact of population factors on economic growth.

There are no officially published systematic data or up-to-date information on the status of China's demographic changes or population dynamics. While various rounds of national population censuses have provided information about population changes, a lack of consensus on some important parameters governing China's demographics—such as the actual total fertility rate (TFR)[1]—has ensured that no authoritative projections of population change, including predictions of the magnitude and age structure of the population, have been regularly publicized. Neither the public nor academia, therefore, have updated information about trends in population developments, and many even believe that the peak of population growth will be reached around 2040, after which the total population in China may total as many as 1.6 billion (for example, see Lau, 2010). More specifically, most scholars ignore the fact that the growth of China's working-age population (those aged 15 to 59) has been slowing for many years, plateauing in 2010. The result of this plateau was that the demographic foundation of an unlimited labor supply has been shaken, and so certain analysts are unwilling to accept the arrival of the Lewis Turning Point associated with a diminishing demographic dividend.

It is obvious that an undistorted understanding of the status of and ongoing trends in China's demographic transition will help scholars and policy researchers better understand the state of the labor market, and will also serve as a foundation for policy decisions regarding the sustainability of China's economic growth. This chapter argues that the country's demographic transition and dual economy development have a common starting point, share similar characteristics in the developmental stages, and to a certain extent have overlapping processes, so that the demographic window of opportunity in which a demographic dividend can be obtained is necessarily one of the stages of dual economy development. Accordingly, the theoretical and empirical work and reasoning regarding a diminishing demographic dividend and the coming of the Lewis Turning Point serve as a stone with which to kill two birds at once. Specifically, this chapter examines the logical relationship between the country's demographic transition and the development of a dual economy based on the examples already provided by international experiences, and, by analyzing various sources of statistics, also depicts China's process of demographic transition along with its impact on economic growth.

4.1   THE DEMOGRAPHIC DRIVER OF ECONOMIC GROWTH

Even before Lewis's prominent paper first appeared, the mature form of the demographic transition theory had already been published.[2] Corresponding to periods of pre- and post-industrialization, demographic transition is categorized into three stages, respectively characterized by (1) a high birth rate, high death rate, and low natural rate of population growth, (2) a high birth rate, low death rate, and high natural rate of population growth, and (3) a low birth rate, low death rate, and low natural rate of population growth.

Although we cannot judge whether Lewis was aware of prevailing theories in demography, there is no lack of demographic assumptions related to the theory of demographic transition in his description of the development of a dual economy. For example, while defining an unlimited supply of labor—the key concept behind the theory of a dual economy—he explains: "unlimited supply of labor may be said to exist in those countries where population is so large relatively to capital and natural resources, that there are large sectors of the economy where the marginal productivity of labor is negligible, zero, or even negative" (Lewis, 1954). The connotative assumption of this statement is that a typical dual economy characterized by unlimited supply of labor is at the second stage of demographic transition—that is, the natural growth rate of the population is high as a result of decreased mortality and consistently high birth rates. Since agriculture is the primary sector for production, it is the first place where the abundant population and surplus labor force accumulate.

The key to comprehending the logical and empirical relationship between demographic transition and the development of the dual economy is to explore how a demographic dividend is engendered and obtained. In the early literature of demography and economics, the population–development nexus was discussed by focusing on the relationship between the economic growth rate and the population growth rate, while the discussion of demographic transition primarily analyzed demographic subjects such as population quantity, birth rate, and death rate, but was not closely related to economic growth. What's more, mainstream growth theory, while incorporating the population growth rate into endogenous growth, has usually neglected characteristics of the demographic transition into a dual economy.

After long ignoring the relationships between economic development and the structural characteristics of a given population—particularly those relationships between the population age structure and the labor supply—demographers have become more conscious of population aging and its consequences as developed countries and many newly industrialized economies successively completed their demographic transition process. Economists are further interested in the ongoing change in the working-age population, or dependency ratio, that goes with fertility decline, as well as its effect on sources of economic growth (Williamson, 1997).

The interrelation between the population growth pattern and changes in the country's age structure can be depicted as follows. First, in the time span between an earlier decline in the mortality rate and a later decrease in the birth rate, the natural rate of growth of the population usually rises quickly, with the ratio of children to the general population also increasing. Second, after a certain period of time, as fertility decreases and the baby boomers grow up, the proportion of the working-age population grows accordingly. Third, the continued decline in fertility as a result of economic and social developments causes a decrease in the natural growth rate of a population, while the structural consequence of such a dynamic is population aging. In short, following a reversed U-shape pattern—namely, the natural growth rate of a population first increases and then declines after a turning point, with an interval of about one generation—the growth rate of the working-age population presents a similar pattern of change.

During the period in which the country's age structure is most productive, an adequate supply of labor coupled with a high savings rate may afford an extra source of economic growth and, thus, form a demographic dividend. Consequently, once the demographic transition exceeds this stage—namely, once the age structure of the population becomes less and less conducive to economic growth—as a result of rapid aging, such conventionally defined demographic dividends gradually disappear. Since

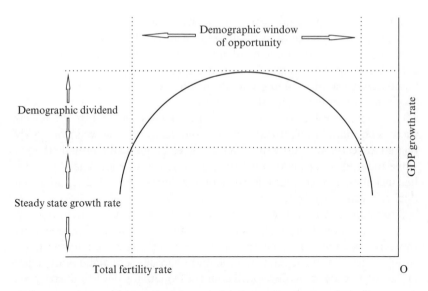

Figure 4.1   The relationship between fertility and economic growth

the stages of demographic transition can be sufficiently characterized by changes in the total fertility rate, one can theoretically expect the following relationship between demographic transition and economic growth (Figure 4.1): the stage of high TFR coincides with a steady state of low growth rate; as the TFR falls, a more productive population age structure emerges, with demographic dividends promoting economic growth at a higher rate; when the TFR further drops to a low level and the population ages, economic growth rates again shrink to low, steady states. Thus, at a certain stage of demographic transition when the TFR declines rapidly and the population age structure becomes more and more productive, there forms a demographic "window of opportunity."

It is worth noting that factors impacting the performance of economic growth are multifold and are not just related to population. This is also true in explaining both the steady state of the growth rate of low-income economies, known for poverty traps, and the steady state of the growth rate in high-income economies struggling on the frontier of technological innovation. For example, in the empirical works defending the neoclassical growth theory, economists have found more than 100 explanatory variables that are statistically significant in unveiling determinants of growth performance, but none is sufficient and exclusive in and of itself (Sala-i-Martin, 1996). For simplicity, we have also put aside the retroactive effect of economic growth on the country's demographic transition[3] in order to focus on the straightforward relationship between fertility and economic growth. Following the assumption made above, this interrelation between fertility and growth can first be deduced from the theory of demographic dividends and then confirmed empirically.

The panel data from the World Development Indicators enable us to picture a descriptive relationship between annual GDP growth rates and TFR levels among countries from 1960 up through recent years. For those countries and years in which data are available, annual GDP growth rates have ranged from −51 to 106 percent. To avoid the complication of explaining the outliers, we ignore these extreme numbers and only investigate those between 0 and 10 percent, which are assumed to represent a normal span of annual GDP growth rate. According to the preceding discussion, the relationship between economic growth rate and fertility is not a simple linear one, but instead follows the algebraic relationship of a quadratic function. That is, as the TFR declines, the economic growth rate first increases and then declines. In Figure 4.2, according to the functional relationship between GDP growth rate, the TFR, and the square term of the TFR, we present the fitted value of the annual growth rate of GDP with a 95 percent confidence interval.

Figure 4.2 depicts a reversed U-shaped pattern of GDP growth rate against

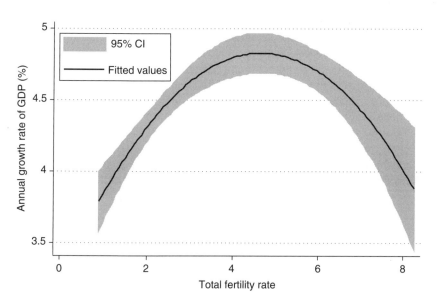

Source: Calculation based on dataset of World Development Indicators.

Figure 4.2   The empirical relationship between the TFR and GDP growth

Table 4.1   Regression results: the relation between the TFR and growth

	Coefficient	Standard error	t value	P>| t |
TFR	0.6852	0.1133	6.05	0.000
TFR squared	−0.0736	0.0137	−5.38	0.000
Constant term	3.2359	0.1909	16.95	0.000
Observations	3380			

a decline in the TFR—countries at the lower stages of demographic transition characterized by a high TFR usually suffer from poor economic performance; as their TFR levels fall, economic growth speeds up; after a certain point, as the TFR further declines and the demographic transition enters the later stage characterized by a very low TFR, economic growth then tends to slow down. Such a simplified empirical curve is perfectly consistent with the theoretical prediction described previously. To further examine the statistical significance of the relationship between the TFR and economic growth, we regress the GDP growth rate on the TFR and the squared term of the TFR (Table 4.1) by assuming nonlinear correlation and using the same data. The regression results illustrate the reversed U-shaped relationship between GDP growth and the TFR by revealing the significantly positive sign of the TFR coefficient and the negative sign of the squared term of the TFR.

While the more precise explanation—based on both economic theory and empirical evidence—requires much more work, the relationship shown here between fertility and economic growth is a sufficient framework by which to investigate the actual relationship between the demographic transition perceived in demography, the demographic dividend coined by demographic economists, and the Lewis Turning Point deduced from development economics, all based on the Chinese experience. In the next section, we will analyze the formation and anticipated disappearance of the demographic dividend and draw a verdict on the advent of the Lewis Turning Point in the process of China's economic development.

4.2   THE CHINESE DEMOGRAPHIC TRANSITION

In 1957, when Professor Ma Yinchu delivered his speech—the contents of which were later published as a book, titled *New Population Theory* (Ma, 2002)—suggesting the implementation of a population control policy by the central government, his arguments were based on the 1st Population Census conducted in 1953, which showed an increasingly rapid growth in the Chinese population. He correctly noted that it was socioeconomic development that had driven up the birth rate and down the death rate in the early years of the People's Republic of China. Given his incomplete knowledge at the time, however, he failed to apply demographic transition laws to future trends of fertility and population growth.

Population changes in China have actually followed and attested to the laws of demographic transition. In the first two decades following the establishment of the People's Republic of China in 1949, the economy recovered rapidly and people's living standards improved, which pushed China's demographic transition into the second stage. That is, eliminating the abnormal years between the late 1950s and the early 1960s, mortality fell substantially while the birth rate remained at a consistently high level, with the result being that the natural growth rate was persistently high. The TFR remained as high as 6 until the early 1970s, only to decline dramatically afterwards (Figure 4.3).

The fastest decline of the TFR, however, had already occurred before the one-child policy was formally implemented. The TFR dropped from 5.8 to 2.3 in the decade from 1970 to 1980, when the government was carrying out only a voluntary birth control policy—that is, encouraging late marriage, fewer children, and a longer interval between births—while

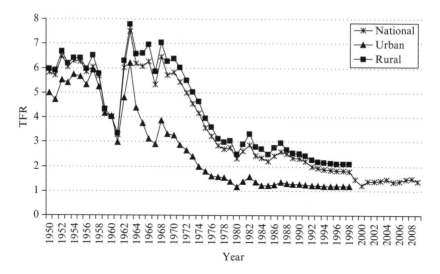

Source: The regional TFR for the period before 1998 was calculated using data from the China Center for Population Information database; the national TFR post-1998 was calculated on the basis of various population surveys and/or census data.

Figure 4.3   The reduction in total fertility rates: aggregate, urban, and rural

it remained unchanged during the entire decade of the 1980s, when the central government announced its compulsory population control policy. In the more than two decades since then, the TFR dropped dramatically, until the present day, when the TFR is accepted as 1.4 to 1.6, both of which figures are well below the replacement level of 2.1.

It is not accurate to characterize the policy governing the Chinese population as a ubiquitous one-child policy. Considering diversity in socioeconomic development and culture, China's population policies differ between rural and urban areas, between the Han majority and other minority ethnicities, and among regions. According to differentiated birth policies, the one-child policy applies to 36 percent of the Chinese population, the one-and-a-half child policy applies to 52 percent of the population, a policy allowing two children to 10 percent, and one allowing three children to 2 percent. That is, the policy-determined fertility rate is a little more than 1.4 (China Development Research Foundation, 2012).

According to both demographic theory and historical experiences, a country enters the phase of low fertility once its TFR drops to below 2.1. While the Chinese government has set a goal for its TFR to be below 1.8 (Task Group of the National Strategy on Population Development Studies, 2007), most scholars believe that the TFR in China has actually been 1.5—well below 1.8—since 1998. The United Nations put China's TFR for 2006 at 1.4 in its *World Fertility Pattern, 2009*, thereby placing the country among others with low fertility rates. International comparison shows that, in terms of demographic transition, China has been well ahead of its stage of development, as its TFR (1.4) is not only lower than the world average of 2.6 and the average of less-developed countries (excluding the least-developed countries) of 2.5, but also lower than the average level of developed countries (1.6) from 2005 to 2010 (United Nations, 2010).

Scholars and policy researchers have tried to determine families' desired number of children. In other words, in assessing the effectiveness of and possible adjustments to the population policy, decision makers want to know whether it is the birth control policy or socioeconomic development that has resulted in the substantial decline in fertility in China.

There are three examples that help to illuminate the issue. First, according to surveys of childbearing intentions conducted in Jiangsu province in 1997, 2001, and 2006, the intended fertility rate was 1.74, 1.70, and 1.73 respectively for these years (Zheng, 2011). Those desired numbers of children are not significantly higher than either the policy-set TFR or the current TFR, but they are significantly lower than the replacement level of TFR. Second, a quantitative study found that the rapid decline in the TFR in China can be attributed to the implementation of the population policy, enhancement of per capita GDP, and the accumulation of human capital, and that the marginal effect of birth control on the decline of the TFR has tended to decrease in importance, while the effects of economic development and human capital accumulation on the decline of the TFR have increased over time (Du, 2005). Third, like China, other Asian economies such as South Korea, Singapore, Thailand, and Taiwan, where no mandatory policy has been enforced, have also experienced dramatic declines in fertility, from a high TFR (similar to China's) in the 1950s to as low as below replacement level in the 1990s. Even in India, where economic growth and social development have not performed as well as those of China and other Northeast Asian economies (with demographic transition correspondingly lagging behind), fertility has also been similarly declining (Lin, 2006).

The aforementioned findings confirm the scholarly consensus that economic growth and social development are the driving forces of demographic transition. Given the unprecedented economic growth and social change in the 35 years since it initiated economic reform in 1978, in addition to its unique family-planning policy China has completed its demographic transition from a high fertility pattern to a low fertility pattern within a much shorter period of time than most developed countries. For example, it took about 75 years for England and France to decrease their TFR from 5 to replacement levels, while it took fewer than 30 years for China to accomplish this same reduction in fertility (China Development Research Foundation, 2012).

Empirically, there are two reversed U-shaped curves that characterize the demographic transition. First, as a result of the country's decline in fertility, the natural growth rate of the population initially increases, reaches a peak, and then decreases. Second, lagging about 20 years behind the first curve, the proportion of the working-age population increases from a low level, reaches its peak, and then declines again. As is shown in Figure 4.4, in China the natural growth rate of the population has been in decline since the mid-1960s, while the proportion of the working-age population aged between 15 and 59 continuously increased until it reached a peak in 2010, after which it began to decline. During the time period in which diminishing population growth and an increasing share of the working-age population coexisted, China gained its demographic window of opportunity—namely, that the population factor was in favor of economic growth.

4.3   ACCOUNTING FOR CHINA'S ECONOMIC GROWTH

Throughout the entire period since China's reform and opening-up was initiated in the early 1980s, the country's rapid economic development has

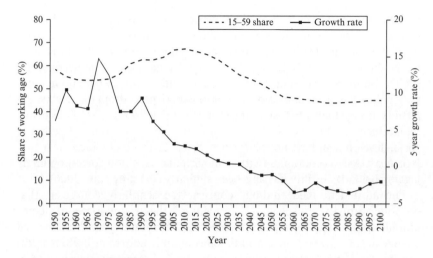

Source: United Nations (2011).

*Figure 4.4   Trends in population growth and share of working-age
            population*

benefited from the demographic dividend, which can be both predicted by
economics theory and proven by statistical evidence.[4] The significance of
demographic transition in contributing to economic growth is manifested
in the following sources of growth.

First, the continual decline in the dependency ratio helps the national
economy maintain a high rate of savings, which lays the foundation for
capital formation crucial to high-rate economic growth. In the planned
economy period, the capital formation rate—namely, the ratio of fixed
asset formation (plus inventory) to GDP—was unusually high. For
example, it was 38.2 percent in 1978, and continued to increase during the
reform period. Between 1995 and 2012, it increased from 40.3 percent to
47.8 percent.[5] More importantly, a sufficient supply of labor has prevented
diminishing return to capital inputs. As can be expected from existing
economics theory, this factor is manifested in the contribution of physical
capital to GDP growth rate when breaking down the sources of Chinese
economic growth.

Second, as the continual increase in the working-age population ensures
an ample labor supply and Chinese workers participate in economic
globalization, China has maintained an obvious low-cost labor advantage.
Furthermore, compared to other developing countries that hold advantageous population age structures, Chinese workers attain significantly

better education, helping enhance the productivity of labor.[6] An estimate based on a survey of manufacturing enterprises shows that an additional year of schooling for workers increases labor productivity by 17 percent. It is both the quantity and the quality of human resource that have allowed China to enjoy an advantage of unit labor costs, which is positively related to the wage rate and negatively to labor productivity (Qu et al., 2010). Those factors positively impacting the Chinese growth rate are manifested in contributions to variables such as labor growth and human capital accumulation.

Third, China's rural areas have lagged behind urban areas in terms of demographic transition and, as the rural surplus labor—accumulated in the planned economy period—moved out of the countryside after the country entered its period of reform and opening up, the efficiency of resource reallocation improved, becoming the main source of total factor productivity (TFP) improvement. For example, in an earlier work, Cai and Wang (1999) estimated that, from 1978 to 1998, labor migration from low-productivity agricultural sectors to high-productivity non-agricultural sectors—namely, a gain of reallocation efficiency—contributed 21 percent of GDP growth, leaving a residual, unexplained 3 percent, which can be viewed as an improvement in technical efficiency and technological progress.

Last but not least, other factors related to demographic transition also serve as a demographic dividend contributing to economic growth. In fact, if the dependency ratio—the ratio of the dependent population to the working-age population—is taken as the proxy for a revealed demographic dividend, then its contribution to economic growth can be seen as a demographic dividend in the purest sense. In other words, if we believe that other factors such as quantity of labor, years of schooling, capital formation, and reallocation efficiency all imply a demographic dividend, we can view the dependency ratio as a residual of the demographic dividend.

In existing economics literature, most studies employ the dependency ratio as a proxy variable to estimate the contribution of pure demographic factors to economic growth. For example, in his groundbreaking paper, Williamson (1997) found that, from 1970 to 1995, the demographic dividend denoted by the dependency ratio contributed from one-fourth to one-third of the overall growth of East Asian economies. Based on the data of 17 countries in Europe and North America, he also found that, between 1870 and 1913, the extra growth rate of those countries of the new world that exceeded the growth rate of European countries can be almost all attributed to the former's lower dependency ratio.

Based on a production function approach, Cai and Zhao (2012) analyzed the rate of economic growth since China initiated reform, aiming to explore

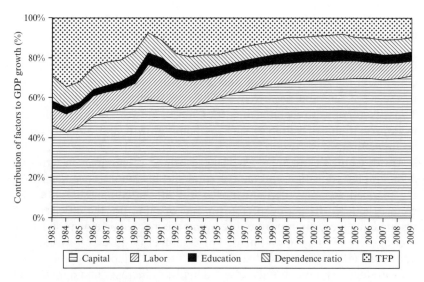

Source: Cai and Zhao (2012).

Figure 4.5   Relative contributions of different factors to GDP growth over time

the contributions of various factors. Variables incorporated in the equation include fixed asset formation (capital), total employment expansion (labor), the number of years of schooling of workers (human capital), the dependency ratio (demographic dividend), and TFP. The findings show that, to the average GDP growth rate in the period from 1983 to 2009, capital input contributed 71 percent, labor input 7.5 percent, education 4.5 percent, the dependency ratio 7.4 percent, and TFP 9.6 percent.

Patterns in each factor's contribution to GDP growth over time are presented on an annual basis in Figure 4.5. To exhibit continuous patterns free from short-run fluctuations, here we use one year's data to estimate the relative contributions for the year 1983, two years' data for 1984, and so on, with 27 years' worth of data for 2009. Therefore, the actual trends in changes should be more apparent than what is shown in Figure 4.5. To summarize, (1) the contribution of capital increases over time but is not sustainable, (2) the contributions of labor input and the dependency ratio tend to diminish as the population's age structure changes, (3) the contribution of human capital is relatively stable and smaller, and (4) the contribution of TFP is not as significant as it was expected to be, but it is the most sustainable source of economic growth.

4.4 THE DISAPPEARANCE OF THE DEMOGRAPHIC DIVIDEND

The rapid demographic transition contributed to unprecedented economic growth during the period when the working-age population grew and the dependency ratio declined. Since 2010, however, population trends have altered their direction—that is, the working-age population aged 15 to 59 has started to shrink and the dependency ratio to increase, implying the disappearance of the demographic dividend.

Based on the total amount of the working-age population and the absolute level of the dependency ratio, some scholars argue that the demographic dividend will not disappear for at least a decade or even longer. According to a UN prediction, in 2025 the working-age population will total 895 million, compared to 880 million in 2005, and the dependency ratio will stay at 0.59, compared to 0.60 in 1995 (United Nations, 2011). However, such an argument can be shown to be untenable in terms of both empirical evidence and policy implications. After all, the concept of a demographic dividend can only be understood within the framework of a growth theory other than demography. As is illustrated in section 4.3, the demographic dividend is not only realized in a sufficient labor supply and low dependency ratio, but also embodied in an increasing return to physical capital, growing human capital, and the reallocation of production factors between the agricultural and non-agricultural sectors. Taking into account the changes across all variables (or growth sources), we can foresee a diminishing potential for economic growth.

First of all, in terms of the contributions made by labor growth and the dependency ratio to GDP growth, the directions of their changes are much more vital than the magnitude of the changes themselves. For example, in econometric estimation practices, when researchers assert certain contributions of those variables to the GDP growth rate, they mean that 1 percentage point of change in a variable will contribute a certain number of percentage points of change in the growth rate. Therefore, as the working-age population shifts from growth to reduction and the dependency ratio from decline to an increase, the demographic dividend inevitably witnesses a shift from a positive to negative contribution to economic growth.

Secondly, as the growth rate of the working-age population diminishes and eventually shifts into the negative, the Chinese will encounter the famous phenomenon of a diminishing return on capital. As Arthur Lewis, the founding father of the dual economy theory, put it:

[T]he key to the [dual economy development] process is the use which is made of the capitalist surplus. Insofar as this is reinvested in creating new capital, the capitalist sector expands, taking more people into capitalist employment out of the subsistence sector. The surplus is then larger still, capital formation is still greater, and so the process continues until the labour surplus disappears. (Lewis, 1954)

The key to understanding such a statement is that economic growth can break the economic law of diminishing returns on capital only because of the existence of surplus labor. Following the assumption of the neoclassical theory of growth, the labor supply is limited, therefore, when capital inputs exceed a certain level, diminishing returns occur, which in turn prevents any sustainability of growth solely driven by factors inputs. While the only solution neoclassical economists suggest for sustaining economic growth is to continually increase TFP, the property of an unlimited supply of labor enjoyed by dual economy development—by curbing diminishing returns to capital—allows (labor and physical capital) inputs-driven growth to be sustainable until a labor shortage eventually emerges and returns to capital start diminishing.

As the Chinese economy has passed successively through the Lewis Turning Point and the turning point of the shift in the working-age population from growth to decline, the diminishing return on capital inevitably accelerates, which is confirmed by a series of econometric studies.[7] As is shown in Figure 4.6, before it peaked in 2010 the growth of the working-age population aged between 15 and 59 had already been decreasing. As a response to such a population trend, the growth of capital investment aiming to apply more capital-intensive technologies and to form a more capital-intensive industrial structure accelerates, which tends to increase the capital–labor ratio, and as a result marginal return to capital diminishes.

Finally, as the surplus laborers in agriculture gradually dry up, room for labor mobility's ability to gain reallocation efficiency tends to narrow, which is bound to lower the growth of TFP. In addition, the narrowing technological gap between China and more advanced countries also tends to slow TFP growth. According to a study (Kuijs, 2009), the contributive share of TFP growth to the potential GDP growth of China declined from 30.9 percent in 1978–1994 to 28.4 percent in 2005–2009, and will further decline to 27.4 percent in 2010–2015, while the contributive share of the capital–labor ratio to potential GDP growth increased from 29.9 percent in 1978–1994 to 57.9 percent in 2005–2009, and will further increase to 64.3 percent in 2010–2015. Given the ongoing diminishing returns on capital, this type of altered growth pattern will hardly sustain China's economic growth.

Taking into account the substantial changes in those factors driving economic growth, one can fully expect the Chinese economy to have slowed

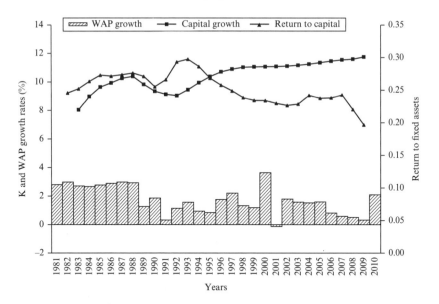

Note: K—capital; WAP—working-age population.

Source: Data on capital growth and the marginal return to capital from Cai and Zhao (2012); data on the working-age population from Cai and Lu (2013).

Figure 4.6 Dynamics of the working-age population, capital growth, and capital return

down after 2010, since that year signaled the turning point at which the country lost its demographic dividend. Based on measurements in economic and population growth, researchers have estimated China's potential GDP growth rates at different periods so as to identify the slowdown of the economy. For example, one of the very first studies showed that, on average, the potential GDP growth rate per annum will decline from 9.9 percent in 1978–1994 and 9.6 percent in 1995–2009, to 8.4 percent in 2010–2015 and 7.0 percent in 2016–2020 (Kuijs, 2009).

In studying the cyclical phenomenon of the macroeconomy, economists usually predict GDP growth for the following period, which is, in general, based on previous trends and the expected short-term shocks across the years predicted. Such predictions are hardly helpful in foreseeing long-term growth trends, especially of developing countries, however, because they cannot capture the change in the stages of economic development, which are usually accompanied by changes in growth potentials. Estimation of the potential growth rate, however, can serve to

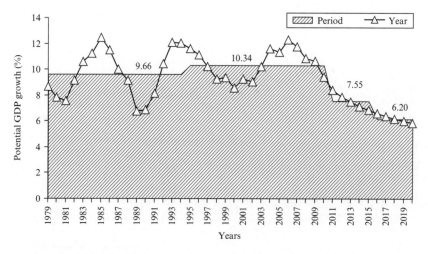

Source: Cai and Lu (2013).

Figure 4.7   Estimated potential growth rates by year and period

predict future growth trends by taking into consideration the changes in
the relative scarcity of production factors—namely, the supply capacities
of labor and capital—as well as the trend of productivity enhancement.
In China's case, the key to such assessments is to accurately capture the
shifting dynamics of population change.

By considering the shrinkage of the working-age population, which
negatively impacts labor supply and reallocative efficiency, and the resultant slowdown of investment growth and TFP growth, estimated potential GDP growth rates for different periods predicted by Cai and Lu
(2013) suggest that the potential annual growth rate in China is currently
undergoing a decline from 10.3 percent in 1995–2010 to 7.6 percent in
2011–2015, and 6.2 percent in 2016–2020 (Figure 4.7). That is clear and
straightforward proof for the disappearance of the demographic dividend.

4.5   CONCLUSION

In quite a short period of time, China has passed through two important
turning points—the Lewis Turning Point in 2004 and the turning point
of demographic dividends in 2010—which signals the exhaustion of the
conventional sources of economic growth. The implications are threefold.
First, the disappearance of the demographic dividend inevitably leads to

economic slowdown, which is a natural outcome of changes in the stages of economic development. Second, if the new economic engines cannot restart within a reasonable time span after the old drivers of the economy have stalled, the economic slowdown will be long-lasting and economic development delayed. Third, any policy mistakes made in coping with the slowdown may lead to long-term stagnation, which, for China, means succumbing to the fate of the middle-income trap.

According to international experiences drawn from countries considered to be stuck in the middle-income trap (and even from certain developed countries, such as Japan), there is a great possibility that such a slow-down can become stagnation as a result of unsound policy implementation. In China, while enterprises and investors respond to the changes in resource endowment by adjusting their production and technological structure—which is carried out on the basis of signals from the production factor markets—the government has, on the other hand, strengthened its intervention in investment activities for the purpose of exploring new comparative advantages, a solution which tends to artificially drive up the capital–labor ratio. Such strengthened governmental activity and its consequences can be closely tied to what economists have documented as a recurrence of the old developmental model.

For example, Fan and Wu found that, after the mid-1990s, when China initiated the strategic restructuring of its state-owned sector, administrative power over resources allocation and intervention in the production factors market were consolidated, particularly through control over the so-called "strategic industries" (Fan and Wu, 2010). Facing the economic slowdown that resulted from the passage of the two turning points, the government also intended to stimulate the economy through macroeconomic policies, industrial policies, and even regional strategies, all of which may cause distortion of prices and thus an ultra-increase in the capital–labor ratio.

The single most important function of economic theories is to predict events that have not yet happened. Although there are no ready theories in the toolbox of conventional economics that touch upon the simultaneous arrival of the two turning points, recognizing the inevitable, ongoing disappearance of the demographic dividend and conceptualizing the existing facts through realistic examination are necessary in order to adopt sound policy measures to tackle the slowdown of the Chinese economy. That enables us to distinguish between short-term, cyclical macroeconomic shocks and long-term, structural change when the slow-down occurs, so that we know the only way to tackle it is to find a new growth engine, which requires a shift from an input-driven growth pattern to a productivity-driven growth pattern. That is the task assigned to the following chapters.

NOTES

1. Conducted in 2000, the 5th National Population Census shows that China's TFR was 1.32, which is even lower than the policy-allowable level of 1.51. Many doubt such a result (e.g. Yu, 2002). Since then, debates on the actual TFR of China have existed among scholars and policy researchers. Generally speaking, the government departments responsible for implementing the population control policy tend to believe in a higher TFR, whereas scholars believe in a lower TFR. In spite of the disagreement, the estimates mostly fall in the range 1.4 to 1.8, which are all significantly lower than the replacement level of 2.1.
2. Whereas Thompson first identified the three stages of demographic transition and another scholar added a further two later stages, neither was considered the father of the theory of demographic transition, because they did not provide a standard theoretical explanation of the decline of fertility. See Thompson (1929). That honor was later awarded to Notestein (1945). For a brief history of this field, see Caldwell (1976).
3. In an econometric study, Du found that population policy, per capita GDP, and level of human capital are the decisive factors driving down China's fertility, and empirically identified the different effects of these three factors. See Du (2005).
4. As is illustrated by literature, the demographic dividend is delivered through a number of mechanisms, including labor supply, savings, and human capital. See Bloom et al. (2002).
5. This calculation is based on nominal GDP and the value of fixed assets. Because the GDP deflator was greater than the price index of fixed assets, if GDP and fixed asset formation are deflated, respectively, by differentiated deflators this ratio may demonstrate an even faster increase.
6. For example, the average years of schooling of the working-age population in China were 33 percent higher than those in India. See Niu and Wang (2010).
7. For studies that consistently cover both the high return to capital during the fast-growing period of the Chinese economy and the accelerating trend of diminishing return to capital since the 1990s, see Bai et al. (2006) and Cai and Zhao (2012).

REFERENCES

Bai, Chong-En, Chang-Tai Hsieh, and Yingyi Qian (2006), *The Return to Capital in China*, NBER Working Paper No. 12755, Cambridge, MA: National Bureau of Economic Research.

Bloom, David, David Canning, and Jaypee Sevilla (2002), *The Demographic Dividend: A New Perspective on the Economic Consequences of Population Change*, Santa Monica, CA: RAND.

Cai, Fang, and Yang Lu (2013), "The End of China's Demographic Dividend: The Perspective of Potential GDP Growth," in Fang Cai, Ross Garnaut, and Ligang Song (eds.), *China: A New Model for Growth and Development*, Canberra: Australian National University E Press, pp. 55–74.

Cai, Fang, and Dewen Wang (1999), "The Sustainability of Economic Growth and the Labor Contribution," *Economic Research Journal*, 10, 62–68.

Cai, Fang, and Wen Zhao (2012), "When Demographic Dividend Disappears: Growth Sustainability of China," in Masahiko Aoki and Jinglian Wu (eds.), *The Chinese Economy: A New Transition*, Basingstoke: Palgrave Macmillan, pp. 75–90.

Caldwell, John (1976), "Toward a Restatement of Demographic Transition Theory," *Population and Development Review*, 2, 321–366.

China Development Research Foundation (ed.) (2012), *China Development Report 2011/12: The Changes of Population Trend and Reform of Population Policy*, Beijing: China Development Press.

Du, Yang (2005), "The Formation of Low Fertility and Its Impacts on Long Term Economic Growth in China," *World Economy*, 12, 14–23.

Fan, Shitao, and Jinglian Wu (2010), "Beyond the East Asian Miracle: Looking Back and Future Prospects for China's Economic Growth Model," in Cai Fang (ed.), *Transforming the Chinese Economy*, Leiden: Brill, pp. 241–277.

Kuijs, Louis (2009), *China through 2020—A Macroeconomic Scenario*, World Bank China Research Working Paper No. 9, Washington, DC: World Bank.

Lau, Lawrence (2010), "The Chinese Economy: The Next Thirty Years," presented at the Institute of Quantitative and Technical Economics, Chinese Academy of Social Sciences, Beijing, January 16.

Lewis, Arthur (1954), "Economic Development with Unlimited Supply of Labor," *Manchester School*, 22 (2), 139–191.

Lin, Justin Yifu (2006), "Development Strategy, Population and Population Policies," in Yi Zeng, Ling Li, Baochang Gu, and Yifu Lin (eds.), *China's Population and Economic Development in the 21st Century*, Beijing: Social Sciences Academic Press, pp. 3–10.

Ma, Yinchu (2002), *New Population Theory*, Beijing: Population Publishing House.

Notestein, Frank (1945), "Population—The Long View," in Theodore Schultz (ed.), *Food for the World*, Chicago: University of Chicago Press.

Niu, Jianlin, and Guangzhou Wang (2010), "Composition and Development of the Chinese Education System," in Fang Cai (ed.), *The China Population and Labor Yearbook*, Vol. 2: *The Sustainability of Economic Growth from the Perspective of Human Resources*, Boston, MA: Brill, pp. 43–61.

Qu, Yue, Fang Cai, and Yang Du (2010), "Population Dividend: Continue or Alter?," in Fang Cai (ed.), *The China Population and Labor Yearbook*, Vol. 2: *The Sustainability of Economic Growth from the Perspective of Human Resources*, Leiden: Brill, pp. 15–27.

Sala-i-Martin, Xavier (1996), "The Classical Approach to Convergence Analysis," *Economic Journal*, 106, 1019–1036.

Task Group of the National Strategy on Population Development Studies (2007), *The Report on China's National Strategy on Population Development*, Beijing: China Population Press.

Thompson, Warren (1929), "Population," *American Journal of Sociology*, 34 (6), 959–975.

United Nations (2010), *World Fertility Pattern 2009*, http://www.un.org/esa/population/publications/worldfertility2009/worldfertility2009.htm.

United Nations (2011), *World Population Prospects: The 2010 Revision*, CD-ROM edn., New York: United Nations, Department of Economic and Social Affairs, Population Division.

Williamson, Jeffrey (1997), *Growth, Distribution and Demography: Some Lessons from History*, NBER Working Paper No. 6244, Cambridge, MA: National Bureau of Economic Research.

Yu, Xuejun (2002), "Estimation on Magnitude and Structure of 5th National Population Census," *Population Research*, 26 (3), 9–15.

Zheng, Zhenzhen (2011), "Studies of Fertility Desire and Implication," *Academia Bimestris*, 2, 10–18.

5.   Growing old before getting rich

Extend the care of the aged in one family to that of all families. (Mencius)

When describing properties of the population's age structure by employing graphs of population pyramids, early textbooks of demography usually use as examples one developing country and one developed country. The age structure of the developing country is characterized as a typical pyramid with a broad base of youth and a sharply tapering top of the elderly, whereas the age structure of the developed country is quite the opposite, characterized by a narrower base of youth and broader top of the elderly. The latter case results from low fertility and population aging. More recently, drawing the population pyramids of China in different years, say 1982 and 2010, is sufficient to compare these contrasting phases of demographic transition.

The change in the population age structure in China not only reflects the population aging that results from economic and social developments in general, but also indicates a population that is aging more rapidly than the speed of income growth. Such a gap in the progress between the demographic transition and income growth in China can be expressed as "growing old before getting rich." This chapter is intended to describe this unique feature of China's demographic transition and to discuss the special challenges it poses to the sustainability of China's economic growth.

5.1   THE PREMATURELY AGING POPULATION

Population aging is an inevitable demographic consequence resulting from general economic and social developments. First, accompanying the transition from rates of high fertility to low fertility, the population growth rate is the first to diminish, followed by the working-age population's growth accelerating, slowing down, and then shrinking before the total population peaks at an absolute number. Second, an improvement in life expectancy as a result of socioeconomic development is a result of not only the lowered mortality of infants and the overall population that accompanies socio-economic development, but also of the increased longevity of the elderly; it therefore increases the proportion of the aged population to the total population. China has recently experienced both processes of population transformation and is steadily entering into an aging society.

Observers all over the world have long harbored growing concerns over China's enormous population and associated population growth. Few have noticed, however, that declined fertility has caused population growth to slow down dramatically. According to the 6th National Census, we can draw some important conclusions about China's population in 2010: (1) the total population totaled 1.34 billion and it will be unlikely to exceed much more than 1.4 billion at its peak if the present TFR does not change significantly, (2) the average life expectancy at birth was 74.8 years, a level comparable to high human development countries, and (3) the working-age population between 15 and 59 reached its peak and afterwards began to shrink.

Consequently, the Chinese population is aging rapidly. In 2010, the proportion of the population aged 60 and older was 13.3 percent, while the proportion of the population aged 65 or older was 8.9 percent. According to the general definition—namely, that a country can be seen as an aged society if those two proportions exceed 10 percent and 7 percent respectively—China is already an aged society. Figure 5.1 vividly shows

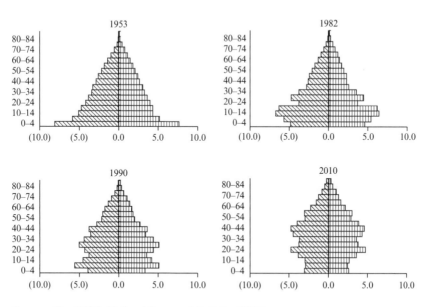

Source: Fan (1995); National Bureau of Statistics (2012).

Figure 5.1   Changes in the age structure of China's population

the dramatic change in the shape of the population age structure, from a typical age pyramid in the earlier years to a barrel-shaped pyramid in 2010.

The United Nations' (2011) prediction regarding the age structure of the country indicates an ever-severer population aging rate in China. According to this source, the proportion of the Chinese population aged 65 and older is 9.4 percent, and it is predicted to increase to 13.6 percent in 2020, 18.7 percent in 2030, 26.8 percent in 2040, and 30.8 percent in 2050, at which time China will make up 14.4 percent of the world's population and 22.5 percent of the world's elderly. International comparison shows that as a result of a rapid decline in fertility followed by the decline in 2010 of the proportion of the country's youth population—namely, the population aged 14 and younger—the speed at which the population began to age in China exceeded that of other less-developed countries after 1970, and it began to exceed that of more-developed countries after 2010 (Figure 5.2). These figures admit no room for doubt that China will soon catch up with its more developed counterparts in terms of population aging.

No matter the criteria, China is ranked among developing countries. For example, based on per capita GDP, the World Bank categorizes countries into low-income groups, lower-middle-income groups, upper-middle-income groups, and high-income groups. By this criterion, China

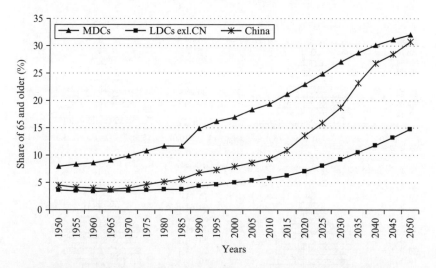

Note: MDCs—more-developed countries; LDCs excl. CN—less-developed countries excluding China.

Source: United Nations (2011).

Figure 5.2   An international comparison of China's population aging

is now in the upper-middle-income group, at least among developing countries. In 2010, the proportion of the population aged 65 and older constituted 19.4 percent of the total population in more-developed countries, 5.8 percent in the less-developed countries excluding China, and 9.4 percent in China itself. That China has a significantly higher proportion of an elderly population than other developing countries implies its uniqueness in regard to demographic transition, which we phrase in this chapter as "growing old before getting rich."

Generally speaking, the extent of the phenomenon of population aging is positively correlated to per capita income. Although the achievements in tackling population aging differ among countries, those that are ranked as high-income countries—being at the frontier of technological innovation and having matured in terms of a social welfare system—have so far managed to avoid the crisis of population aging. International experiences suggest that it is vital for China to cope with its rapid population aging by sustaining its economic growth and thus becoming a high-income country. In other words, since the process of demographic transition is irreversible—that is, even the relaxation of the country's population policy cannot significantly put off population aging—the gap of "growing old before getting rich" in China can only be narrowed or eliminated through an increase in per capita income.

One may use Figure 5.2 to comprehend how such a mechanism would function. For example, while China is numbered among developing countries and its population was significantly older than its peer counterparts in 2010, if China manages to become a developed country (by any metric) sometime between 2020 and 2030 (which can be reasonably predicted if its per capita income continues to experience a reasonable growth rate), its population will be relatively younger than those of its peer countries in the high-income group. In short, China is unable to change the fact that it is "growing old," but it can "get rich" faster so that the reference groups to which it compares will be changed in a somewhat more favorable direction.

5.2   CAN THERE BE A SECOND DEMOGRAPHIC DIVIDEND?

It is apparent that the uniqueness of its demographic transition poses significant challenges to China's economic growth, including a more rapid disappearance of the demographic dividend, difficulties confronting the so-called second demographic dividend, and a lack of resources to support the elderly. In what follows, we will illustrate the relationship between population aging and the disappearance of the demographic dividend in a

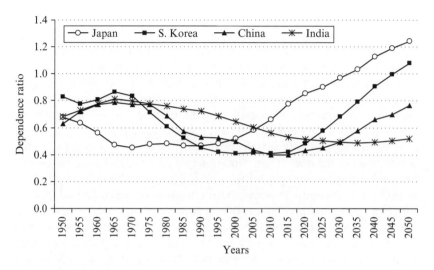

Source:　United Nations (2011).

*Figure 5.3　International comparisons of turning points of the dependence
　　　　　　ratio*

comparative manner by looking into the change of the dependence ratio
(the ratio of the population aged 14 and younger and 65 and older to the
population aged between 15 and 64), since this indicator can reflect both
the labor supply and the savings rate alike (Figure 5.3).

In general, despite the fact that China has enjoyed a demographic
dividend during its fast-growing period over the past three decades, its
economic growth is not particularly favored by population factors when
compared to its Asian counterparts, both developing and developed.

To begin with, we will compare China with Japan. The dependence
ratio in Japan reached its lowest point in around 1970 and remained low
for more than 20 years, until it rapidly increased in the early 1990s. When
Japan's turning point of demographic transition—namely, an increase in
the dependence ratio—arrived in the early 1990s, however, the country was
much richer than China is today in terms of per capita GDP. On the other
hand, Japan is typical of a country whose economy has stagnated as a
result of the disappearance of the demographic dividend, which may hold
lessons for China as it enters a similar stage.

Secondly, we will compare China with South Korea. The decline of the
dependence ratio in South Korea started earlier and lasted longer than that
in China. Namely, as a more advanced country, South Korea had reaped
a demographic dividend even after it became a high-income country, until

its dependence ratio began to rise in about 2010, in which year China's dependence ratio began to increase as well.

Thirdly, we will compare China to India, a latecomer country in terms of per capita GDP. Compared to that of China and South Korea, India's dependence ratio began to decline around the same year (1965), but the decline has been at a much lower rate, which will allow India to witness the turning point of the dependence ratio from a decline to an increase roughly around 2035. That is, India will enjoy a demographic dividend for the 25 years after China began to lose its demographic dividend in 2010. As China's comparative advantage in labor-intensive industries diminishes, India, along with other countries that have advantageous population structures, will become potential competitors with China.

Some scholars argue that, even after the conventional demographic dividend signaled by the stagnation of the working-age population and an end to the decline in the dependence ratio—which tends to end the era of an unlimited labor supply and high savings rate—has vanished, there could potentially be a second demographic dividend generated by individuals and families motivated to save as a precaution for their old age (Lee and Mason, 2006). Motivation for saving, however, cannot parallel the conventionally called demographic dividend on its own, since the latter involves not only capital accumulation, but also labor supply, human capital, and reallocation efficiency.

In understanding what causes the aging of a population, it has been well documented that the demographic transition from the initial phase of a juvenile population to the phase of a working-age population decreases in succession, so that the proportion of the aged population is enhanced; the role of a given population's increasing life span in enhancing life expectancy, however, is often neglected. Assuming that there is not a significant change in the population age structure—namely, the diminishing share of the youth population and working-age population coupled with an increasing proportion of the elderly population—the extent of population aging defined as a larger proportion of the elderly population to the total population can still be increased as long as the elderly live longer.

Thanks to economic and social developments, Chinese life expectancy has risen from 67.8 years in 1982 to 74 years in 2010. Given healthy longevity as a precondition, the elderly should be viewed as no less precious for human resources and human capital than any other age group; therefore, the second demographic dividend takes on a remarkable significance only in consideration of the labor supply and the accumulation of human capital.

It is worth stressing that the use of a demographic dividend is conditional, particularly as it requires a specific series of institutional conditions.

Numerous existing literatures indicate that, for developing countries, the key to catching up with developed countries is simply through promoting faster economic growth than that of the developed countries, thus resulting in a convergence. This convergence is conditional convergence, however, insofar as various latent features of developing countries can become practical sources of economic growth by simply meeting a series of material and institutional conditions, thus realizing a quicker economic growth (Sala-i-Martin, 1996).

The drop of China's population dependency ratio began in the mid-1960s, but only the reform and opening-up initiated in the late 1970s created the conditions under which the first demographic dividend could be utilized. The second demographic dividend required further conditions, which come down to reforms of the educational system, employment system, household registration system, social security system, and other similar social and policy structures.

In fact, the demographic dividend is not only a concept coined by economists to take into account population factors as a separate variable in economic growth, but also a catalyst that allows other variables to contribute to economic growth throughout certain periods of time. Therefore, in a growth accounting that incorporates demographic factors, the variable dependence ratio can only cover a residual of the demographic dividend, while many other variables—including capital formation, labor input, human capital accumulation, and TFP—are all closely related insofar as they reflect a demographic dividend.

Therefore, both the first and second demographic dividends should be understood and exploited in the same way—that is, by taking advantage of beneficial population properties to maximize the utilization of all growth sources. The difference might be that, while the first demographic dividend primarily allows for an inputs-driven growth model characterizing the dual economy development, the second demographic dividend should spur a TFP-driven growth model characterizing the neoclassical growth period.

For different countries in different stages of global development, the first demographic dividend both arrives and departs at different points in time; on the one hand, if it comes early, then it also goes sooner, while, on the other, if the dividend arrives later in a country's development, then it also lasts for a longer period of time. In fact, in many countries experiencing early development, the obvious effects of a demographic dividend were not observed, since the demographic transition there had been progressing very slowly and smoothly.

Along with the arrival of its era of aging, therefore, China does not necessarily have a particular problem with a demographic debt compared to other countries. Although China has indeed enjoyed the contribution of the demographic dividend to its economic growth, it only needs to avoid a "vacuum period" of demographic dividends between the acquisitions of a first and second demographic dividend. If China continues on this route, which simultaneously extends the first demographic dividend while creating the conditions for a second demographic dividend, it may avoid the negative influence brought about by the aging of its population to economic growth and thereby maintain sustained economic growth.

5.3 MOTIVES FOR SAVING AND THE PENSION SYSTEM

In terms of the general life cycle, a person is first counted among the juvenile dependent population, then becomes a member of the productive working population through employment after reaching an appropriate working age, and ends as a member of the elderly dependent population after withdrawing from the labor market.

Correspondingly, the primary period of employment is mainly between the ages of 20 through 60, with the actual commencement of employment being postponed for four to five years after the citizen in question initially reaches a working age in order to obtain further education. Irrespective of whether a person obtains income from labor, however, the person's consumption actually occurs throughout his/her entire life.

The life cycle pattern for Chinese urban households is depicted in Figure 5.4, from which the life cycle of an individual's labor income and consumption can be characterized as follows. Firstly, relatively invariable consumption is maintained throughout a lifetime. Secondly, income from labor only begins when a person reaches about 20 years old, is rapidly enhanced afterward, and remains stable at the highest level during the ages between 25 and 40. Thirdly, labor income steadily drops after the age of 45, until it vanishes at about 60 years old.

Because of the asymmetrical nature between income and consumption over a given life cycle, the individual, family, and even society must make provision in order to balance relatively invariable consumption with inconsistent incomes during different periods of life. Therefore, in a period of time characterized by an increase in the working-age population and a decreasing dependence ratio, a high savings rate can be realized in order to help with capital formation. In China's period of rapid economic development, while the dependence ratio has declined, the savings rate—namely, the ratio of capital formation to total GDP—has continued to increase. In addition to other factors—for example, biased distribution of national

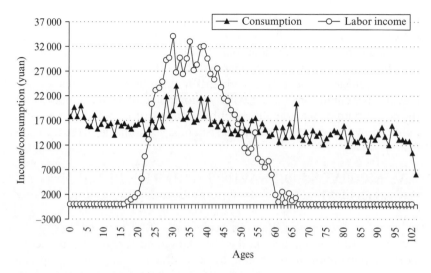

Source: Author's calculation based on CULS in 2010.

Figure 5.4 Life cycle of individual's labor income and consumption

income among individuals, enterprises, and the state, lack of social security, and people's propensity to save—demographic factors have laid a
foundation for maintaining a high savings rate in China during the reform
period.

As the absolute number of the working-age population falls, one of the
most severe challenges facing the economic growth of an aging society is
that a high savings rate can no longer be sustained. To this day, there have
been many critiques of China's high savings that may soon become irrel-
evant, whereas less attention is paid to how China will be able to maintain
its capital formation as its population ages.

As can be predicted, in an environment predicated on an aging population, people's behaviors governing production, consumption, and saving
will be built on the basis of precaution for old age, which tends to induce
a new motive to save. Whether such a motivation can bring about a high
savings rate, however, relies on institutional arrangements. Typically, the
family-based elderly support model and pay-as-you-go public pension
model, both of which rely on an intergenerational transfer of resources,
are insufficient to generate the motivation to save for old age. Instead, a
public pension system based on full accumulation motivates saving, and,
when the accumulated funds enter the capital market, such a saving can be
transformed into capital. As those conditions need to be created through

long-term institution building, however, as is the case in mature market economies, China has a long way to go to obtain such a new source of savings.

First of all, to a large extent, support for China's elderly still comes from families. As a result of the incompleteness of a public elderly support system—namely, the relatively low coverage rate and participation rate of pension programs, especially for urban non-employed residents, informal employees, and migrant workers and rural residents—a large proportion of the Chinese elderly have to rely on financial support from other family members. According to a nationwide survey conducted in 2009, 34.4 percent of the elderly (22.2 percent of male and 46.4 percent of female respondents respectively) live off the support of other family members (Department of Population and Employment, National Bureau of Statistics, 2010).

Second, China's basic pension system is primarily of the pay-as-you-go type—that is, the pooled pension funds collected from incumbents are immediately paid to the retirees without accumulation. Theoretically, China presently implements a two-pillar pension system for urban employees, which is supposed to allow for the coexistence of a social pooling program characterized by both a pay-as-you-go and a partially funded system with an individual account separated from the social pooling account. Because of the lack of funds, however, the two accounts have long been mixed, such that participants' contribution to the individual accounts is not accumulated but used as an expenditure of the social pooling account. As a result, accumulation in an individual's personal account was virtually zero until 2001, when a pilot reform aiming to inject money into the individual account was initiated in Liaoning, a northeast province.

As the result of this pilot reform, first in Liaoning province and then in several follow-up provinces, there has been an increase in the accumulation of the overall pension fund (or the difference between revenue and expenditure) since 2001 (Figure 5.5). Owing to the low contribution rate and limited number of provinces that have implemented the reform, the general accumulation in the pension fund in terms of both absolute quantity and ratio to the amount of overall expenditure is still too small to declare a partially funded system.

Looking into the accumulation of individual accounts, for example, researchers found that, in 2011, only 270.3 billion *yuan* had been accumulated in the account, compared to the bookkeeping figure of 2085.9 billion *yuan*, and that there was a gap of 2215.6 billion *yuan* between what would be expected and what actually existed (Zheng, 2012, p. 2). The balance shown in Figure 5.5 amounts to 1949.7 billion *yuan*, a much bigger surplus than that which had been accumulated in the individual account; one of

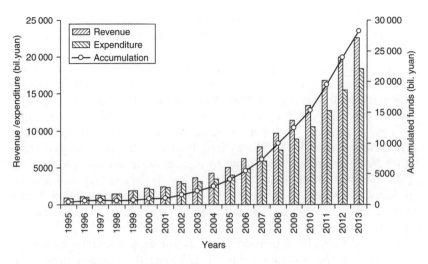

Source: National Bureau of Statistics (2014).

Figure 5.5   Revenue, expenditure, and accumulation of pension funds

the reasons that the surplus could not be transferred into the empty individual account is because the social pension system is not yet a nationwide pooling program and the accumulated balance is highly concentrated in a few provinces.

In 2012, for example, seven provinces held 55.9 percent of the total balance—namely, the difference between the revenue and the expenses of the pension fund. In an extreme case, Guangdong—a developed coastal province and the primary destination for migrant workers—contained 16.2 percent of the country's total pension balance, owing to the fact that it receives a huge contribution from migrant workers without having to expend resources on them, since they are mostly young and highly mobile among regions.

With the pay-as-you-go nature of the system, not only is China's pension system incapable of inducing a new motive for saving and/or source of capital formation, but it is also bound to give rise to a crisis of support for the elderly in the future. The pay-as-you-go system is usually established and operated based on the availability of a large-scale working-age population or, to put it simply, on a low dependence ratio. If such conditions no longer exist, at least one of the following adjustments must be done. That is, if a society cannot increase labor productivity at the same pace as the dependence ratio changes, it has no choice but to increase the contribution rate, reduce the payment level, or raise the retirement age in response to the pending crisis (Turner, 2006). For a country like China that is characterized by growing old before getting rich, however, all these are painful adjustments and hard tasks.

Lastly, the capital market is not developed, and indirect financing still occupies a leading position in China. This can be seen by comparing the composition of financial assets between China and the United States. In 2008, the ratio of bank deposits to GDP was 166 percent in China and 65 percent in the US, the ratio of the market value of the stock market to GDP was 66 percent in China and 135 percent in the US, and the ratio of corporate bonds to GDP was 50 percent in China and 216 percent in the US. Pension funds and life insurance companies in China held 3 percent of the total market value of the stock market, compared to 30 percent in the United States (Howe et al., 2009). More generally, in a 2013–2014 international comparison of competitiveness, China's financial development was ranked as 54th among 148 countries and territories (Schwab, 2014). As a matter of fact, that China's capital market is unable to maintain or increase the value of its accumulated pension funds is one of the primary reasons that the reform aiming to enrich the individual account has made so little progress.

5.4 RETIREMENT AGE AND THE LABOR SUPPLY

As a result of the demographic transition, the aging of a population reflects not only the relative changes in the proportion of different age groups to each other but also the prolongation of a population's average life expectancy, particularly as a result of enhanced longevity. Jointly considering the two factors of healthiness and human capital accumulation (including education, training, and learning-by-doing), the effective working age should be extended as life expectancy increases. If this should occur, it would mean enhanced labor force participation through the postponement of the actual retirement age.

The calculation is simple. On the basis of the United Nations' predictions regarding China's population age structure (United Nations, 2011), the postponement of the actual retirement age will, in roughly ten years, significantly reduce the number of the retired population who depend on the support of working-age adults. For example, according to such calculations, if the actual retirement age can be postponed from 55 to 60 or 65, in 2030 the number of the retirement-age population for every 100 of the working-age population aged 20 and older will be, respectively, reduced from 74.5 under a retirement age of 55 years old to 49.1 under a retirement age of 60 years old and 30.4 under a retirement age of 65 years old. That will not only help close the gap in pension funds but also enhance labor force participation.

It is important to note that the legal retirement age is different from the actual retirement age, such that, even given a fixed legal retirement age, there could be a large deviation in the actual retirement age following labor market conditions. Researchers find that, presently, the actual retirement age of Chinese urban workers is 53 years, which is substantially different from the legal retirement age of 60 years for men and 50 or 55 years for women. If changes are made only to the legal retirement age but the labor market is unable to fully support these populations, it would mean that the choice between employment and retirement would effectively be revoked and that this population group would possess a critically fragile status in the labor market.

It is true that, in many developed countries, raising the legal retirement age has become a widespread option for tackling the labor shortage and for filling the pension gap. In 2010, for example, the average retirement age in OECD countries was 62.9 for male workers and 61.8 for female workers (OECD, 2011). A comparison of two important conditions between China and developed countries, however, would not suggest an immediate increase to the retirement age for China.

First, people in different income groups have different life expectancies after retirement. Life expectancy is the most comprehensive indicator that reflects a given population's health condition, which is influenced by their level of economic and social development at the aggregate level and is closely associated with the income, medical services, and even educational level of the individual within different population groups. Therefore, different groups within the population with a similar retirement age have different remaining life expectancies after retirement; thus the time span for drawing a pension varies.

For example, even in the United States, where overall income and levels of medical service are relatively high, for the remaining life span of the population aged 65 years in 1997, women could, in general, expect to live as many as 19.2 years after retirement, while the population as a whole averaged 17.7 years, but men in low-income groups lived, on average, only 11.3 years after retirement (Weller, 2000). The difference in life expectancy can be expected to be much more pronounced in China. As for the disparity among regions, in 2010 the average life expectancy was 80.3 years in Shanghai but only 68.1 years in Qinghai, one of the poorest provinces. Although the life expectancy data for certain age groups are unavailable, the remaining life expectancies of the retired may hold enormous disparities among population groups, because China has greater income inequality and social security coverage is very low compared to the US.

Second, the overall endowments of human capital in China are remarkably mixed among population age groups. The feasibility of postponing the retirement age with the aim of increasing labor force participation is that an older worker's education attainment is not at a significant disadvantage compared to that of the younger worker; with their additional work experiences, older workers retain competitiveness in the labor market. While this is more or less the reality for most developed countries, it is not for China. For example, among the US's working-age population, the average number of years of schooling of the 20-year-old population is 12.6 years, while that of the 60-year-old population is 13.7 years. Quite different, at present, is China's working-age population, in which the older the population group the lower their educational level. For example, the average number of years of schooling drops from close to 10 at 24 years old to 6 at 60 years old (Figure 5.6).

Any given public policy is operable only if it contains a fair idea at the beginning of its design. At present, Chinese workers approaching the retirement age are a transitional generation, shouldering the legacy from the country's earlier planned period. That is, their human capital endowments put them in a disadvantageous competitive position in the labor market. Once the retirement age is extended, workers in the older group will be more likely to be unemployed or drop out of the labor force, as

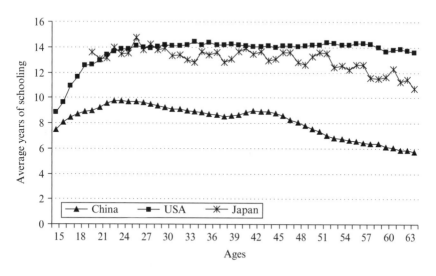

Source: Niu and Wang (2010).

Figure 5.6 International comparison of years of schooling by age

is expected through the "discouraged worker effect." In addition, being unable to receive pension benefits before reaching the postponed legal retirement age and living shorter life spans as a low-income group, they will benefit significantly less over their entire life spans than they would have under the current policy.

In recent years, although employment pressure has decreased as a result of a tighter labor market, the competitive position of this particular group of workers has remained relatively unchanged. Based on 2010 Population Census data, while the labor force participation rate of Chinese non-agricultural workers reached its peak of 86 percent at the ages between 30 and 35, and then rapidly decreased, only 57 percent of those between 50 and 55 and 13.8 percent of those aged between 60 and 65 participated in the labor force (Cai, 2013). In conclusion, the conditions for postponing the retirement age have not yet been achieved.

5.5 CONCLUSION

The commonly discussed demographic dividend refers to a productive population age structure, which provides a window of opportunity for extra sources of economic growth through the labor supply, savings rate, return to capital investment, and TFP performance. Stemming from this notion, we can assert that, after China passed through the turning point characterized by the dependence ratio going from a decline to an increase, its demographic dividend virtually began to disappear. The reason many scholars and policy researchers do not accept such an assertion is that they are reluctant to admit the possible exhaustion of the growth potential in China, which has been experiencing a miraculous economic performance for the past 35 years. In holding to such wishful thinking, however, they may fail to recognize new opportunities that are necessary for China's future growth.

As a researcher who has insistently warned of the imminent disappearance of the demographic dividend, I myself am not a pessimist regarding the prospect of the Chinese economy, but believe that only when we face up to the ongoing changes to the stages of economic development will China find its way to soundly sustaining long-term economic growth. The next stage of development following the Lewis Turning Point is that of so-called neoclassical growth, in which sustainable economic growth is decisively dependent on the enhancement of TFP. In the United States and developed European countries, for example, GDP growth is sustained because the TFP there continues to grow, whereas, in countries considered to be stuck in the middle-income trap, economic growth stagnates because TFP performances are unsatisfactory.

While the specific feature of growing old before getting rich presents special challenges to China, as long as there is still a wide gap in technologies and innovations compared to more developed countries, creating a unique opportunity window, the country will continue to catch up at a reasonably high rate through the advantage of backwardness. That is, assuming correct policy reforms are carried out, it can take advantage of the potential offered by the growth rate, which includes the exploitation of the second demographic dividend.

In an aging society, whether savings can be motivated by and transformed as capital accumulation depends on a series of institutional settings, particularly in the realm of a support system for the aged (Lee and Mason, 2006). In China specifically, appropriate social support systems for the elderly should be built on a multilayered and multi-pillar foundation that can simultaneously expand coverage and motivate saving. Such a system should include at least two components: first, to establish a social pension program that universally covers every senior citizen with basic financial support; and, second, to transform the current pay-as-you-go system to a partially funded system in order to provide an incentive for saving and the financial sustainability of pension funds.

Based on a policy option simulation, for example, Cai and Meng (2004) suggest that if the social old age support system can be completely transformed from the currently implemented pay-as-you-go type into a fully funded type—namely, a fully filled individual account—a much greater proportion of retirees will not rely on the country's social pooling pension provision in the future and, as a result, the social financial burden of supporting the elderly will be substantially reduced.

Expanding the overall labor force and reducing the social burden of supporting the elderly should not be done at the expense of those currently approaching the retirement age, however. At present, a more feasible policy option is not to postpone the retirement age but to create human capital conditions for the younger generations of workers so that they will be able to adapt their skills in the process of industrial upgrading and to work longer before they reach retirement.

The demographic dividend, which has benefited the fast growth of the Chinese economy, not only involves a sufficient supply of labor but also encompasses the expansion of education and skills for workers. Changes in the population age structure have also created several new, positive conditions, which would be advantageous to expanding and deepening education and may be regarded as the second demographic dividend created by the accumulation of human capital.

The changes in China's age structure caused by the country's demographic transition can be observed through the declining percentage of the elementary education-level population (that is, aged 5–14 years). Along with this tendency towards the decline of certain age demographics is the lagging change in the working-age population, namely, that the latter change is represented first by an anticipated rise, then stabilization, and finally a subsequent drop. The change in the relationship between the variations of these two age groups will bring about a drop in the ratio of the school-age population to the working-age population. The economic result of this phenomenon is that existing constraints on educational resources will experience obvious alleviation following the change in the population age structure; thus the country, society, and families may put more resources towards education. Chapter 9 will go deeper into the discussion of human capital accumulation.

REFERENCES

Cai, Fang (2013), *Demystifying the Chinese Economic Development*, Beijing: China Social Sciences Press.

Cai, Fang, and Xin Meng (2004), "Demographic Change, System Transition, and Sustainability of Social Pension Model," *Comparative Studies*, 10, 179–206.

Department of Population and Employment, National Bureau of Statistics (2010), *China Population Statistical Yearbook 2009*, Beijing: China Statistics Press.

Fan, Jingjing (ed.) (1995), *China's Population Structure by Age and Sex*, Beijing: China Population Publishing House.

Howe, Neil, Richard Jackson, and Keisuke Nakashima (2009), *China's Long March to Retirement Reform: The Graying of the Middle Kingdom Revisited*, Washington, DC: Center for Strategic and International Studies and Prudential Foundation.

Lee, Ronald, and Andrew Mason (2006), "What Is the Demographic Dividend?," *Finance and Development*, 43 (3), 16–17.

National Bureau of Statistics (2012), *Tabulation on the 2010 Census of the People's Republic of China*, Beijing: China Statistics Press.

National Bureau of Statistics (2014), *China Statistical Yearbook 2014*, Beijing: China Statistics Press.

Niu, Jianlin, and Guangzhou Wang (2010), "Composition and Development of the Chinese Education System," in Fang Cai (ed.), *The China Population and Labor Yearbook*, Vol. 2: *The Sustainability of Economic Growth from the Perspective of Human Resources*, Boston, MA: Brill, pp. 43–66.

OECD (2011), *Pensions at a Glance 2011: Retirement-Income Systems in OECD and G20 Countries*, Paris: OECD.

Sala-i-Martin, Xavier (1996), "The Classical Approach to Convergence Analysis," *Economic Journal*, 106, 1019–1036.

Schwab, Klaus (ed.) (2014), *The Global Competitiveness Report 2013–2014*, Geneva: World Economic Forum.

Turner, Adair (2006), "Pension Challenges in an Aging World," *Finance and Development*, 43 (3), 36–39.

United Nations (2011), *World Population Prospects: The 2010 Revision*, CD-ROM edn., New York: United Nations, Department of Economic and Social Affairs, Population Division.

Weller, Christian (2000), *Raising the Retirement Age: The Wrong Direction for Social Security*, Briefing Paper, Washington, DC: Economic Policy Institute.

Zheng, Bingwen (2012), *China Pension Report 2012*, Beijing: Economy and Management Publishing House.

6.   The risk of a middle-income trap

Either one goes forward, or he'll be left behind; either one becomes joyful,
or he'll be sad; either one gets what he wants, or he'll lose it.
(Deng Xi [545–501 BC])

Based on the view that East Asia is the most dynamic region in the world,
the World Bank conducts a thematic study of the East Asian economy
every four years to summarize its unique experiences and lessons in development and to expose specific problems and challenges facing it over
defined periods of time. In its 2007 report, *An East Asian Renaissance:*
Ideas for Economic Growth, the World Bank raised the issue of a "middle-
income trap" for the first time. The report shows that "middle-income
countries have grown less rapidly than either rich or poor countries" (Gill
and Kharas, 2007).

Since then, the concept of the middle-income trap has been increasingly
discussed among economists. It has been used to illustrate the predica-
ments of certain Latin American and Asian economies and is applied as
a reference for passing judgment on China's economic prospects. Its
relevance to China's particular case, meanwhile, has drawn more attention since the Development Research Center of the State Council and the
World Bank jointly conducted a study on how China can overcome such
a middle-income trap (World Bank and Development Research Center of
the State Council, People's Republic of China, 2013).

Meanwhile, many researchers disagree on the very use of the concept
of the middle-income trap itself. Although systematic research is not yet
available, we can summarize the expression of such disagreements as they
have appeared in media and public discussions. First and foremost, some
researchers who are not familiar with the term "trap" in economics literature suggest that it connotes a "conspiracy theory." That is, if one literally interprets the term "trap," it would be difficult to understand that an
economy can be framed through the usage of such a term. What's more,
economists whose thinking is influenced by neoclassical theory believe
that, unlike the theory of the poverty trap or the identifiably vicious
circle of poverty, there is not yet an economic theory available that can
adequately and fully explain the many phenomena related to the so-called
middle-income trap. Additionally, certain schools of thought that interpret

the situation on the ground in a manner differently than those adhering to the middle-income trap as portrayed in this investigation suppose that the middle-income trap theory lacks empirical evidence. Last but not least, researchers who have only superficial knowledge of the Chinese economy doubt the issue's relevance to China.

A concept or proposition is worth bringing to the forefront so long as it can be analyzed through theoretical frameworks and has both significant empirical evidence and specific relevance, so that a more thorough discussion and studies can be carried out. For that reason, this study supports the basic concept of the middle-income trap and holds that relevant studies should be expanded. This chapter reviews relevant economic theories—theories of economic growth in particular—and demonstrates that the middle-income trap can certainly be included in existing frameworks of economic growth analysis or, further, has the potential for forming a special framework of its own. It then introduces several empirical studies and statistical proofs of the middle-income trap and summarizes relevant characteristics of the concept. By introducing characteristics of China's economic development phase, it discusses the implications of the concept of the middle-income trap to China's sustainable economic growth.

6.1 THE THEORETICAL BASIS OF THE MIDDLE-INCOME TRAP

Traditionally, the word "trap" is used to describe an economic state of hyper-stable equilibrium that is beyond a comparable static equilibrium and cannot be changed by normal short-term outside forces. For example, after the effect of a given factor that helps improve per capita income is fully brought to bear, because it is somewhat unsustainable, other restraining factors will begin to work and offset that effect, bringing per capita income back to the original level.

The pessimistic views of Thomas Robert Malthus on the relationship between population growth and economic development are reflected in the "Malthusian trap" or the "Malthusian equilibrium." R.R. Nelson went further to combine the Malthusian model with the Harrod–Domar growth model to form a development theory, which is expressed as a low-level equilibrium trap being indicative of less-developed countries.[1] Moreover, not only is absolute poverty an equilibrium state; some economic historians have put forward the hypothesis of a "high-level equilibrium trap" as they try to explain China's historical development and solve the Needham Puzzle (Elvin, 1973). Therefore, the use of the term "equilibrium trap" has a long history in development economics.

The concept is conducive to deducing policy implications from theoretical analyses. Based on the low-level equilibrium trap hypothesis, development economics has developed the "critical minimum effort" and the "big-push" theories, among other explanatory hypotheses, as well as corresponding policy implications. Another example can be found in the hypotheses of Theodore W. Schultz, who sees the traditional agriculture that is *de rigueur* in developing countries as a state of equilibrium in and of itself. Based on this, he derives policy suggestions for reforming traditional agriculture through the introduction of new factors of production to break the equilibrium (Schultz, 1964).

However, the aforementioned development economic theories concerning equilibrium state analysis have not been fully incorporated into mainstream growth theories. In reality, mainstream economists have long separated the neoclassical analysis of economic growth from the development factors that can be observed based on the previously mentioned hypotheses. Despite this, Hansen and Prescott (2002) attempt to meld the Malthusian equilibrium model and Solow's neoclassical growth model and analyze them using a unified theoretical framework. Hayashi and Prescott (2008) also notice that there is a transitional phase from the Malthusian model to the Solow model, the key to which is to eliminate barriers deterring labor migration.

Compared with the early industrialized countries whose economic growth is a homogeneous process, those countries still economically catching up, as it were, have a distinct characteristic—namely, a dual economic structure. In reality, the dual economy defined by Arthur Lewis is just a transitional state between the Malthusian poverty trap and the Solow neoclassical growth model, and is prevalent in developing countries. In this phase, economic growth has gone beyond the vicious poverty cycle in which income growth leads to a population increase, which, in turn, drags the income level down to a basic subsistence level, and entered a phase characterized by the modern sectors continually absorbing agricultural surplus labor until the economy encounters the Lewis Turning Point, so that there is no longer an unlimited supply of labor and the system becomes more and more neoclassical-like.

Economist Masahiko Aoki divides economic development in East Asia into the Malthusian phase of the poverty trap (M-phase), the government-led development phase (G-phase), the Kuznets process—in which development is realized through structural shifts—(K-phase), the human capital-based development phase (H-phase), and the post-demographic transition phase (PD-phase) (Aoki, 2012). In fact, what he phrases as the Kuznets phase can also be called the Lewis development phase, though the former focuses more on structural change and the latter on labor reallocation.

The division of development phases in such a way reveals that the shift from one development phase to another means a jump or breach, or, in other words, while shaking off the poverty trap is an important step, the shift from middle-income to high-income levels (from the K-phase to the H-phase and, ultimately, the PD-phase) is an equally important, thrilling jump. If the latter is so challenging that some economies have long failed to break through this phase, and the phenomenon is so widespread that it has had statistical significance and entails important theoretical and policy implications, then it is logical for us to use the concept of the middle-income trap.

Although it is not necessarily in the immediate context of the middle-income trap, researchers have found and tried to conceptualize some stylized facts that may help economists to form an initial theoretical framework for the middle-income trap.

According to the economic growth convergence hypothesis, economic growth depends on multiple factors (or determinants) such as investment rate, human capital accumulation, government functions, infrastructure conditions, and system and policy environments (Barro and Sala-i-Martin, 1995). In other words, at the initial development phase of low per capita income, improvements in these factors push forward economic growth convergence. The accumulation or improvement of those growth-favorable elements is, however, also subject to the law of diminishing marginal effects; when all the "low-hanging fruits" have been harvested, those forces pushing economic growth, while still being necessary conditions, will gradually lose their luster unless the economy successfully shifts to an endogenous growth model driven mainly by TFP.

Some studies find a link between the middle-income trap phenomenon and globalization. For example, Eeckhout and Jovanovic compare the economic growth of various economies before and after globalization, and find that, in the era of globalization, the long-term growth rate of those economies (if they are ranked using the criterion of per capita income) would be U-shaped. An explanation in the study is that laborers in rich countries possess better technologies and skills, so the number of high-skill positions has grown, particularly with the global shift in economic structures, whereas poor countries do not have the same level of skills, but the number of unskilled jobs have increased; those countries in between, meanwhile, do not have either of these labor resource advantages (Eeckhout and Jovanovic, 2007). Garrett goes further to explain that, when rich countries become increasingly affluent as a result of their accelerating technological advancement, the poorest countries have achieved faster growth in their manufacturing, but those countries in between fail to make headway in either direction (Garrett, 2004).

This, in reality, hints at a generalized theoretical explanation for the middle-income trap; that is, countries at higher economic development stages obviously gain from globalization owing to their comparative advantages in capital-intensive and technology-intensive industries thanks to their technological innovation capabilities, if we consider comparative advantage to be the source of productivity enhancement. Those at lower economic development stages also gain from globalization given their comparative advantages in labor-intensive industries as a result of their rich labor resources and low labor costs. The middle-income countries in between, however, gain less from globalization because they do not have comparative advantages in either aspect. We summarize the scenario as a "comparative advantage vacuum," which, although not completely accurate, helps to illustrate the awkward situation the middle-income countries are facing.

In addition, such hypotheses can generally apply to economies that have entered the high-income-country phase. First of all, economists believe that TFP growth is a difficult task even for developed countries. For example, Cowen (2011) thinks that, since the 1970s, the United States has been stuck on a "technological plateau," which slows its growth rate. Hayashi and Prescott (2002) suggest that it was the slow growth of productivity that caused the Japanese economy to plateau. Secondly, some researchers also explore the loss suffered by workers in developed countries as a result of international labor relocation (see Samuelson, 2004).

Therefore, there is no easy way to achieve higher productivity performance and to cope with a potential loss in the economic globalization for all countries at any given stage of economic development, and countries in the middle of transition in particular are bound to face extraordinary challenges. As the 2007 World Bank report points out, development strategies and policies that are starkly different from previous ones must be adopted during a country's transition from the middle-income to the high-income phase (Gill and Kharas, 2007), which requires a series of hard choices and a breathtaking leap forward.

6.2 INTERNATIONAL LESSONS AND EMPIRICAL EVIDENCE

According to categorizations by the World Bank in recent years and calculated by the "atlas method" that is similar to the one used for market exchange rates, in 2010 those countries with a per capita gross national income (GNI) of less than US $1005 are in the low-income group, whereas those with per capita GNI of US $1006 to US $3975 are categorized as belonging to the lower-middle-income group; those with per capita GNI of US $3976 to US $12275 belong to the upper-middle-income group, and those with per capita GNI of more than US $12276 are high-income countries (World Bank, 2012). Of course, these standards of categorization are dynamic. Based on similar dynamic standards, if a country steps into the rank of middle-income countries but fails to graduate and become a high-income country after a long period of growth, then it falls into the middle-income trap.

According to such standards, if countries that have become rich through oil exports are excluded, apart from the developed economies such as the USA and European countries, so far only a handful of economies such as Japan, South Korea, Singapore, Taiwan, Hong Kong, and Macao have successfully surpassed the middle-income stage. Many Latin American countries which once had similar levels of development to European countries, as well as some Asian countries that have long been middle-income countries, have failed to become members of the high-income club. Even some Latin American countries whose per capita incomes once crossed the demarcation line between middle-income and high-income groups have ultimately retrogressed to the middle-income levels.

Thanks to technological advancement, institutional innovation, and strengthened resource mobilization capabilities, the world's production frontier has been expanding over time. Therefore, it is more appropriate to use relative, instead of absolute, per capita income to categorize income groups and, in particular, to examine the middle-income trap as a phenomenon of lingering growth. Some economists use the purchasing power parity method suggested by economic historian Angus Maddison to estimate the per capita GDP of particular economies and to compile the catch-up index (CUI), with values presented as a percentage of the US level of per capita GDP (Woo, 2012). Using this method, the authors can prove the existence of the middle-income trap to an extent.

To be exact, this study defines those with a CUI higher than 55 percent as high-income countries, those with a CUI between 20 and 55 percent as middle-income countries, and those with a CUI lower than 20 percent as low-income countries. Among the 132 countries being compared, there were 32 middle-income countries in 1960 and 24 in 2008. Changes in the group show that there is a 50 percent possibility of the middle-income countries falling into the middle-income trap. Considering cross-group movement, the possibility of moving to the lower level is higher than that of moving upward. Although there are countries from other groups moving into the middle-income group, the number of countries moving upward from the low-income group doubles that of those moving downward from the high-income group.

There are studies that reveal the formation of the middle-income trap from a dynamic perspective. For example, they summarize statistics regarding the concerned economies and find that, in the middle-income phase, a country's economic growth could not and would not maintain its growth momentum forever. Therefore, the study of those phases in which economic growth generally slows down can verify the existence of the middle-income trap. Based on the findings of economic historian Angus Maddison, one such study suggests that, over the past 100 years, 40 economies have seen their per capita GDP reach the turning point of US $7000, 31 of which saw their growth rates decline by 2.8 percentage points on average after reaching that turning point (Ho et al., 2009).

Among numerous such studies, the Nobel laureate Michael Spence finds that 13 economies in developing Asia, Latin America, and Africa had achieved annual growth rates of 7 percent or higher in the 25 or more years following the 1950s. However, with the exception of Japan and the Asian Four Tigers—namely, South Korea, Hong Kong, Taiwan, and Singapore—none of them sustained this fast growth upon entering the middle-income group (Spence, 2011).

There are also studies that attempt to prove that the middle-income trap is non-existent. Among them, investment bank economist Jonathan Anderson chooses ten "middle-income countries" with a per capita income of US $8000–10 000 and ten "low-income countries" with a per capita income of US $1000–3000 and compares their long-term economic performance (Anderson, 2011). His findings can be summarized as follows. First, "middle-income countries" performed well in the first decade of this century, despite the fact that they had stagnated during the previous decade. Second, "low-income countries" have failed to show better growth performance compared with their middle-income counterparts. Third, the average growth rates of the countries in the two groups are almost the same. From these findings, Anderson comes to the conclusion that the middle-income trap does not exist. However, his data and interpretation are not adequate to come to such a conclusion.

Firstly, his categorization of the two groups of countries differs from that of typical income-based categorization. For example, his grouping of "middle-income countries" includes both former planned economy countries and those Latin American and Middle East countries heavily dependent on their oil resources for growth, as well as Brazil, Russia, and South Africa, the richest of the BRICS countries (the others are India and China). Generally speaking, they are the richest countries among the middle-income bloc. The "low-income countries" in his categorization are almost all those that have already fallen into the middle-income trap or still risk falling into it.

Secondly, the middle-income trap is a historical concept and might not necessarily match the economy realities of today. Those middle-income countries that had been in trouble before the start of this century were nothing but examples of falling into the middle-income trap. Although some of them have performed well over the past ten years, they have not necessarily made the prerequisite shift necessary for overcoming the middle-income trap. Studies show that the soaring demand for a bulk stock of energy and raw materials, in which Latin American countries have a comparative advantage, leads to deindustrialization in those countries. For example, according to an article in Argentine newspaper *Clarín*, while the growth rate of primary product exports in Latin America in the period from the 1990s to the first decade of the twenty-first century increased from 2.6 percent to 11.4 percent, the growth rate of exports of medium-technology-intensive products declined from 16.3 percent to 4.7 percent, and that of high-technology-intensive products declined from 35 percent to 3.8 percent, resulting in a substantial trade deficit in those countries.[2]

No one is sure at the moment that those countries that have benefited from surging demand as a result of China's strong economic growth and are heavily reliant on the exports of their resource products and growth of preliminary industries will have sufficient growth sustainability to become high-income countries. There are quite a few such historical examples where a country temporarily became a high-income economy but, ultimately, was forced back into a lower-income bracket. Take Argentina, for example. According to World Bank data, Argentina registered a per capita GNI of US $8140 in 1997. However, it subsequently fell below that level for many years. In 2004, its per capita income was only 44 percent of its 1997 level. Since then, its economic growth has been accelerating, with its per capita income reaching the level of 1997 in 2010.

Thirdly, the middle-income trap model does not assume absolute convergence, and, therefore, the fact that the growth performance of lower-middle-income countries fails to significantly surpass that of upper-middle-income countries does not necessarily mean it is illogical; rather, it is an indication of the middle-income trap. We use the concept of the middle-income trap simply and exactly to indicate that countries hoping to possess rich economies face the challenge of breaking through the middle-income equilibrium trap, just as those hoping to shake off poverty need to overcome the low-income equilibrium trap.

Chinese academics and policy researchers often relate the middle-income trap to particular phenomena in certain countries. For example, the middle-income trap and Latin American trap are considered synonymous. Such discussions tend to focus on the consequences of countries falling into the middle-income trap, while they pay less attention to the causes that

Table 6.1　Catch-up index and Gini coefficients in selected countries

	1960–1984		1984–2008	
	Change in CUI	Gini coefficient	Change in CUI	Gini coefficient
Argentina	−12.17	43.8 (1981)	−1.64	45.8 (2009)
Brazil	2.46	58.6 (1983)	−2.45	54.5 (2008)
Chile	−12.79	55.5 (1984)	17.39	52.3 (2009)
Colombia	−1.03	50.8 (1988)	−0.71	58.5 (2006)
Mexico	2.77	48.5 (1984)	−5.03	51.7 (2008)
Venezuela	−42.29	51.2 (1984)	−8.87	43.5 (2006)
The Philippines	−2.22	45.5 (1985)	−1.43	44.0 (2006)

Source:　Woo (2012); dataset of World Development Indicators.

put the countries in the trap in the first place. In what follows, we look into both the consequences and the causes of the middle-income trap.

Income inequality is a typical phenomenon associated with the middle-income trap. Taking some Latin American countries as typical examples of countries stuck in the middle-income trap, one can clearly see that they are more likely to suffer severe income inequality across various periods of time. In Table 6.1, we compare the experiences of catching up with the United States and Gini coefficients in those countries identified by Woo (2012) to be stuck in the middle-income trap. It shows that the biggest Gini coefficients exist typically in the middle-income trap countries, which are located mainly in Latin America.

Such an unequal distribution of income significantly lowers the actual level of human development. For example, in 2010, the calculated human development index of Latin America as a whole was 0.704, but, taking into consideration the income inequality index, the adjusted human development index for the region was only 0.527. That is, the extent of income inequality made Latin America lose over 25 percentage points from the measure of its human development (UNDP, 2011).

After examining the experiences of those countries that are considered to be stuck in the middle-income trap, we can summarize four steps necessary and sufficient for a country to fall into the trap. First, a fast-growing economy inevitably experiences a shift towards slowdown as a result of the disappearance of its traditional comparative advantages. Second, misguided policies, which were intended to tackle the slowdown but fail to grasp the cause of it in the first place, render the economy into one of long-term stagnation. Third, the absence of favorable, sound incentives will lead to unchecked rent-seeking activities, which contribute to the formation of an unfair and unequal pattern of resources and income distribution and, in turn, solidify the power of already-vested interests. Fourth, in order to maintain the existing pattern of distribution, the vested interest groups make every effort to formalize and preserve existing institutions and resist any reforms that are necessary for the public interest.

What is described above can be viewed as either four sequential steps or four phenomena that exist concurrently. Therefore, countermeasures have to be adopted to sever the link from one step to another and to solve the four individual problems simultaneously. In the next section, we discuss the implications of the middle-income trap for China by framing the four phenomena as a point of reference.

6.3   IMPLICATIONS FOR CHINA'S ECONOMIC GROWTH

In 2010, China became the world's second-largest economy, and its per capita GDP reached US $4382, which means that it has become an upper-middle-income country as categorized by the World Bank. Even though the World Bank study predicted that the size of the Chinese economy measured by purchasing power parity would overtake the United States' economy in 2014 to become the world's largest (Giles, 2014), China's per capita GDP still remains in the upper-middle-income group. In addition, where China stands in terms of its distance to the innovative frontier confirms its middle-income position.

For example, China was ranked the 29th most competitive country in the world by *The Global Competitiveness Report 2013–2014*. This high rank, however, is mainly due to non-science-and-technology attributes like the stability of the macroeconomy and the size of the domestic market. In other pillars of the competitive index, China was ranked much lower—for example, 70th in higher education and training, 54th in financial market development, and 85th in technological readiness (Schwab, 2014).

With a rapid and sizable increase in expenditure on research and development, scientific articles published and patents registered in China have grown much faster than in most parts of the world. While China is near the top in total numbers of such achievements, their quality and applicability are still far behind those of the developed countries. For example, measuring the scientific articles published by Chinese scholars by the ratio of those published to the total number cited suggests that China is not yet at the frontier of science and associated technologies (Hatakenaka, 2010; Dutta and Lanvin, 2013).

An upper-middle-income country, China has entered a period of time in which its growth rate is expected to slow down according to the criteria used in scholarly studies. Namely, in terms of per capita GDP, the Chinese economy has already fallen into the interval between the turning point of economic slowdown suggested by Ho et al. (2009) and the turning point of slowdown suggested by Eichengreen et al. (2011). Those authors warn that, because of many hidden problems and unsustainable factors in its economic growth, there is a 70 percent possibility of China being subjected to the inexorable law of economic slowdown. In fact, this predicted economic slowdown had already begun as of 2012 and is expected to continue.

Seen from the perspective of existing economic growth models, China can also be situated in a special development phase. If we use the analytical framework of Hansen and Prescott (2002) and insert the Lewisian dual economy development phase in between the Malthusian growth phase and the Solow growth phase, then it is evident that, as the number of rural surplus laborers decreases, a standing labor shortage has become normal while at the same time the wage level of ordinary workers has been on the rise. As a result, China's economy has passed the Lewis Turning Point and has started to shift to the Solow neoclassical growth pattern.

The migrant worker shortage has become noticeable and drawn public attention since 2004. Meanwhile, the wages of ordinary workers, most noticeably those of migrant workers, have risen continually from 2004 until today, which is in stark contrast with the previous decades, when wage growth virtually stalled. In the period from 2004 to 2013, the real growth rate of migrants' wages was 11.8 percent, whereas the real per capita GDP growth rate was only 9.4 percent, with a declining trend, indicating that the growth rate of ordinary workers' wages tends to be faster than the growth rate of labor productivity.

As a result, rising labor costs started gradually weakening China's comparative advantage and international competitiveness in labor-intensive manufacturing commodities. According to a report on the website of French newspaper *Le Figaro*, given the great pressure of wages inflation and the relatively slower growth of labor productivity in China, its gap in the cost of production to the United States has closed to less than 5 percent.[3] The loss of its comparative advantage is leading China's labor-intensive manufacturing to transfer from the coastal area to inland areas, or even to countries with lower labor costs, as the flying geese paradigm in economics literature suggests.

In conclusion, the economic slowdown resulting from the disappearance of a demographic dividend tends to be a self-reinforcing process: the slower the economy grows, the greater the gap in the growth rates between wage rates and labor productivity, which makes the economy lose its comparative advantage even faster at the same time as its growth slows. To break such a potentially vicious cycle requires being very aware of what causes the initial slowdown and where the new engine of growth can be found.

Even before economic growth decelerated, the income gap in China had become very wide as measured by international standards. Not only is China's Gini coefficient very large, but the income gap between rural areas and urban areas is considered to be the widest in the world. Since that income distribution pattern has been formed partially by the labor market and partially by the unfair distribution of resources and unequal access to public services among different groups of residents, the vested interest groups make various efforts to resist reforms that are intended to change the distributive pattern. This not only sets obstacles for narrowing the income gap but also impedes the improvement of allocation efficiency, which is a sustainable engine of economic growth (especially after the demographic dividend disappears).

Although it has lost much of its comparative advantage in labor-intensive industries, China has yet to gain a comparative advantage in the technology-intensive and capital-intensive sectors, which means the country is facing a "comparative advantage vacuum." China has been one of the biggest beneficiaries of economic globalization, and its further economic growth cannot proceed without opening to the outside world.

Given that China shares almost all the typical challenges facing middle-income countries, raising concerns about the problems of the middle-income trap and a thorough study of related phenomena—as well as the experiences of other economies—are useful for Chinese policy makers.

6.4   CONCLUSION

The concept of the middle-income trap can be explained within an economic analysis framework, verified from economic development experiences, and is relevant to the sustainability of China's economic growth. Therefore, it is useful for academics and policy makers who are concerned with the Chinese economy. In order to investigate the position of the middle-income trap theory in a development economics framework and its relevant policy implications, we may examine the whole process of long-term economic development as portrayed in Figure 6.1, from which one can glean the necessary tasks required to break through the poverty equilibrium trap and the middle-income trap and to make a transition to becoming a high-income economy.

In the process of economic development, an economy is initially faced with the vicious cycle of poverty. Its per capita output growth can be offset by a population increase—namely, per capita income is diluted by

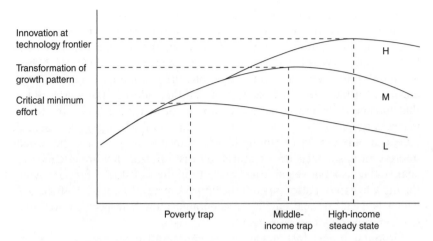

Note: H—high; M—middle; L—low.

Figure 6.1   Turning points of economic growth and breaking-through strategies

the growth of the population. As a result, the standard of living can be maintained only at a subsistence level at best, with savings being hard to accumulate. Even if a technological advancement in the traditional sense occurs, the "critical minimum effort" of escaping the equilibrium trap cannot be made until there is a revolutionary technological and institutional breakthrough, such as the application of technologies and market-scale expansion resulting from an industrial revolution, which makes new technologies profitable (Hansen and Prescott, 2002). Only then can such a state of equilibrium be broken.

Unlike the United States and European countries, which rely on independent innovation at the frontier of science and technology, most of the latecomer countries do not necessarily rely on technological breakthroughs of their own; as long as they can eliminate institutional obstacles that deter the application of new technologies, technologies needed can be obtained through imitating, borrowing, purchasing, and foreign direct investment (Romer, 2010).

In most developing countries whose economic growth can be understood through a dual economy framework, not only is the unlimited labor supply itself an accumulation of one of the necessary production factors, but demographic dividends help to maintain a high savings rate and prevent a diminishing return to capital so as to accelerate capital formation. The changes in industrial structure characterized by labor mobility both between sectors and between rural and urban areas also give rise to a reallocation of resources and improvement in TFP. Therefore, in the process of globalization, the dual economy is capable of bringing about high-rate economic growth. While such an extraordinary growth, however, ends with the advent of the Lewis Turning Point and the loss of the demographic dividend, the economy experiencing it faces a future economic slowdown and, under some conditions, the risk of falling into the middle-income trap.

An indispensable prerequisite for breaking the bottleneck brought about by the Lewis Turning Point and the loss of a demographic dividend in avoiding the middle-income trap is to upgrade the pattern of economic growth from one driven by production factor inputs and resource real-location effects caused by the transition from the agricultural to the non-agricultural sectors to one driven by an improvement in total factor productivity and labor productivity. Once such a shift is made, long-term economic growth will be built on innovation and will become sustainable. In this sense, a host of theoretical models, international experiences, and policy suggestions are significant in helping China cope with the challenges posed by the middle-income trap.

In the next chapters, we will discuss the urgency of improving TFP and the significance of accelerating human capital through education and training. Above all, according to international experiences, a successful transition from the middle-income stage to the high-income stage depends vitally on a host of institutional changes. Kharas names some areas of necessary reform, including the development of the capital market, acceleration of innovation and higher education, improvement of urban management, building of livable cities, formation of an agglomerative effect, the effective rule of law, decentralization, and anti-corruption (Kharas, 2010). Despite the assertion that the effects of those reforms mentioned above may need a decade or so to become manifest, as we will see in the following chapters, some changes to economic reform can actually have an immediate effect on the rapid growth of the Chinese economy.

NOTES

1. For a literature review, see Hayami and Godo (2005).
2. Quoted from a secondary source: "The China Growth Leads to Deindustrialization in Latin America," *Cankao Xiaoxi* [参考消息], August 9, 2011.
3. Quoted from a secondary source: "The Gap in Costs of Production between the United States and China Has Become Negligible," *Cankao Xiaoxi* [参考消息], April 27, 2014.

REFERENCES

Anderson, Jonathan (2011), "Chart of the Day: Is There Really Such a Thing as a 'Middle Income Trap'?," UBS Investment Research, Emerging Economic Comment, July 21.

Aoki, Masahiko (2012), "The Five Phases of Economic Development and Institutional Evolution in China, Japan, and Korea," in Masahiko Aoki, Timur Kuran, and Gérard Roland (eds.), *Institutions and Comparative Economic Development*, Basingstoke: Palgrave Macmillan, pp. 13–47.

Barro, Robert, and Xavier Sala-i-Martin (1995), *Economic Growth*, New York: McGraw-Hill.

Cowen, Tyler (2011), *The Great Stagnation: How America Ate All the Low-Hanging Fruit of Modern History, Got Sick, and Will (Eventually) Feel Better*, New York: Dutton.

Dutta, Soumitra, and Bruno Lanvin (eds.) (2013), *The Global Innovation Index 2013: The Local Dynamics of Innovation*, Ithaca, NY, Fontainebleau, and Geneva: Cornell University, INSEAD, and WIPO.

Eeckhout, Jan, and Boyan Jovanovic (2007), *Occupational Choice and Development*, NBER Working Paper No. 13686, Cambridge, MA: National Bureau of Economic Research.

Eichengreen, Barry, Donghyun Park, and Kwanho Shin (2011), *When Fast Growing Economies Slow Down: International Evidence and Implications for China*, NBER Working Paper No. 16919, Cambridge, MA: National Bureau of Economic Research.

Elvin, Mark (1973), *The Pattern of the Chinese Past: A Social and Economic Interpretation*, Stanford, CA: Stanford University Press.

Garrett, Geoffrey (2004), "Globalization's Missing Middle," *Foreign Affairs*, 83 (6), 84–96.

Giles, Chris (2014), "China to Overtake US as Top Economic Power This Year," *Financial Times*, April 30.

Gill, Indermit, and Homi Kharas (2007), *An East Asian Renaissance: Ideas for Economic Growth*, Washington, DC: World Bank.

Hansen, Gary, and Edward Prescott (2002), "Malthus to Solow," *American Economic Review*, 92 (4), 1205–1217.

Hatakenaka, Sachi (2010), "The Role of Higher Education in High-Technology Industrial Development: What Can International Experience Tell Us?," in Justin Yifu Lin and Boris Pleskovic (eds.), *People, Politics, and Globalization*, Washington, DC: World Bank, pp. 233–265.

Hayami, Yujiro, and Yoshihisa Godo (2005), *Development Economics: From the Poverty to the Wealth of Nations*, 3rd edn., Oxford: Oxford University Press.

Hayashi, Fumio, and Edward Prescott (2002), "The 1990s in Japan: A Lost Decade," *Review of Economic Dynamics*, 5 (1), 206–235.

Hayashi, Fumio, and Edward Prescott (2008), "The Depressing Effect of Agricultural Institutions on the Prewar Japanese Economy," *Journal of Political Economy*, 116 (4), 573–632.

Ho, Ernest, Qing Wang, and Stephen Zhang (2009), "Chinese Economy through 2020: It's Not Whether but How Growth Will Decelerate," Morgan Stanley China Economy, Morgan Stanley Research Asia/Pacific, September 20.

Kharas, Homi (2010), "China's Transition to a High Income Economy: Escaping the Middle Income Trap," in Edwin Lim and Michael Spence (eds.), *Thoughts and Suggestions for China's 12th Five-Year Plan from an International Perspective*, Beijing: China CITIC Press, pp. 470–501.

Romer, Paul (2010), *Which Parts of Globalization Matter for Catch-Up Growth?*, NBER Working Paper No. 15755, Cambridge, MA: National Bureau of Economic Research.

Samuelson, Paul (2004), "Where Ricardo and Mill Rebut and Confirm Arguments of Mainstream Economists Supporting Globalization," *Journal of Economic Perspectives*, 18 (3), 135–146.

Schultz, Theodore William (1964), *Transforming Traditional Agriculture*, Chicago: University of Chicago Press.

Schwab, Klaus (ed.) (2014), *The Global Competitiveness Report 2013–2014*, Geneva: World Economic Forum.

Spence, Michael (2011), *The Next Convergence: The Future of Economic Growth in a Multispeed World*, New York: Farrar, Straus and Giroux.

UNDP (United Nations Development Programme) (2011), *Sustainability and Equity: A Better Future for All*, New York: Palgrave Macmillan.

Woo, Wing Thye (2012), "China Meets the Middle-Income Trap: The Large Potholes in the Road to Catching-Up," *Journal of Chinese Economic and Business Studies*, 10 (4), 313–336.

World Bank (2012), *World Development Report 2012: Gender Equity and Development*, Washington, DC: World Bank.

World Bank and Development Research Center of the State Council, People's Republic of China (2013), *China 2030: Building a Modern, Harmonious, and Creative Society*, Washington, DC: World Bank.

7. The new engine of economic growth

The new emerges out of the destruction of the old. (Han Yu [AD 768–824])

As a result of the decrease in the working-age population and an increase in the population dependency ratio, the demographic dividend enjoyed by the Chinese economy over the past 30 years began disappearing in 2010. It is worth noting that the end of the demographic dividend is always embodied in a reduction in the supply of production factors, especially a reduction of the absolute labor supply, a diminishing return on capital, and a decline of the TFP growth rate resulting from the slowed rate of rural-to-urban migration.

As can be expected by the neoclassical theory of growth, when the traditional engine of growth stalls, the future growth of the Chinese economy is bound to rely on the enhancement of TFP: a new engine powered by technological innovation and improved allocation of resources. For a country in which the government is heavily involved in economic activities, however, the government tends to take action in response to the vanishing of its comparative advantages and the slowdown of the growth rate. One such response—often seen in countries that have experienced similar changes in their development stages—is to stimulate capital investment in the hopes of improving labor productivity through an increase in the capital–labor ratio. When such policies fail, these government efforts usually invite retaliation by the law of diminishing return on capital.

Instead of following up on all aspects of growth sources, this chapter intends only to discuss the necessity of and ways to tackle the phenomenon of a diminishing return on capital in the post-demographic dividend stage of economic development that is of particular relevance to China. Based on an analysis of the challenges currently facing the Chinese economy and existing international lessons, it points out the double tasks facing the transition of the country's economic growth pattern from the dual economy development type to the neoclassical growth type—namely, to retain traditional comparative advantages as long as possible while also seeking a new driver to power economic growth in the long run. These tasks require: (1) formulating a domestic "flying geese paradigm"— namely, transferring labor-intensive manufacturing from coastal to inland regions; and (2) forming a policy climate of creative destruction in order to let enterprises with subpar productivity contract and those with good performance expand so that technological progress is activated.

7.1 THE LAW OF DIMINISHING RETURN ON CAPITAL

The prevailing theory of growth is too simplified to comprehend types of economic development other than that of the neoclassical model. As it is unable to adequately expound upon economic growth (or, more to the point, stagnation) of the Malthusian-type economic development that has dominated most of human history, when the neoclassical theory of growth strips land from factors of production in its model and fails to include the demographic dividend (Hansen and Prescott, 2002), it neither correctly interprets China's miraculous growth over the past decades nor grasps the key points about the challenges currently facing China and those that it is going to face in the near future. There is a classic analogue between the ways in which neoclassical theorists debate the East Asian miracle and how they view the present problems in the Chinese economy.

In its 1993 report, the World Bank used the phrase "East Asian miracle" for the first time to refer to the outstanding economic achievements and growth patterns of the East Asian economies, especially of the Four Tigers (Hong Kong, Singapore, South Korea, and Taiwan). The World Bank's praise of the East Asian experience has touched off the debate over whether East Asian growth can be said to be a miracle as well as whether or not it can be sustained. Based on findings about the East Asian economies by leading economists—most notably Lawrence Lau and Alwyn Young— Paul Krugman asserts that the economic growth in this region is nothing more than the same error the Soviet Union made during its own period of rapid economic growth in the 1950s. Specifically, he believes that growth both in East Asia and in the Soviet Union was driven mainly by labor and capital but little by TFP growth, and therefore the East Asian growth—as in the Soviet Union before it—was not sustainable (Krugman, 1994).

Not all empirical results support the opinion represented by Krugman, however. Research findings on the performance of the TFP of the Four Tigers and other Asian economies have routinely come back with wildly different results, even to the point of complete contradiction. For example, Young's estimate of the annual growth rate of TFP in Singapore during the period 1970 to 1985 was as negligible as 0.1 percent, whereas Marti's estimation for the period 1970 to 1990 was 1.45 percent, the latter being 15 times that of the former (Young, 1994; Marti, 1996). The conflicting findings not only result in different policy implications, but also lead to uncertainty as to the method of measuring TFP and assessing economic performance itself (Felipe, 1997).

Instead of the economic collapse predicted by the "Young–Krugman curse," the Four Tigers have ultimately all joined the high-income group of economies and serve as role models of the successful avoidance of the middle-income trap. The reason why Krugman's prophecy on the fate of East Asian growth was wrong is that he and his fellow economists who firmly held to neoclassical assumptions—namely, that of a labor shortage and hence diminishing return on capital—did not take into account the unique role of the demographic dividend in the economic growth of Asian economies.

A series of studies on the contribution of the demographic dividend to East Asian economies followed the debates taking place on the East Asian miracle, serving as a helpful extension of neoclassical theory and the empirics of growth and offering a more convincing explanation of the growth in those Asian economies concerned (for example, Bloom and Williamson, 1997; Williamson, 1997). In addition, the improvement of econometric techniques and the availability of data have helped people gain a better understanding of those East Asian economies that have successfully modernized (Bhagwati, 1996). That is, their excellent growth performances can be attributed to the contribution both of conventional production factors and of the improvement of TFP. And while, in the early stages of development, TFP growth was mainly gained from taking advantage of the advantage of backwardness resulting from the technological gap with more advanced countries through foreign direct investment and the importation of equipment, it became more and more reliant on independent innovation until it ultimately contributed an overwhelming part to the GDP growth rate at the later stage of development.

In a sense, Professor Krugman's repeated warnings only become meaningful when a country begins shifting its growth patterns from dual economy development to a neoclassical growth model. When Japan and the East Asian Tigers passed through their Lewis Turning Points—characterized by the loss of their comparative advantage in labor-intensive industries—they all experienced a transition of growth patterns and succeeded. As China is now at a similar crossroads, if it is not able to transform its economic growth to a TFP-driven pattern, the diminishing return on capital will ultimately make its growth unsustainable.[1]

For economists, inquiries into sustainable sources of economic growth are always inspirational. Despite the fact that land, labor, and capital were each given significant importance in early economic theories, labor productivity has traditionally been considered an inexhaustible source of economic growth and the cornerstone of the wealth of nations.

Particularly when a country is successively extricated from the Malthusian and Lewisian stages and is moving towards the Solowian stage of development, its continuing economic growth relies heavily on the improvement of labor productivity.

One way to improve labor productivity is to raise the capital–labor ratio. The faster the growth of physical capital relative to the growth of labor, the more it works to develop the deepening of the capital of an enterprise or sector and usually helps to improve labor productivity overall. In reality, this is realized through enterprises purchasing machinery to replace workers in response to the increase in labor cost. Raising the capital–labor ratio, however, is constrained by the diminishing return on capital, as efficiency of production can be decreased as more machinery and equipment are used while skills and technology remain unchanged. This suggests that another way of improving labor productivity—that is, to enhance TFP—has to be phased in.

During the first decade of the twenty-first century, as return to capital investment diminished in China, the relative contribution of factors that drove labor productivity have changed significantly. According to a study by Louis Kuijs, in the period from 1978 to 1994 TFP growth contributed 45.9 percent to the growth of labor productivity, while the increase of the capital–labor ratio contributed 45.3 percent to labor productivity growth. In the period from 2005 to 2009, the share TFP contributed declined to 31.8 percent, and that of the capital–labor ratio increased to 64.7 percent. If such a trend continues, the TFP contribution will further decline to 28.0 percent and the contribution of the capital–labor ratio will increase to 65.9 percent in the period from 2010 to 2015 (Kuijs, 2010).

As a country that has already gone through this process, Japan set a negative example in its alternative between the improvement of TFP and the deepening of capital. In the early 1990s, as a response to the disappearance of the demographic dividend indicated by the precipitous rise in the population dependence ratio, the Japanese economy experienced a deepening of capital through heavy investment, whereas its TFP performance was relatively poor. It turned out that, in its increase in the average productivity of labor, the share contributed by the capital–labor ratio increased from 51 percent in 1985–1991 to 94 percent in 1991–2000, whereas the share of TFP declined from 37 percent to −15 percent during the same period (Asian Productivity Organization, 2008).

Both economic theory and actual experiences in economic development tell us that the effect of raising the capital–labor ratio towards the improvement of labor productivity is constrained by the law of diminishing return on capital. On the other hand, TFP growth is the fountainhead fuelling labor productivity. The defining feature of TFP, which makes it a durable engine of economic growth, is that it has little to do with the input of production factors. Instead, it is the efficiency gained by holding factor input levels constant, and is therefore an inexhaustible source of growth by offsetting the effects of diminishing returns on any tangible factors of production.

Statistically—as a residual of the growth contributions (after deducting the contributions made by inputs of factors)—TFP consists of two parts. First is the reallocative efficiency of resources, which mainly comes from the mobility of production factors between enterprises, sectors, and regions. Second is technological progress and other forms of innovation. While, in general, the secret of TFP growth lies in how to improve these two areas, the reallocation of resources is a fundamental mechanism of TFP improvement, because it rewards the good performance, or punishes the bad performance, of technological innovation.

Resource reallocation efficiency may be obtained through structural readjustment and industrial upgrading. In addition to the well-recognized pattern that labor mobility from low-productivity to higher-productivity sectors creates reallocative efficiency, there is the reallocation of resources among enterprises within sectors themselves—that is, those enterprises with higher productivity win the competition for more factors of production while being an important source of TFP.

During China's period of dual economy development, TFP growth has been overwhelmingly attributed to resource reallocative efficiency through the labor mobility between rural and urban areas. For China at its present stage—characterized by rapid aging at the middle-income level—the potential for economic growth relies on both speeding up innovations and tapping traditional sources of TFP improvement.

7.2   THE DOMESTIC FLYING GEESE PARADIGM

In China, the massive labor migration from rural to urban areas during the reform period, particularly after the country's entry to the WTO in 2001, has contributed significantly to GDP growth. As labor migration decelerates as a consequence of the arrival of the Lewis Turning Point, TFP growth tends to slow down. That suggests that China has to face two formidable tasks if it wants to continue its growth: (1) in terms of growth pattern, it must make the leap from an inputs-driven pattern to a TFP-driven pattern; and (2) in terms of TFP growth, it must undergo a transformation from reliance on resource reallocation efficiency to reliance on technological innovation. However, that does not imply that the potential for reallocation efficiency has disappeared altogether.

It is doubtless true that the country's labor shortage and wage inflation indicate the diminished comparative advantage of labor-intensive
manufacturing, which seems to suggest that the manufacturing center for
labor-intensive goods will be transferred from China to other developing
countries with lower labor costs—the so-called "flying geese paradigm."
Industrial transfers depicted by the flying geese paradigm are directly
engendered by changes in dynamic comparative advantages. That is, as per
capita income increases, resource endowment changes over time. When
advanced countries upgrade their industrial structure—say, from labor-
intensive to capital-intensive industries—the lagging countries take over
the industries discarded by the former and receive foreign investment in
those industries in turn.[2]

As China is a large economy, however, and in addition to its longstanding dual economy characteristics, its turning point should not be
expected to come all at once, but in such a way that some regions experience it sooner and others later. Similarly, the characteristics of the Chinese
economy may also change the traditional pattern of industrial transfer as
revealed by the flying geese theory—that is, industrial transfers consistent
with changes in comparative advantage will not follow a pattern of moving
country to country, but rather region to region within the country.

What we have observed about the industrial transfers from Japan, a
"leading goose," and the Four Tigers in the 1970s and 1980s is that small
economies are characterized by homogeneity in resource endowments and
industrial structure among their regions. In contrast, the primary characteristic defining China as a large economy is heterogeneity of resource
endowment and industrial structure between regions. For a long time,
the mobility of production factors, especially of capital and labor, was
restricted by institutional barriers among the Chinese regions; persistent
domestic disparities in a relative scarcity of production factors and other
key conditions for development have prevented regions from converging in
economic growth.

Accordingly, when some of the regions reach a higher development
stage, others may remain stagnant at a lower stage. In what follows, we
examine the different stages of demographic transition and wage levels
among the eastern, central, and western regions in China in order to
evaluate an apparent domestic flying geese pattern, as opposed to an
international one.

Since socioeconomic development is a major driving force in demographic transition, the huge disparities in socioeconomic development
levels lead to a corresponding difference in demographic transition
among Chinese regions, which serves as evidence of regional heterogeneity and thus supports a domestic flying geese pattern in China. The

2010 National Census shows that, while the natural growth rate of the population—that is, the difference between the birth rate and the death rate—of the country as a whole was 0.505 percent per annum, it was 0.468 percent in the eastern regions, 0.473 percent in the central regions, and 0.678 percent in the western regions.

Because of the mass population migration from the central and western regions to the eastern regions, however, the age profiles of the three regions do not reflect this difference in demographic transition. In 2013, migrant workers—defined as those who left their home township for six months or longer—totaled 166 million, and flocked mainly from rural to urban areas and from the central and western provinces to the eastern provinces. Of the 64.2 million migrant workers originating in the central provinces, 89.9 percent migrated to the eastern regions, while, of the 28.4 million migrant workers originating in the western provinces, 82.7 percent migrated to the eastern regions.

As migrant workers are, on the whole, much younger than other population groups, such population mobility has flattened out the disparities of population aging among regions by increasing the proportion of the working-age population in the eastern regions and decreasing the proportion of the working-age population in the central and western regions. To eliminate such an effect, we can use data from the 2000 census to examine the different age structure among three regions, as these data only count migrants who left their place of origin for one-year stints in other regions. As is shown in Figure 7.1, in 2000, the old age support ratio (ratio of the population aged 65 and older to the population aged between 15 and 64) was 10.15 for the country as a whole, 10.9 percent for the eastern regions, 9.76 percent for the central regions, and 9.53 percent for the western regions.

Two implications can be drawn from the circumstances under which migrant workers work in places other than their home province. First, the existing *hukou* system prevents them from permanently settling in the place to which they have relocated, and therefore they lack equal access to public services. Second, even with the *hukou* reforms already proposed by the Chinese leadership, a majority of migrant workers who have emigrated from the central and western regions to the eastern regions cannot expect to be granted citizenship as *hukou* residents in their destination cities,[3] a fact which also pushes them back to their place of origin.

Migrant workers must therefore expect to return to their province of origin by a certain age. Based on survey data, Meng finds that, on average, migrants' work in cities lasts for nine years, while their individual earnings can increase for up to 24 years after they first enter cities. That is, they quit the urban labor force long before their productivity is exhausted

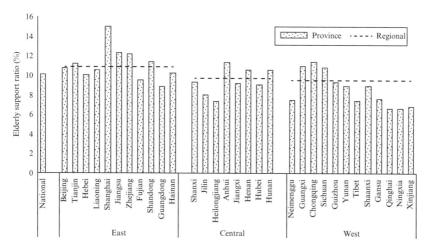

Source: Data of 5th National Census in 2000 from official website, http://www.stats.gov.cn.

Figure 7.1   Old age support ratio by region

(Meng, 2013). On the other hand, those returned migrant workers will be ready to take jobs in those industries that have transferred from coastal to inland areas.

True, wage rates have converged among the eastern, central, and western regions as a result of a nationwide labor shortage and greater labor mobility. In 2012, the ratio of the average wage in the central regions to the average wage in the eastern regions was 98.7 percent, while the ratio of the average wage in the western regions to the average wage in the eastern regions was 97.4 percent. This, however, did not completely erase the comparative advantage of labor costs in the central and western regions, for several reasons.

First, there are factors that tend to reduce the relative wage rates in the inland regions. Those migrant workers who originate from the central and western provinces can enjoy lower costs of living and lower costs of migrating if they find a job without having to move long distances to the coastal regions. The fact that young rural laborers migrate not only for the purpose of finding a job but also to see the world tends to expand the supply of migrant workers in the large-sized coastal municipalities. As the number of new entrants to the labor market shrinks over time, the age structure of migrant workers also changes, with the wage rate in the eastern regions expected to inflate faster than that in the central and western regions.

Second, the current wage rates are more acceptable in the central and western regions than in the eastern regions, which puts pressure on the wage inflation of the latter. As can be observed from public data, the reported numbers of incidences of labor disputes, which are overwhelmingly triggered by clashes over wages, are disproportionally concentrated in the more developed eastern provinces (Cai and Wang, 2012). That implies that the eastern regions will suffer significant pressure as wages surge in the years to come.

In addition to the cost of production factors, the agglomeration effect influencing firms' costs of production and transactions also determine the physical location of industries. Based on a census-type survey for large-scale manufacturing enterprises from 1998 to 2008, a study finds that while the physical location of labor-intensive industries was determined predominantly by the agglomeration effect before 2004—namely, that they were clustered in the eastern regions—it has been more and more determined by the overall cost both of operations and of production factors, areas in which the central and western regions have the advantage (Qu et al., 2012).

Given the existing and expected differentials in the costs of production among regions, the ongoing industrial transfer has predictably occurred mainly inter-regionally in China rather than between China and other countries in recent years. Examining the labor-intensive manufacturing of the country as a whole, the share of output values in the eastern regions peaked at 88.9 percent in 2004 and then declined to 84.7 percent in 2008; in the same vein, the share of assets in the eastern regions peaked at 83.3 percent in 2006 and then declined to 81.6 percent in 2008. Despite the limited availability of data allowing us to observe the changes over just a few years, we can speculate that these trends will continue for some years before more cases of industrial transfer occur between China and other low-cost countries.

7.3   THE MECHANISM OF CREATIVE DESTRUCTION

Since Robert Solow, a Nobel laureate in economics, published his pioneering work (in which the most important contribution is his distinction of total factor productivity as the only sustainable driver of economic growth from factor inputs[4]), economics literature has supported and added to his findings, based on abundant experiences in economic development. In a production function, TFP growth is formulated as a residual—that is, the difference between output growth and factor growth. From what has been observed in the economic development of a variety of countries, both developed and developing, one can summarize three types of TFP growth which have significant implications for China's future growth.

First, in the development of a typical dual economy, an overwhelming part of TFP improvement comes from reallocative efficiency through labor mobility from low-productivity agriculture to the higher-productivity non-agricultural sectors. It is this source of TFP that has made the neoclassical predictions on East Asian and Chinese growth injudicious. While the unprecedented economic growth in China has so far benefited a great deal from resource reallocation, such a source of TFP growth tends to shrink as the pool of surplus laborers dries up.

Second, at any given time and place, scientific and technological innovation is always an inexhaustible source of TFP growth, but it is particularly true under the neoclassical growth scenario as defined by Solow. While for developing countries the existence of a technological gap with developed countries allows them to benefit from "the advantage of backwardness," for developed countries it is practically independent technological innovation alone that determines how fast their economic growth can be achieved. When a country begins the transition to neoclassical growth, as China has, its growth potential becomes more and more dependent on independent innovation.

Third, in both developed and developing countries, resource reallocation among enterprises within sectors can significantly improve efficiency. As differentials in productivity exist among enterprises within sectors, the mobility of factors of production from low-productivity firms to high-productivity firms (which allows more efficient enterprises to survive, expand, and develop, while enterprises that have proven inefficient in the long run are eliminated) could improve national productivity.

As is well documented in economics literature, in a mature market economy like the United States, a so-called "creative destruction" mechanism can create the allocative efficiency relating to the entry, expansion, contraction, and exit of firms within narrowly defined sectors, contributing one-third to one-half of national productivity growth (Foster et al., 2008). In addition, a more recent work by Chang-Tai Hsieh and Peter J. Klenow has demonstrated that, by reallocating capital and labor to equalize marginal products among manufacturers to the extent observed in the United States, China's manufacturing sector could gain a 30–50 percent increase in its TFP (Hsieh and Klenow, 2009).

Generally speaking, resource reallocation as a process of enhancing TFP in dual economy development can be viewed as a "Pareto improvement"—that is, one economically meaningful change can at least benefit one group without harming any others, because the reallocation of laborers between the agricultural and non-agricultural sectors can benefit both sectors at no expense to any part of the economy.

First, the outflow of surplus laborers from farming increases both the agricultural productivity of labor and the income of rural households, thus narrowing the rural–urban income gap. In the period from 1978 to 2012, the annual growth rate in real terms was 6.1 percent for the agricultural productivity of labor—namely, agricultural value added per unit of laborers actually engaged in the sector—and 7.5 percent for the average income of rural households.

Second, the inflow of migrant workers into urban sectors meets the roaring demand of the industrial sectors for labor without creating a reduction in jobs for urban workers. As has been widely discussed in labor economics literature regarding the issue of whether migrant workers compete with or complement local workers in the labor market, research on the Chinese labor market came to a similar conclusion, that—given their status of being latecomers without an urban *hukou*, that is, there is a degree of discrimination against them—migrant workers usually take the jobs that are more complementary to than competitive with those of local workers.

In addition, there is a particular demographic characteristic that ensures migrant workers are more complementary than competitive. For various reasons (for example, the demographic transition in rural areas has lagged behind that of urban areas, and those rural laborers who have more advantageous demographic characteristics are more likely to migrate to cities), rural-to-urban migrant workers are much younger than urban resident laborers (Figure 7.2). The complementarities in the job market can therefore derive from such complementarities of age between migrant and local workers.

On the other hand, the practice of improving TFP beyond labor reallocation between the rural and urban sectors requires creative destruction so that there is little opportunity for further Pareto improvement. As Schumpeter (2003, p. 83) put it, the process of creative destruction is the essential fact of capitalism. In a neoclassical scenario of growth, the overall enhancement of TFP in any country as a whole is not realized through the improvement of productivity in every individual enterprise, but through the expansion of enterprises with high productivity and contraction of enterprises with low productivity. Only when better-performing enterprises dominate the economy will overall productivity grow.

Japan has succeeded in the transition from middle-income country to high-income country, but it is a bad example of enhancing TFP after its demographic dividend disappeared and the technology gap with other developed economies narrowed. A study finds that the poor performance of TFP was caused by a policy that subsidized inefficient firms and

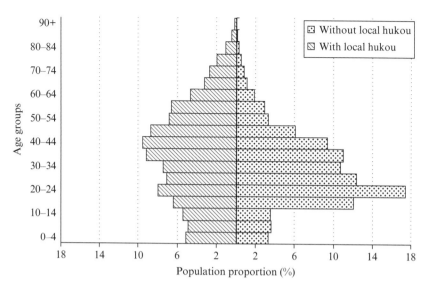

Source: National Bureau of Statistics (2012).

Figure 7.2 Complementarities between locals and migrants in urban China

declining industries and, as a result, created a large number of zombie firms, which may largely account for the Japanese "lost decade of growth" (Hayashi and Prescott, 2002).

To allow more productive enterprises to expand and less productive enterprises to decline or even die is the way that "creative destruction" works. Although the potential remains for China to encourage resource reallocation among sectors and regions, its continuous economic growth becomes more and more dependent on competition among enterprises and the innovation of science and technology, all of which require creative destruction. Nevertheless, in the final analysis, exploiting both traditional and new sources of growth is preconditioned by the elimination of institutional barriers to improving TFP—namely, when buckling down to economic reforms, the first order of business is to prevent any mistakes in policy making in response to the economic slowdown.

7.4 AVOIDING POLICY DISTORTIONS

Both the central and the local governments have played active roles in China's successful economic growth over the past three decades, which can primarily be viewed as a transition period from the low-income stage of economic development to the upper-middle-income stage. Because there were many opportunities for economic growth of which the country could take advantage, and as there was a significant technological gap between China and developed countries in the early period of China's contemporary economic growth, it was not only feasible but necessary for the different levels of government to play a role in spurring the investment-driven growth of GDP.

However, as China begins its journey towards the transition from the upper-middle-income stage to the high-income stage—which requires productivity growth through mass innovations by individual enterprises but not by governments—the old economic growth model must be abandoned. What governments should do at the new stage of economic growth is, instead, create a competitive environment and abolish institutional obstacles preventing the application of new technology.

In general, TFP performance can explain why there are significant divergences in the rise and fall of nations' economies, sustainable growth and abnormal slowdown, and the successful transition to high income and entanglement in the middle-income trap. For countries that face a transformation of growth patterns, sustaining the necessary TFP growth to spur a reasonable rate of economic growth is a challenging task and, in some cases, is an almost impossible mission, not only as a result of the old practices that stand in the path of success, but also because of frequent mistakes made by a government facing policy choices. That is the reason that so many countries have stumbled at the point of transition from middle-income to developed country status.

Such a task is especially challenging for China for two reasons. One, China is likely to be the victim of its own success. Massive investments led by the central and local governments have spurred impressive—though overreaching and inefficient—growth in the past few years, and that experience tends to overextend governments. Two, as the Chinese governments (central and local) have proven very capable of stimulating growth by means of expansionary fiscal policy, loose monetary policy, and investment-led industrial and regional policies, when a policy is wrongly chosen in the face of economic slowdown it can cause massive distortions.

Take the acceleration of industrialization in the central and western regions, for example. Such an acceleration has two driving forces. First of all, this process itself is the outcome of the industrial transfer from coastal to inland regions in response to the inflation of labor costs in the coastal areas. Since it is carried out mainly by market forces, it causes little distortion. Another force driving industrial development in the central and western regions is the implementation of various regional policies in the name of strategies of "Going West" (西部大开发战略), of "Revitalizing the Northeast and Other Old Industrial Bases" (东北等老工业基地振兴战略), and of "Raising the Central Regions" (中部崛起战略), which involve massive government-led, investment-oriented programs and tend to cause distortions.

In implementing these regional strategies, the central government has invested in and provided transfer payment to the central and western regions through various channels, such as the construction of infrastructure, the construction of production capacities, subsidizing social security programs, and other fiscal support programs, giving rise to a substantial alteration in the distribution of financial resources among regions. For example, the share of the central and western regions in China's total fixed assets investment increased from 41.2 percent in 2000 to 51.4 percent in 2010. Along with this change, the state-owned sectors in these areas increased as well. In the same period, the share of state-owned fixed asset investment in the central and western regions increased from 47.0 percent to 60.9 percent.

That this uneven investment led to a strengthening of the state-owned sectors can be confirmed by official statements. At the International Conference on Improving the Investment Environment and Revitalizing the Northeast held in January 2006, for example, a high-ranking official in charge of the implementation of the Revitalizing the Northeast strategy asserted that the state's powers of control and influence had substantially strengthened as state investments became more concentrated in strategic sectors in the northeast provinces (Hu and Sun, 2006).

The governments' efforts aiming to narrow the regional disparities are necessary, and industrial policies aiming to promote growth in lagging regions must be proactive. Regional strategies should not divert industrial development from any comparative advantages that may already exist in a specific region, however. Differentials in regional development measured by per capita income imply a difference in resource endowments among regions. That is, developed regions endowed with a relative abundance of capital have a comparative advantage in capital-intensive industries, while less-developed regions with an abundance of labor have a comparative advantage in labor-intensive industries.

The industrial structure of each region is essentially formed in accordance with its comparative advantages, assuming there are properly functioning factor markets. The large disparities in resource endowments among the eastern regions and the central and western regions provide opportunities for lagging regions to catch up with their advanced counterparts if the central and local governments implement appropriate industrial policies and regional strategies.

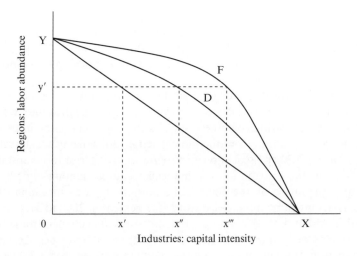

Figure 7.3   Regional comparative advantages and industrial choices

In Figure 7.3, we show how industrial development can follow or defy existing comparative advantages. Following the principle of comparative advantages, a perfect match between regions and industries should be on the straight line *YX*, namely, labor-intensive industries are allocated to the relatively less-developed regions, since they have a comparative advantage of labor, while capital-intensive industries or technology-intensive industries are allocated to the more-developed regions, since they have a comparative advantage in capital and technology. For example, for a region with labor abundance *y'*, the ideal corresponding industry chosen is *x'*.

Since industrial policies are intended to predict and line up with dynamic comparative advantages—which allows for the choosing of potential industries in advance—and the less-developed regions demand more investments in infrastructure, industrial policy-related investments tend to be allocated to more capital-intensive sectors. Therefore, the more forward-looking match-up between resource endowments and industrial choice can be indicated on the line *YDX*. That is, in a region with labor abundance of *y'*, industry with capital intensity of *x''* may be chosen in order to adequately pair resources and advantages.

It is not easy to define the proper limits for industrial choice based on the dynamics of comparative advantages. If reasonable boundaries are exceeded, say the resource endowment/industry matching moves to line *YFX*, then industrial choice will deviate from the comparative advantage of a given region. As is shown in Figure 7.3, for the same region with labor abundance y', industry with capital intensity x''' may be too capital-intensive to be efficient in resource allocation.

The catching-up industrialization in China's central and western regions that has shown a deviation from those regions' comparative advantages is more or less indicative of the case depicted above. Because enterprises and sectors that defy the prevailing comparative advantage must suffer a tremendous loss of allocative efficiency, they can only survive through government subsidies.

The capital intensity of manufacturing in the central and western regions as measured by the capital–labor ratio has begun to increase at a more rapid pace than that of the eastern regions since the implementation of the "Going West" strategy at the beginning of the twenty-first century, witnessing a steep surge in 2003–2004, and surpassing that of the eastern regions in absolute terms in 2007: for example, the capital–labor ratio of manufacturing in the central regions and the western regions was 20.1 percent and 25.9 percent respectively higher than that in the eastern regions.

At some point, those newly invested processes that adopt more advanced technologies and equipment help enhance TFP and productivity of labor, as long as the growth of productivity is faster than that of the wage rate and thus the unit labor cost—namely, the ratio of wages to labor productivity—can be reduced or at least remain unchanged.[5] As the demographic dividend for China as a whole disappears, however, the development of highly capital-intensive heavy industry will eventually cause a diminishing return on capital in the economic growth of the central and western regions.

A government-led growth pattern works against the creative destruction mechanism, however, and thus impedes the improvement of TFP. Even after 35 years of reform, the share of state investment is still significant, and state-held companies hold a monopoly in certain sectors, whereas small and medium-sized private enterprises are unfairly treated in access to registration, entry to sectors, financing, and other conditions of operation. In 2012, state-holding companies spent 36.2 percent of the domestic fixed assets investment of the country as a whole. In the secondary sector, state-owned and state-holding firms possessed 40.6 percent of total assets and 43.0 percent of total liabilities, but they generated only 26.4 percent of revenue from their principal business and 24.5 percent of total profits.

While the state firms tend to be over-protected, on the one hand, and the small and medium-sized private enterprises discriminated against, on the other, the lack of the mechanism of creative destruction inevitably reduces firms' efficiency at the micro level and thus the economy's healthiness at the macro level.

According to China's industrial policies and industrial organization regulations, some sectors and industries are awarded a strategic status to which the entry of private enterprises is not encouraged. For example, the state sectors are required to hold "absolute control" over the so-called strategic industries such as military industries, electric power and the electric grid, oil and petrochemical industries, telecommunications, coal, air transportation, and the shipping industry, and to hold "strong control" over certain basic key industries such as equipment manufacturing, automotive manufacturing, the electronic information industry, construction, the iron and steel industry, nonferrous metal industries, and the chemical industry. In the cases of "absolute control" and "strong control," state sole proprietorship, absolute shareholding, or conditional relative shareholding is required (Ren and Liu, 2006).

The monopoly of state-owned firms means that not only are private firms not encouraged to enter into those industries because of institutional barriers, but also state-owned firms need not exit even if they operate poorly. In some cases, the state sector enjoys profitability by virtue of its monopolistic position regardless of its performance or productivity, while in other cases it is protected and allowed to survive because of the governments' concern for GDP growth, tax revenue, employment, and therefore social stability.

By its very nature, such a monopolistic status confined to the state sector is bound to impede the application of new technologies. At the present stage of development, there is an increasing sense of urgency to shift the development of enterprises and the growth of the Chinese economy to more reliance on technological progress. At both the level of enterprise and the level of the economy, the main constraint on the improvement of productivity is not the availability of new technologies, but the incentive to apply available technologies and the appropriateness of choosing them. Economics literature suggests that the world's stock of experiences, ideas, scientific knowledge, and technological know-how can be shared across countries and enterprises; it is therefore institutional barriers that prevent enterprises from applying existing knowledge, and hence that impede the improvement of TFP in economies (for example, see Parente and Prescott, 2002). As is suggested by both international and domestic examples, the existence of monopolies and state protection gives rise to a lack of incentives in the application of technology and an inappropriateness of technological choices.

Figure 7.4 can help us understand this. Given the existing stock of technologies, their application to economic growth does not necessarily require that all enterprises innovate at the technological frontier, but rather go through a process of searching, purchasing, borrowing, and adapting.

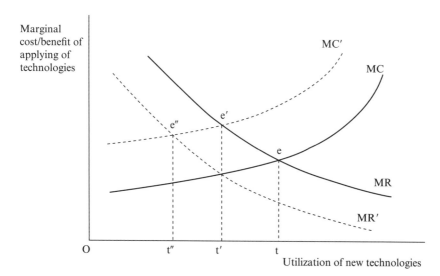

Figure 7.4   How monopoly impedes technology application

Whether, and to what extent, enterprises employ those available technologies, however, depends on a comparison between the marginal benefits and the marginal cost of adopting them. Namely, individual enterprises make decisions in accordance with the principle of maximization of the net marginal benefit of applying a technology. Since the pursuit of applying new technologies is motivated by competitive pressure and any consideration of the cost of applying new technologies is constrained by enterprises' budgets, the lack of competition tends to lower marginal benefits, and soft budget constraints tend to increase marginal (opportunity) costs.

As state-owned firms enjoy a privileged status in the obtainment of investment, land, and natural resources, as well as in preventing competition, they tend not to apply more efficient technologies to the optimal degree, or they are more likely to make inappropriate technological choices given that the prices of production factors are distorted, which in turn leads to a combination of low-efficiency technologies being used by enterprises. That is, for enterprises' decision making, three cases—namely, that the marginal cost of applying new technologies increases, the marginal benefit of applying new technologies declines, or both occur simultaneously—make applying technology non-optimal.

China's extant experiences during its reform period have confirmed the theoretical hypothesis explained above. Despite the monopolistic status possessed by the state sector that allows for profitable production, the efficiency of those protected, state-owned firms is significantly lower than that of non-state enterprises in more competitive sectors. A study by Brandt and Zhu finds that, during the period from 1978 to 2007, the annual growth rate of TFP was 1.36 percent in the state sector and 4.74 percent in non-state sectors (Brandt and Zhu, 2010). The poor performance of the state sector in productivity has substantially depressed its return on investment. Another study shows that the average rate of return on capital for private enterprises is 50 percent higher than that of wholly state-owned enterprises (Dollar and Wei, 2007).

7.5 CONCLUSION

Since Robert Solow laid the foundation underpinning the neoclassical theory of growth, the decisive role that TFP plays in breaking the law of diminishing return on capital—and therefore in sustaining long-term growth—has been well recognized in theoretical and empirical works. Those studies demonstrate that the performance of TFP can sufficiently explain the differentials in per capita income among countries, the collapse of the former Soviet economy, the "lost decades" of the Japanese economy, and the slowdowns that have been observed in many previously fast-growing economies.[6]

It is worth noting that TFP is no doubt an important factor in explaining why some countries have been stuck in the middle-income trap, others currently face the risk of falling into such a trap, and a handful of economies have successfully avoided this fate.

Thanks to the unique window of opportunity of the reallocation of resources seen in the development of a dual economy, TFP performance in China during its reform period has been sufficient and has contributed a reasonable portion to the country's extraordinary growth. Just as traditional policies that have been proven effective in helping speed the transition from poverty to middle-income status no longer work in aiding the transition from upper-middle-income to rich country status, TFP improvement will be able to continue only by finding new sources rooted in a new growth pattern. Therefore, fully understanding the role of, as well as methods of exploiting, TFP will certainly contribute to the transition of China's economic growth pattern.

Involved in an advisory role in China's 12th Five-Year Plan, Paul Romer, an American economist and pioneer of the endogenous growth theory, suggested that the Chinese central government should evaluate local governments by their ability to promote local economic development through TFP instead of GDP (Romer, 2010). Now that local Chinese governments not only have strong incentives to promote economic growth but also are disciplined and motivated to follow the guidance of the country's central leadership, such a change in the evaluative criteria of the central government in assessing local governments' behaviors and achievements would have a significant impact.

Experiences in Singapore suggest that it does matter whether a government recognizes the vital role of TFP and seeks ways of encouraging enterprises to improve it. Even though Singapore was not willing to accept criticism of the East Asian growth model prevailing in the early 1990s, its government did recognize the important role of TFP growth in sustaining its economic growth and subsequently set a national goal requiring 2 percent annual TFP growth (Felipe, 1997). Perhaps it is because of this that the economic development of Singapore eventually broke the prophecy made by Paul Krugman.

In China, there is still great potential for improving TFP through reallocating factors of production between the rural and urban sectors, among industries within the secondary and tertiary sectors, and among firms within individual industries, if certain conditions—such as human capital accumulation and institution building—can be met. In the following chapters, we will analyze these conditions and the necessary reforms enabling China to sustain and accelerate its TFP growth.

NOTES

1. As a matter of fact, Krugman made such a warning again by predicting that the Chinese model was about to hit its Great Wall after it hit the Lewis Turning Point. See Krugman (2013).
2. For a brief history of the flying geese paradigm and its extension and application, see Kojima (2000).
3. In some famous cases of pilot *hukou* reforms in cities such as Guangzhou, Shenzhen, and Chengdu, the municipal authorities selectively grant local *hukou* identity only to intra-provincial migrant workers, while excluding those from other provinces.
4. For example, see Solow (1956).
5. For related studies, see Cai et al. (2009).
6. The most representative works include Krugman (1994), Hayashi and Prescott (2002), Parente and Prescott (2002), and Eichengreen et al. (2011).

REFERENCES

Asian Productivity Organization (2008), *APO Productivity Databook 2008*, Tokyo: Asian Productivity Organization.
Bhagwati, Jagdish (1996), "The Miracle That Did Happen: Understanding East Asia in Comparative Perspective," keynote speech at the conference on "Government and Market: The Relevance of the Taiwanese Performance

to Development Theory and Policy" in honor of Professors Liu and Tsiang, Cornell University, May 3.

Bloom, David, and Jeffrey Williamson (1997), *Demographic Transitions and Economic Miracles in Emerging Asia*, NBER Working Paper No. 6268, Cambridge, MA: National Bureau of Economic Research.

Brandt, Loren, and Xiaodong Zhu (2010), "Accounting for China's Growth," Working Paper No. 395, Department of Economics, University of Toronto.

Cai, Fang, and Meiyan Wang (2012), *Labour Market Changes, Labour Disputes and Social Cohesion in China*, OECD Development Centre Working Paper No. 307, Paris: OECD Development Centre.

Cai, Fang, Dewen Wang, and Yue Qu (2009), "Flying Geese within Borders: How Does China Sustain Its Labour-Intensive Industries?," in Ross Garnaut, Ligang Song, and Wing Thye Woo (eds.), *China's New Place in a World in Crisis: Economic, Geopolitical and Environmental Dimensions*, Canberra: Australian National University E Press, pp. 209–232.

Dollar, David, and Shang-Jin Wei (2007), *Das (Wasted) Kapital: Firm Ownership and Investment Efficiency in China*, NBER Working Paper No. 13103, Cambridge, MA: National Bureau of Economic Research.

Eichengreen, Barry, Donghyun Park, and Kwanho Shin (2011), *When Fast Growing Economies Slow Down: International Evidence and Implications for China*, NBER Working Paper No. 16919, Cambridge, MA: National Bureau of Economic Research.

Felipe, Jesus (1997), *Total Factor Productivity Growth in East Asia: A Critical Survey*, EDRC Report Series No. 65, Manila: Asian Development Bank.

Foster, Lucia, John Haltiwanger, and Chad Syverson (2008), "Reallocation, Firm Turnover, and Efficiency: Selection on Productivity or Profitability?," *American Economic Review*, 98 (1), 394–425.

Hansen, Gary, and Edward Prescott (2002), "Malthus to Solow," *American Economic Review*, 92 (4), 1205–1217.

Hayashi, Fumio, and Edward Prescott (2002), "The 1990s in Japan: A Lost Decade," *Review of Economic Dynamics*, 5 (1), 206–235.

Hsieh, Chang-Tai, and Peter J. Klenow (2009), "Misallocation and Manufacturing TFP in China and India," *Quarterly Journal of Economics*, 124 (4), 1403–1448.

Hu, Tao, and Yingwei Sun (2006), "State Economy Control Strengthens Significantly after Two Years of Implementation of the Strategy of Revitalizing the Northeast," http://www.gov.cn/jrzg/2006-01/16/content_160944.htm, January 16.

Kojima, Kiyoshi (2000), "The 'Flying Geese' Model of Asian Economic Development: Origin, Theoretical Extensions, and Regional Policy Implications," *Journal of Asian Economics*, 11 (4), 375–401.

Krugman, Paul (1994), "The Myth of Asia's Miracle," *Foreign Affairs*, 73 (6), 62–78.

Krugman, Paul (2013), "Hitting China's Wall," *New York Times*, July 18.

Kuijs, Louis (2010), *China through 2020—A Macroeconomic Scenario*, World Bank China Research Working Paper No. 9, Washington, DC: World Bank.

Marti, Christa (1996), *Is There an East Asian Miracle?*, Economic Research Working Paper, Zurich: Union Bank of Switzerland.

Meng, Xin (2013), "Rural–Urban Migration: Trend and Policy Implications (2008–2012)," in Ross Garnaut, Fang Cai, and Ligang Song (eds.), *China: A New Model for Growth and Development*, Canberra: Australian National University E Press, pp. 179–197.

National Bureau of Statistics (2012), *Tabulation on the 2010 Census of the People's Republic of China*, Beijing: China Statistics Press.

Parente, Stephen, and Edward Prescott (2002), *Barriers to Riches*, Cambridge, MA: MIT Press.

Qu, Yue, Fang Cai, and Xiaobo Zhang (2012), "Has the 'Flying Geese' Phenomenon in Industrial Transformation Occurred in China?," in Huw McKay and Ligang Song (eds.), *Rebalancing and Sustaining Growth in China*, Canberra: Australian National University E Press, pp. 93–109.

Ren, Fang, and Bing Liu (2006), "SASAC: State Sectors Have to Hold Absolute Control over 7 Industries," http://www.gov.cn/jrzg/2006-12/18/content_472256.htm, December 18.

Romer, Paul (2010), "Notes on Optimizing China's New Pattern of Growth," in Edwin Lim and Michael Spence (eds.), *Thoughts and Suggestions for China's 12th Five-Year Plan from an International Perspective*, Beijing: China CITIC Press, pp. 572–587.

Schumpeter, Joseph A. (2003), *Capitalism, Socialism, and Democracy*, Taylor & Francis e-Library.

Solow, Robert (1956), "A Contribution to the Theory of Economic Growth," *Quarterly Journal of Economics*, 70 (1), 65–94.

Williamson, Jeffrey (1997), *Growth, Distribution and Demography: Some Lessons from History*, NBER Working Paper No. 6244, Cambridge, MA: National Bureau of Economic Research.

World Bank (1993), *The East Asian Miracle: Economic Growth and Public Policy*, Oxford: Oxford University Press.

Young, Alwyn (1994), "Lessons from the NICs: A Contrarian View," *European Economic Review*, 38 (3–4), 964–973.

8. Macroeconomic policies in transition

Haste makes waste. (*The Analects of Confucius*)

John Williamson, the first person to coin the term "Washington Consensus," feels wronged by criticisms from certain theoretical circles and the public. He not only believes that there is nothing wrong with his original proposal regarding Latin American countries' transition to sustainable economic growth tracks, but also adds several new points focusing in particular on macroeconomic stabilization (Williamson, 2004). Michael Spence sees the widely prevailing generalization of the Washington Consensus—namely, that it is to "stabilize, privatize, and liberalize"—as a simplified misinterpretation of Williamson's original proposition (Spence, 2011). The question remains, however, as to how much these debates on the Washington Consensus actually encapsulate significant differences in institutional settings and thus in the conditions of macroeconomic stability both between developed and developing countries and between those countries with mature market mechanisms and countries in system transition.

It is apparent that western economics, especially those theories on which the Washington Consensus are based, have proven unable to adequately explore the roles that a variety of economic policies have played in China's economic growth, to say nothing of accurately depicting the ways in which China's macroeconomic stability has been accomplished and what principles should be followed in the future when deciding economic policies.

One of the greatest challenges facing the Chinese economy in its present period of economic transition (which is characterized by rising labor costs) is to sustain economic growth by exploring new comparative advantages. Over-involvement by governments, however, has its own potential risks given that, in order to realize their objectives within a foreseeable period of time, governments tend to overuse industrial policies, regional strategies, and massive stimulus packages, which can lead to the persistence of traditional growth patterns, resulting in the imbalance, discoordination, and unsustainability of economic growth. This chapter discusses the potential risks inherent in implementing these instruments of policy and presents the implications for existing and potential policies.

8.1   WHERE DOES THE IMBALANCE IN THE CHINESE ECONOMY LIE?

For some economists and politicians active in international affairs, global economic imbalance is a perpetually fruitful topic. More often than not, many of them blame the situation on China's growth pattern, which is characterized by a mass trade surplus to the United States and Europe and over-reliance on investment for growth. It is unfair, however, to criticize China for manipulating the exchange rate and causing the subsequent global imbalance. Being at the stage of dual economy development that is characterized by an unlimited supply of labor, the Chinese economy, at the early stage of promoting growth and embracing globalization, is bound to gain comparative advantages in labor-intensive manufacturing. On the other hand, developed economies, suffering high costs of labor and even the phasing out of manufacturing, cannot compete with China in the labor-intensive sectors. That is how trade imbalances are formed. As for the high leverage and low savings rate in the American economy, it is a domestic problem all on its own.

The controversial debate turns on the point that many politicians in western countries raise questions about imbalances in the world economy from the vantage point of their own interests, while economists in those countries can always supply whatever theoretical evidence is needed to support these political explanations. For example, certain prominent American economists who have always declared themselves advocates for free trade and economic globalization, now recognizing that the United States is not the exclusive, or even the primary, beneficiary of globalization (as a result of suffering weakening competitiveness in manufacturing, jobless recovery, and widening income inequality), often revise their previously held views.[1]

Policy makers in China have realized that economic growth which is heavily reliant on exports is not sustainable and have made efforts towards transforming such a model of growth. For years, as the pattern of the world economy has changed and the comparative advantage of China in labor-intensive manufacturing has weakened, the growth model of China has changed significantly. For example, after experiencing steady and moderate appreciation in the years from 1994 to 2004, the Chinese renminbi (RMB) began a rapid revaluation in 2005 until the global financial crisis—set off by the subprime mortgage crisis in the United States—burst in 2008. Since then, as a result of the deceleration of exports, the trade surplus has substantially decreased and the contribution of net exports to economic growth has often been nil. In 2012, the International Monetary Fund (IMF) admitted that China had undergone a significant reduction in

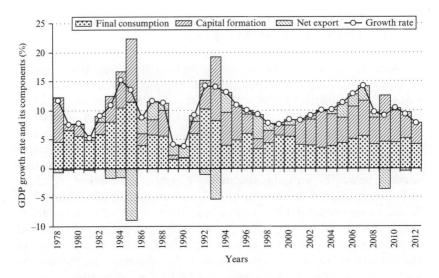

Source: National Bureau of Statistics (various years).

Figure 8.1 GDP growth rate and contributive components of demand factors

its current account surplus since peaking in 2007, and as a result the RMB is now only moderately undervalued (IMF, 2012). In May 2015, the IMF declared that China's currency is "no longer undervalued" (Mitchell and Donnan, 2015).

In fact, the imbalance of the Chinese economy is mainly a domestic matter. That is, China's economic growth has been driven by investment rather than by exports for quite some time. As is shown in Figure 8.1, since the mid-1990s, final consumption, which consists of resident consumption and government consumption together, has been a relatively stable contributor to GDP growth. Because the share of resident consumption declines over time while the share of government consumption remains steady, the contribution of final consumption to growth has been weak in the past few years. On the other hand, the contributions of net exports and investment to GDP growth have been volatile and offset each other—namely, once changes in the world economy cause a reduction in Chinese exports, increased capital formation (domestic investment) is usually stimulated with the intention of maintaining a target GDP growth.

For example, the contribution of net exports to GDP growth was greatest during 2005, 2006, and 2007, achieving 22.2 percent, 16.7 percent, and 18.0 percent of the total, respectively. After the world financial crisis broke out, with the weakening of the comparative advantage of Chinese labor-intensive commodities, the contribution of net exports dramatically declined and thereafter remained at zero or negative. Meanwhile, the contribution of capital formation increased to 88.5 percent in 2009 and has remained stable since then.

When the Chinese leadership called for a transformation of the economic growth pattern, three objectives were established—that is, the transformation from factor input-driven growth to productivity-driven growth, from export- and investment-led growth to consumption-led growth, and from a manufacturing-reliant industrial structure to a service-oriented industrial structure. As is shown in Figure 8.1, although growth's reliance on exports has decreased considerably, investment still serves as a fairly significant factor in the GDP growth.

The greatest difficulty facing the transformation of growth patterns lies in the government's determination to maintain a high speed of economic growth and hence heavy involvement in economic activities. In other words, it is the government that employs various economic policies to achieve a desired growth rate, which in turn makes it more difficult to accomplish the transformation of the growth pattern.

Under this growth pattern, in which the government plays a significant role, whether a desirable objective can be achieved or not depends in large part on stimulus policies—or, said in another way, exercisable leverages which the government can achieve through implementing economic policies and assessing the effects that follow. For the central government, in aiming to promote economic growth under a traditional growth pattern, there seems to be both tangible and practical means by which to act, means which include monetary policies and fiscal policies to stimulate the macroeconomy, industrial policies to nurture the so-called strategic industries, and regional strategies to boost massive investment to lagging areas. In tackling the world financial crisis—primarily in 2009–2010—all these policies were implemented simultaneously in the hope of killing three birds with one stone—namely, spurring growth, revitalizing strategic industries, and balancing regional development.

For local governments in China, which are characterized in the academic literature as entrepreneurial governments, their direct involvement in activities such as negotiating foreign direct investment, lobbying for project approval, guaranteeing credit loans, and even distorting the prices of production factors has been a typical method of promoting the growth of the local economy.

For both central and local governments accustomed to acting in the ways described above, it seems that the transformation of the growth pattern might result in the loss of certain forms of leverage beneficial to promoting economic development. In theory, under a pattern of productivity-driven, consumption-led, and sector-balanced growth, the government has an important role to play. For example, improving human capital, increasing public spending on research and development, narrowing the income gap, and boosting urbanization and reforms in certain key areas will all accelerate the transformation of the growth pattern. These policy measures, however, require long-term persistent efforts to bring them about, and very often the effects of the necessary economic reforms may not be apparent in the short run (Kharas, 2011). As a result, governments tend inherently to chase short-term goals.

This engagement with short-term goals is quite apparent with Chinese central and local governments, which pursue the immediate effect of investment projects on expanding GDP. In general, a strong desire for GDP growth frequently pushes these governments to adopt policies that generate short-term effects. Consequently, the traditional growth pattern recurs again and again while the new growth pattern is consequently held back. As the Chinese economy enters the new stage in which it experiences deceleration of growth, changes in policy desire and policy measures are not only necessary but also urgently important. In what follows, we discuss the appropriate roles and policy measures that can be undertaken by the government by looking into both supply-side and demand-side factors.

8.2   THE POTENTIAL GROWTH RATE FOR CHINA

During the period of dual economy development in China, the property of having an unlimited supply of labor has prevented diminishing returns on capital; the high savings rate brought about by the declining dependency ratio has supported the rapid growth of investment; an adequate supply of factors of production has sustained rapid economic growth; labor mobility from the agricultural to the non-agricultural sectors has generated reallocative efficiency in resources (which contributes significantly to TFP enhancement); the improvement of incentive mechanisms has enhanced technical efficiency at the level of micro-management; and, through foreign direct investment and other learning processes aimed at narrowing the technological gap between China and developed countries, the potential advantage of backwardness has been translated into technological progress of China's own. In short, as a condition of the country's economic reform and opening-up over the past three decades, China has enjoyed a high potential growth rate and, in fact, achieved an equally high speed of actual growth.

With the discontinuation of the growth of the working-age population, however, and a notable reduction of surplus labor in agriculture, the Chinese economy has gradually become less and less characterized as a dual economy and been more and more constrained by neoclassical conditions. That is, labor shortages and the resultant diminishing returns on capital occur, and, while the window of opportunity for resource reallocation between the agricultural and the non-agricultural sectors narrows, it constrains the supply of production factors and reduces the potential for the improvement of TFP. As a result, the potential growth rate in China is inevitably declining.

In Chapter 4, we reviewed the estimations of China's potential growth rate in the coming years. Our own prediction is based on the assumptions of the negative growth of labor, a reduced savings rate, and a slightly lower growth of TFP (Cai and Lu, 2013), which suggests that the estimated declining trend in the potential growth rate (and the ongoing slowdown of the actual growth rate) is caused by changes in supply-side factors. Namely, it is the weakening of the economy's growth capacity that is causing the deceleration of the growth rate in China.

In confronting the economic slowdown, not only are the central and local governments in China inclined to invigorate economic growth by adopting policies aimed at stimulating demand factors, but many economists also suggest policy direction from the demand side. For example, Paul Krugman alleges that, in order to maintain China's economic growth, consumer spending must rise dramatically to take its place (Krugman, 2013). Justin Lin opposes this view by arguing that any increase in consumption cannot be anything but the consequence of the improvement in labor productivity. But Lin did not logically conclude any proposal for improving labor productivity; instead, he suggests that China should further expand its investments in order to boost economic growth (Ni, 2013).

These influential economists either misjudged the cause of the slowdown of the Chinese economy or were not able to distinguish between supply-side factors determining the long-term potential of economic growth and demand-side factors that shock the short-term macroeconomy. Comparing the estimated potential growth with the actual growth rate thus will help to distinguish between long-term growth issues and short-term macroeconomic issues while also shining a light on the real challenges facing a slowed-down economy and finding the correct direction in which to direct economic policies.

Therefore, a combination of long-term and short-term views creates a consistency between theory and practice in judging the macroeconomic situation, foreseeing long-term growth trends, and drawing policy implications. As is shown in Table 8.1, four combinations between the properties of supply and of demand formulate different theoretical scenarios of the

Table 8.1   Macroeconomic scenarios with combinations of different supply and demand factors

	Strong supply	Weak supply
Strong demand	Scenario 1	Scenario 4
Weak demand	Scenario 2	Scenario 3

economy, which correspond to actual scenarios of the growth and macro-economic situation. Such a theoretical abstraction allows us to understand both the nature and the crux of the past, present, and future of China's long-term growth and macroeconomy.

The first scenario is formed by a combination of strong supply and strong demand. By and large, this is the normal scenario at the stage of development where the supply of production factors is sufficient and there is no obvious phenomenon of a diminishing return on capital. That is, it exists as a phenomenon of catching-up at the stage of dual economy development. For China, it is the ordinary state of economic growth and the way the macroeconomy existed before it went through its Lewis Turning Point in 2010.

As can be seen in Figure 8.2, the potential growth rate is estimated to be high during this period thanks to the demographic dividend. For example, China's annual potential growth rate was 10.3 percent from 1978 to 1995 and 9.8 percent from 1995 to 2009 (Cai and Lu, 2013). In the same period of time, a marked increase in resident income, rapid investment growth, and a substantial expansion of exportation have generated a strong demand in order to match the potential growth rate. Despite macroeconomic fluctuations and the occasional growth gap—namely, the differences between the actual growth rate and the potential growth rate, which were not substantial and have tended to diminish over time—both supply-side factors and demand-side factors have helped to achieve an unprecedentedly rapid economic growth in China.

A second scenario is created through the combination of strong supply with weak demand. Typically, in the course of economic catching-up, cyclical shocks caused by economic recessions and/or financial crises depress demand factors from time to time so that the economy grows at a rate below its potential capability, consequently causing cyclical unemployment. For example, in the late 1990s, the macroeconomic downturn and East Asian financial crisis resulted in weak demand, inadequate use of production capacities, and thus massive unemployment. It was only after China entered the World Trade Organization (WTO) and its labor market developed that economic growth went back to its potential rate

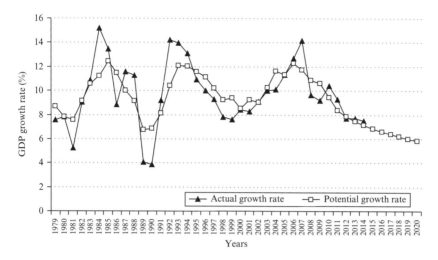

Source: Cai and Lu (2013).

Figure 8.2   Predicted potential GDP growth rates in China

and the macroeconomy returned to the normal state depicted in the first scenario.

A similar case occurred between 1988 and 1989, when the government implemented tight macroeconomic policies in order to curb severe inflation, causing depression; another such case happened from 2008 to 2009, when the world financial crisis hit the real economy. In both cases, the actual growth rates were below potential growth rates.

A third scenario is formed by a combination of weak supply and weak demand. Usually, as the stage of dual economy development approaches its end, conventional drivers of economic growth—namely, the demographic dividend—begin to vanish, which weakens the economy's comparative advantage. As a result, while the potential growth rate decreases, those demands being made by exports and investment are correspondingly reduced. For example, as the result of an overall shortage of labor, diminishing return to capital, and the slowdown of TFP growth, China's potential GDP growth rate declined from 8.4 percent in 2011 to 7.9 percent in 2012 and 7.5 percent in 2013. Since there were no strong demand factors stimulating the macroeconomy, the actual growth rate was 7.7 percent for 2012 and 2013. That is, supply-side factors and demand-side factors coincided perfectly in those years.

One might argue that the reduced demands of the Chinese economy result directly from the weak recovery of the world economy from the

2008–2009 financial crisis. It is true that the weakness of overall demand for exports, especially of labor-intensive consumption commodities, has to do with the slow recovery of developed countries and that China suffers as a result. By examining changes to the comparative advantages of China's labor-intensive manufacturing, however, we can identify whether domestic factors (the weakening of comparative advantages) or external factors (for example, worldwide reductions in exports) most determine the decline in external demand for Chinese commodities.

That is, statistically, looking into the revealed comparative advantage index (denoted by a ratio of the share of the export of labor-intensive manufacturing in the total volume of exports in China to the same share of total world trade), we can rule out the factors of an overall reduction in world trade. Our calculations show that the revealed comparative advantage index for 11 selected commodities, which both are labor-intensive and made up a dominant share of China's exports in 2003, declined from 4.39 in 2003 to 3.41 in 2013. That is to say, the exports of those commodities in China have not kept pace with the overall expansion of exports to world trade because their comparative advantage has declined in China.

A fourth and final scenario is formed by a combination of weak supply and strong demand. Such a situation can occur only when there is government intervention aimed at stimulating investment and/or exports through policy measures. Artificially stimulated demand, however, tends to inflate economic growth beyond its potential rate, leading to inflation, overcapacity, and economic bubbles. In the face of economic deceleration, economists and policy makers often instinctively search for measures from demand-side factors as a way to handle demand shocks. If a final assessment of the actual causes of the slowdown is incorrectly made, however, the price of choosing inappropriate policy tools will be extremely high. Therefore, this scenario presents a huge risk that the Chinese economy must confront in the near future.

8.3   POTENTIAL PRICES FOR STIMULATION POLICIES

Following the general law of economic growth, the Chinese economy has eventually slowed down following the disappearance of its demographic dividend in 2010. In 2012, 2013, and 2014, its annual growth rate was 7.7 percent, 7.7 percent, and 7.3 percent respectively, markedly lower than the average across the period from 1978 to 2011. Because China is still a developing country in terms of per capita GDP, all solutions to its economic constraints and social challenges rely on continual economic growth and thus an increase in standards of living. At this stage of development, therefore, the most likely response of the government to an economic slowdown is to transform its anti-cyclical policies into regularly implemented policies in hopes of spurring long-term economic growth.

One such practice is to combine monetary and fiscal policies, which are supposed to stimulate the macroeconomy while experiencing shocks from the demand side, with industrial policies usually aimed at promoting strategic industries and sustaining long-term growth, which in reality often leads to overstimulation of the macroeconomy. Industrial policies that direct investors to a narrow range of areas by giving them a variety of preferential treatments tend to create a wave phenomenon in investment,[2] which intensifies the discoordination, imbalance, and unsustainability that already exists in the Chinese economy.

In the course of economic catching-up, industrial policies are often considered central to developmental policies. Taken as a set of selectively supportive policies for specific industries and regions, industrial policies have not disappeared from the scene as those representing neoliberal economics and the Washington Consensus wish to see. While the experiences of the East Asian economies and newly emergent markets show that industrial policies are not necessarily doomed to failure (Ghosh, 2012), and China's rapid economic growth is believed to be attributable to its appropriate implementation of industrial policies and regional strategies,[3] there are indeed noticeable flaws in this practice, such as a distortion of the prices of production factors, suppressing competition, and "picking the winners."

It is not appropriate to affirm or negate industrial policies based only on individual experiences. The rationality and effectiveness of their implementation depend on the differing circumstances of individual countries with specific concerns towards their own objectives, means, times, and places, as can be observed in the fact that success is the result in some circumstances while failure occurs in others.[4]

When a country encounters a diminishing comparative advantage in labor-intensive industries owing to an increase in labor costs, investors and enterprises have to make the necessary adjustments by correspondingly shifting the direction of their investment—that is, they usually try to find new sectors and regions according to dynamic comparative advantages and to gain new competitiveness, but, as there is no guarantee that they will make the correct choices, they will also have to bear the possibility of painful failure if they make the wrong decisions.

Therefore, entrepreneurs ought to innovate within an environment of "creative destruction" that allows the successful to thrive and expand while the unsuccessful wither and fail. If such a reward and punishment mechanism does not exist, the magnitude of venture investment will not reach the apex of its own potential. That is to say, it falsely appears that the search for new comparative advantages is an activity with externalities, which private entrepreneurs lack the incentive to conduct. The logical consequence, then, is the government's involvement. That is why governments in so many countries at specific stages are so keen to implement industrial policies of all forms, and governments tend to pursue an increase in the capital–labor ratio in implementing industrial policies.

It is universally observed in catching-up economies that governments tend to be most deeply and directly involved in those investment activities aimed at finding new growth points in sectors and regions that are considered to have dynamic comparative advantages. As can be seen in China, such government interventions manifest themselves as a set of policies and strategies. First, in implementing policies such as making plans for revitalizing certain traditional industries, issuing a directory of so-called strategic industries, and developing regional strategies aimed at lagging provinces, the government adopts various means of subsidizing, encouraging, and protecting enterprises, sectors, and regions. Second, in tackling macroeconomic cycles, the government often dictates or guides enterprises to invest in these prioritized areas through a macroeconomic stimulus plan.

In practice, these two sets of policy measures are jointly implemented in the hope of serving both the stimulation of the macroeconomy and the upgrading of the industrial structure. As we will endeavor to demonstrate, however, these two goals cannot be reached simultaneously and fully.

First of all, in many cases, the government's primary concern is economic growth, while structural adjustment is secondary. For example, in implementing stimulus investment packages to cope with the financial crisis in 2009–2010, for the stimulus package to be supported by tangible projects, the Chinese government approved and implemented several projects that had previously been rejected in accordance with industrial policies. As a consequence, there have been redundant constructions and an overcapacity in the economy and a resurgence of capital- and energy-intensive—and even polluting—industries.

Secondly, the implementation of industrial policies, while promoting the prioritization of certain industries, often causes a wave phenomenon of investment and associated side effects. Under the assumption of economic rationality, tens of thousands of individual investors choose a particular direction for investment and subsequently experience the consequences of their economic choices. While, at the individual level, both success and failure can be independent of each other, at the aggregate level industrial upgrading is the ultimate goal.

On the other hand, when the government becomes deeply involved in investment activities by means of various preferential policies and even direct subsidies, it is more likely that a wave phenomenon will occur. Since government-led investment in certain narrowly defined areas is usually sizable, takes a long time to show any payoff, and carries a bigger risk, the wave phenomenon can cause serious consequences once incorrect investment decisions are made. Moreover, the government—as the last source of responsibility for investment—is unwilling to accept failure and therefore more likely to compound the error than to reduce it.

For example, in coping with the world financial crisis, the Chinese government identified ten industries that were to be supported and revitalized, including textiles, iron and steel, automotive, ships, equipment manufacturing, electronic and information, light industry, petrochemicals, logistics, and nonferrous metals. In 2010, seven industries were selected as strategic or "pillar" industries, including alternative energy, biotechnology, high-end equipment manufacturing, energy conservation and environmental protection, clean-energy vehicles, new materials, and next-generation information technology. The implementation of such industrial policies inevitably led to a deluge of massive investments.

When explaining innovation as the activities of new combinations in groups or swarms, Schumpeter actually implies a wave phenomenon in investment pushed forward by credit expansion (Schumpeter, 1982), which can be intensified through the involvement of governments. Since the beginning of the twenty-first century, particularly after the implementation of an investment stimulus package aimed at tackling the financial crisis of 2008–2009, the supply of broad money alongside loans provided by financial institutions has witnessed a rapid expansion in China (Figure 8.3), which serves to overtly demonstrate the problems caused by the wave phenomenon of massive investment.[5] Not only that, but in what follows one can see both from theories and from experience that not only can loose monetary policy, expansionary fiscal policy, and stimulus industrial policies not reach their intended objective—namely, stabilizing growth—but they can also have a prolonged negative impact on the sustainability of economic growth.

The implication of a decline in the potential growth rate is that the country's weakened comparative advantage prevents the competitive sectors of the real economy from production and investment at the previously seen volumes. Therefore, a loose monetary policy has a very limited effect on expanding real demand. If favored fiscal policies were implemented, it would very likely result in mal-investment and the protection of inefficient enterprises. The lessons from Japan in the late 1980s and early 1990s show that the subsidization and protection of those industries and enterprises that have already lost their comparative advantages and competitiveness can create mass zombie firms, resulting in the stagnation of the productivity of the economy as a whole (Hayashi and Prescott, 2002).

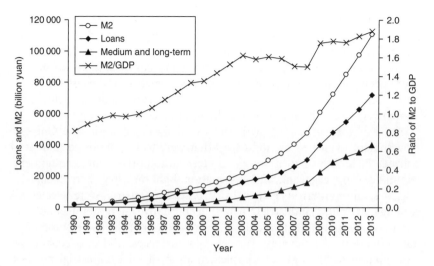

Source: National Bureau of Statistics (various years).

Figure 8.3   Expansions of money supply and credit loans

Shifting the stimulus from competitive sectors to infrastructure, on the other hand, can cause similar problems. That is, since the demand for infrastructure is not formed independently, but is derived by the development of a competitive real economy, blindly investing in infrastructure while demand is sluggish will eventually lead to overcapacity in that area. When the Japanese government tried to rely on large-scale public investment to stimulate its infrastructure, it ran into the awkward situation of being unable to put that investment in place (Miyazaki, 2009). It is not hard to imagine that the money supply released with the intention of investing in the real economy and/or infrastructure was eventually leaked to the real estate market, stock market, overseas property market, and sectors that tend to produce bubbles. After that bubble burst in Japan, it sank into the "lost two decades."

Targeting Keynes's advocacy for a stimulus policy, economist Hubert Henderson wrote in a letter to Keynes in 1933:

> if you were to announce that you were going in for a large 200 million programme, you would not get a single order under that programme for at least a year, whereas the effects on gilt-edged market and the like of the announcement of your intention would be immediate. You might thus easily get a vicious circle wound up before your virtuous circle had begun to operate at all. (Skidelsky, 1992, p. 474)

The Chinese economy may find an analogue in and implications for its own policy choices in those experiences and foresights.

First, the experiences of China's small and medium-sized enterprises (SMEs) indicate that such stimulus policies would hardly sustain long-term growth. Searching for new comparative advantages has to rely on the creative destruction of tens of thousands of SMEs, a process which requires solid financial support. The frequent implementation of stimulus policies tends to intensify macroeconomic volatility, however, and harms the emergence, development, and expansion of SMEs.

SMEs in China always face difficulty in gaining access to credit, while also bearing a high cost of financing no matter what the current direction of macroeconomic policies. During expansionary periods, all policies tend to favor large firms. State-owned enterprises (SOEs) are characterized by soft budget constraints and are not sensitive to the costs of financing; they usually receive a majority of loans from state-owned banks and leave little credit for SMEs. On the other hand, during periods of tight macro-economic policies, SMEs are the first to bear the brunt of credit shortages, a break in money chains, and increased cost of financing. Both SOEs' soft budget constraints and SMEs' lack of access to formal credit lead to a prevalence of shadow banking, potentially causing financial risks.

Second, in the circumstance that local governments take part in various investment activities, they become over-indebted. Because local Chinese governments hold a relatively small share of the fiscal revenue and do not have the right to issue government bonds, since the late 1990s they have been involved in credit activities in a disguised way through government-guaranteed platforms of financing. Especially since 2009, with the implementation of a massive stimulus package to tackle the financial crisis, much of the new banking loans have flooded into the government financing platforms, forming local governments' debts. According to an official report by the National Audit Office of China, as of June 2013 all levels of the Chinese government are liable for the amount of 20.69 trillion *yuan*, of which local (provincial and lower) governments were responsible for 10.88 trillion *yuan* (National Audit Office of China, 2013).

Third, industrial policies often serve as the force behind market over-capacities. Those industries under the guidance of industrial policies are often among the leading sectors in expansion and thus the area where the wave phenomenon is most likely to occur. According to the calculation by Qu (2012), the average capacity use rate of China's industry was 81.9 percent in 2010, whereas those sectors that are chosen as strategic industries and receive government support all have much lower capacity use rates (Figure 8.4). For example, the capacity use rate of the iron and steel industry was 50 percent, while that of nonferrous metal manufacturing

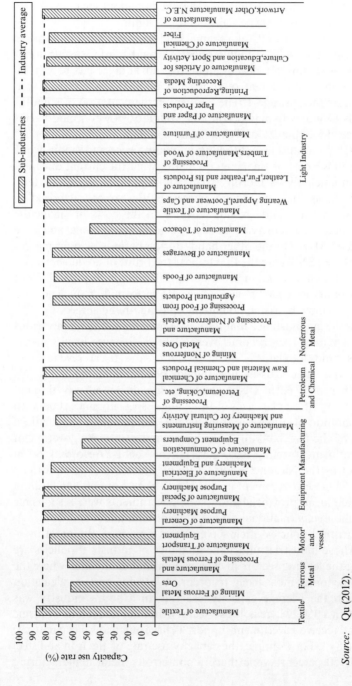

Source: Qu (2012).

Figure 8.4 Capacity use rates by industry in 2010

was only slightly above 70 percent. In addition, as Zhou Xiaochuan, the governor of the People's Bank of China, points out, infrastructure also suffers from overcapacity (Shi and Zheng, 2009).

In circumstances where the economy grows at a rate below its potential capacity as determined by the supply of production factors and improvements to productivity, an expansionist macroeconomic policy is needed to manage demand-side factors. It is, however, unnecessary and dangerous to utilize various stimulus policies to push economic growth beyond its potential rate. To tackle the decline of potential growth, the only appropriate option is to deepen those areas of economic reform that, by their nature, can increase the supply of production factors and productivity.

8.4   CONCLUSION

In the face of the decline in the potential growth rate, there are three options from which policy makers may choose: (1) they may spare no efforts in bringing about an actual growth beyond the potential rate; (2) they can do nothing but accept the slowed economic growth; or (3) they can put forward the necessary efforts to increase the potential growth rate itself. Different choices require the employing of contrary policy measures and result in entirely distinct consequences.

Figure 8.5 depicts the alternative policy options and possible outcomes. Given the existing long-term aggregate supply curve S_1 that corresponds

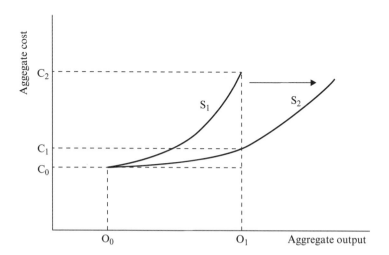

Figure 8.5   Costs for growth under different aggregate supply curves

to a slowed potential growth rate, a larger magnitude of output—namely, a growth rate beyond the potential rate—demands a higher aggregate cost. For example, when the output level is expanded from O_0 to O_1, the aggregate cost correspondingly increases from C_0 to C_2 as a result of a more dramatic increase in marginal costs. In fact, when further extending the cost to include not only direct inputs in the production process but also the price of those factors that cause volatility in the macroeconomy and negatively affect economic growth (say, inflation, carbon dioxide emissions, pollution, distortion of production factors, inefficiency of resources allocation, overcapacities, and so on), one may conclude that any pursuit of a higher growth rate beyond its potential capability is economically costly.

The decline in potential growth rates caused by supply-side factors also has an impact on demand-side factors. First, as the country's comparative advantage in manufacturing weakens, exports of labor-intensive commodities will no longer make as significant a contribution to growth as in the decade after China entered the WTO. Second, as the return on capital investment diminishes, a continual growth relying heavily on investment will further aggravate the imbalance already existing in the Chinese economy. Therefore, at the present stage of development, the overuse of stimulus policies may become the last straw in government failure and should be cautiously avoided.

Alternatively, increasing the potential growth rate is a potentially sound choice. For example, with the adjustment of the price incentives of production factors and refinement of the policy climate, the supply of production factors can be augmented and productivity improved. Supposing the long-term aggregate supply curve moves from S_1 to S_2, output expansion from O_0 to O_1 can be archived at a much smaller aggregate cost—namely, only from C_0 to C_1. In other words, the augmented potential growth rate can support a higher actual growth rate without resulting in a distortion of factor prices or harm to the macroeconomy.

The potential of such reform dividends, however, has not been widely recognized by scholars, the press, or policy makers. While industrial policies, regional strategies, and macroeconomic policies formulated for stimulation are recognized as straightforward measures for the government to obtain a growth rate beyond its potential capability, there seem to be no tangible methods of leverage by which to change potential growth rates. The effects of reforms on the increase in the potential growth rate may only be considered as a theoretical possibility before reforms bring about real benefit. For example, the World Bank economist Kharas (2011), known for defining the concept of the middle-income trap, asserts that reforms aimed to avoid the middle-income trap usually take at least a decade to see any effects, which may make anxious policy makers impatient.

Similarly, many analysts believe that there is a trade-off between reform and growth or, in other words, that China will have to sacrifice a certain degree of rapid growth in order to push forward with reforms. As the old Chinese saying goes, "Choose the greater of two interests, choose the lesser of two evils."

Even supposing there is such a trade-off between reform and growth, the "reform" is the necessary condition for long-term, sustainable growth, while the "growth" here is the root of the country's unsustainable growth pattern. Furthermore, given the existence of institutional obstacles impeding the sufficient supply of production factors and increases in productivity, related reforms aiming to eliminate those institutional obstacles can bring about the immediate effect of increasing the potential growth rate—namely, a reform dividend.

Demand-side factors, though unrelated to the potential growth rate, can help make economic growth more sustainable and the macroeconomy more balanced. Of the troika of demand factors—namely, exportation, investment, and consumption—the latter has served as the stabilizer of the Chinese macroeconomy, while exportation and investment have been more volatile (Figure 8.1). Increasing the share of consumption in the demand factors, therefore, will be conducive to stabilizing the macroeconomy. Statistically, consumption consists of government consumption and resident consumption. In recent years, while the share of resident consumption has declined, the share of government consumption has remained relatively unchanged; as a result, the share of total consumption in regard to GDP has declined. As a result, any reforms that help increase consumption, not least resident consumption, will make the macroeconomy more stable and, thus, growth sustainable.

On the basis of understanding the cause of economic slowdown, of distinguishing between long-term growth and short-term shocks, and, thus, of recognizing those reform dividends coming from supply-side and demand-side factors, the following chapters will identify key areas of reform and discuss approaches to reform.

NOTES

1. Paul Samuelson once regarded the Ricardian theory of comparative advantage as a single theory that is both correct and significant in all social sciences' theories. In recent years, however, he has proved that globalization does not necessarily equally benefit all countries deeply involved in international trade. See Samuelson (2004).
2. Lin (2007) observes that massive enterprises and investors often reach a highly concurrent judgment on dynamic comparative advantages, which gives rise to a wave phenomenon.

3. A short review of the implementation of industrial policies in China can be seen in World Bank and Development Research Center of the State Council, People's Republic of China (2013).
4. The so-called new structural economics, proposed and advocated by Lin (2012), is actually intended to explore how to determine the objectives of industrial policies based on a sound framework of thinking and the specific situation of countries.
5. Many researchers have discussed the negative consequences of the huge stimulus package implemented by the Chinese government at the local and national levels in 2009 and 2010. A review can be read in Lardy (2012).

REFERENCES

Cai, Fang, and Yang Lu (2013), "The End of China's Demographic Dividend: The Perspective of Potential GDP Growth," in Ross Garnaut, Fang Cai, and Ligang Song (eds.), *China: A New Model for Growth and Development*, Canberra: Australian National University E Press, pp. 55–74.

Ghosh, Jayati (2012), "The Continuing Need for Industrial Policy," *Frontline*, 29 (9), 5–18.

Hayashi, Fumio, and Edward Prescott (2002), "The 1990s in Japan: A Lost Decade," *Review of Economic Dynamics*, 5 (1), 206–235.

IMF (International Monetary Fund) (2012), *People's Republic of China: 2012 Article IV Consultation*, IMF Country Report No. 12/195, Washington, DC: International Monetary Fund.

Kharas, Homi (2011), "China's Transition to a High Income Economy: Escaping the Middle Income Trap," in Edwin Lim and Michael Spence (eds.), *Thoughts and Suggestions for China's 12th Five-Year Plan from an International Perspective*, Beijing: China CITIC Press, pp. 470–501.

Krugman, Paul (2013), "Hitting China's Wall," *New York Times*, July 18.

Lardy, Nicholas (2012), *Sustaining China's Economic Growth after the Global Financial Crisis*, Washington, DC: Peterson Institute for International Economics.

Lin, Justin Yifu (2007), "Wave Phenomenon and the Reconstruction of Macroeconomic Theories for Developing Countries," *Economic Research Journal*, 42 (1), 126–131.

Lin, Justin Yifu (2012), *New Structural Economics: A Framework for Rethinking Development and Policy*, Washington, DC: World Bank.

Mitchell, Tom, and Shawn Donnan (2015), "IMF Makes Significant Shift with Vote of Confidence in Renminbi," *Financial Times*, May 27.

Miyazaki, Isamu (2009), *A Personal Experience in Japanese Economic Policy-Making*, Beijing: China CITIC Press.

National Audit Office of China (2013), "Audit Results of Nationwide Governmental Debts, No. 32 of 2013 (General Serial No. 174)," National Audit Office official website: http://www.cnao.gov.cn/main/articleshow_ArtID_1335.htm.

National Bureau of Statistics (various years), *China Statistical Yearbook [year]*, Beijing: China Statistics Press.

Ni, Mingya (2013), "Justin Lin: China's Economic Growth Should Rely on Investment but Not on Consumption," *China Securities Journal*, May 31.

Qu, Yue (2012), "The Rapid Growth Sustained by Mass Investment: Research on Over-capacity of Production," in Fang Cai (ed.), *Demographic Transition and*

Economic Rebalance in China, Reports on China's Population and Labor No. 13, Beijing: Social Sciences Academic Press, pp. 112–128.

Samuelson, Paul (2004), "Where Ricardo and Mill Rebut and Confirm Arguments of Mainstream Economists Supporting Globalization," *Journal of Economic Perspectives*, 18 (3), 135–146.

Schumpeter, Joseph (1982), *The Theory of Economic Development: An Inquiry into Profits, Capital, Credit, Interest, and the Business Cycle*, Piscataway, NJ: Transition Publishers.

Shi, Jinfeng, and Zhi Zheng (2009), "Zhou Xiaochuan: Infrastructure Suffers Certain Overcapacity," *21st Century Business Herald*, November 21.

Skidelsky, Robert (1992), *John Maynard Keynes*, Vol. Two: *The Economist as Saviour, 1920–1937*, London: Macmillan.

Spence, Michael (2011), *The Next Convergence: The Future of Economic Growth in a Multispeed World*, New York: Farrar, Straus and Giroux.

Williamson, John (2004), "A Short History of the Washington Consensus," paper commissioned by Fundación CIDOB for the conference "From the Washington Consensus towards a new Global Governance," Barcelona, September 24–25, http://www.petersoninstitute.org/publications/papers/williamson0904-2.pdf.

World Bank and Development Research Center of the State Council, People's Republic of China (2013), *China 2030: Building a Modern, Harmonious, and Creative Society*, Washington, DC: World Bank.

9. Human capital accumulation

It takes ten years to grow trees but a hundred years to educate people. (Guan Zhong [BC 723 or 716–646])

During the period of Chinese economic development following the arrival of the Lewis Turning Point and the disappearance of the demographic dividend, sustaining economic growth will require a disproportionally rapid expansion of those inputs characterized by increasing returns. Human capital—namely, those skills developed through education, training, and learning-by-doing experience—is one such input of economic growth. The growing shortage of unskilled workers in this specific transition period, however, creates a disincentive to human capital accumulation. If China cannot adequately cope with existing challenges facing human capital accumulation, its future growth will be endangered by two problems: one being the lack of human capital that powers innovation-driven economic growth, and the other being labor market vulnerability alongside social unrest potentially caused by severe structural unemployment.

Education is the most important area in which resources are invested for the purpose of accumulating human capital. As an area with significant externality, education is not only characterized by a regular input–output relationship that correspondingly produces profit motives for private investment, but also governed by a special law that is embodied in the difference between private and social returns. This implies that, for education to sufficiently meet the demands of society, the government itself should assume the responsibility for expanding access to education.

This chapter discusses the growing demand for the transformation of economic growth patterns, particularly of the necessity for upgrading the country's industrial structure. Insofar as the skills and innovative ability of workers are concerned, this chapter refers to the precedent set by international experiences in educational development and examines methods by which to create new drivers for human capital accumulation by defining the role of the Chinese government in educational development.

9.1 INDUSTRIAL UPGRADING AND DEMAND FOR SKILLS

According to general laws governing economic development, China has entered a new stage in which the country's industrial structure and existing technologies are likely to experience rapid advancement as a result of the transformation of growth patterns. While the intrinsic result of such industrial upgrading is to improve labor productivity, it is also manifested in the shifting of industrial structures from labor-intensive industries to capital- and technology-intensive industries and from manufacturing to the service sector, all of which require significantly upgraded skills for workers.

Take, for example, manufacturing, which has until this point put China in the position of the world's factory. Improvements in manufacturing will follow two paths. First and foremost, China's manufacturing must climb the value chain. Despite China being ranked as number one in the world in total manufacturing output, its value-added rate—namely, the share of value added to total output value—is significantly lower than that of many developed countries. As a study published in *China Statistics* indicates (Chen et al., 2014), in terms of manufacturing as a whole, the 2010 value-added rate of China was 23.8 percent compared to 35.2 percent in the United States. This not only reflects the gap in the industrial structure between China and the US—which is to say that China's manufacturing is, in general, at the bottom of the value chain—but also is because the productivity of almost every manufacturing industry in China is lower than that same industry in the US. Surprisingly, the gaps in the value-added rate in labor-intensive manufacturing industries (in which China is supposed to have a comparative advantage) between China and the United States are even larger. For example, the value-added rate in the garment and leatherwear industry is 27.2 percent in China and 64.8 percent in the United States, according to the same sources.

Industrial upgrades to Chinese manufacturing structures will also involve a shift in activities from manufacturing itself to activities in forward- and backward-linked sectors, which include research and development, design, marketing, and after-sales service. As a result, producer services, which require more intensive inputs of information, ideas, know-how, talents, brand recognition, and so on, will be separate from manufacturing and expanded in and of themselves. In discussing the relatively smaller share of China's service sector, it in fact means that the relative underdevelopment of producer services is related to the fact that China's manufacturing is at the low end of industry in terms of technological content.

The status of a given country's industry in the value chain is determined by its overall level of technology, management, and skills, all of which have to do with the endowment of human capital. Therefore, the upgrading of China's industry has to be accompanied by human capital being accumulated at the same pace, if not at a disproportionally more rapid pace.

From what we know about the average levels of workers' educational attainments across different sectors, there are certain minimum requirements of human capital in which we can expect to see labor shifts among sectors following the direction of industrial upgrading. We must first divide non-agricultural industry into four categories—(1) the labor-intensive secondary sector, (2) the labor-intensive tertiary sector, (3) the capital-intensive secondary sector, and (4) the technology-intensive tertiary sector—each of which successively requires workers to have higher educational attainments. At this point, we can then compare the number of years of schooling for average workers in each sector with that attained by average migrant workers by age (Figure 9.1).

Take, for example, an average worker in the labor-intensive secondary sector. It requires an extra 0.5 years of schooling for him/her to shift to the

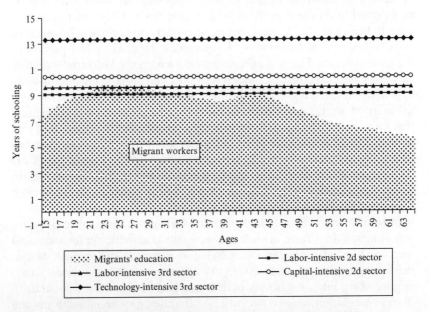

Note: For the details of the categorization of sectors, see Cai and Wang (2012).

Source: Author's calculation based on the 20% sampling micro data of the 1% Population Sampling Survey conducted in 2005.

Figure 9.1   Average years of schooling of non-agricultural workers by sector

labor-intensive tertiary sector, an extra 1.3 years of schooling to shift to the capital-intensive secondary sector, and an extra 4.2 years of schooling to move to the technology-intensive tertiary sector. Presently, the average educational attainment of migrant workers is about the same as that of the average workers engaged in the labor-intensive secondary and tertiary sectors; therefore, migrant workers have to climb those human capital ladders if they shift to higher levels of employment.

The additional years of schooling required to change jobs are by no mean insignificant, because it takes quite a long time to increase the total number of years of schooling for the labor force overall. For example, according to data from previous population censuses, the number of years of schooling for the Chinese population aged 16 and older increased from 6.24 in 1990 to 7.56 in 2000 and to 8.90 in 2010. That is, the educational attainments of Chinese adults increased by only 2.66 years in those 20 years, during which time China experienced the introduction of universal compulsory education and the mass expansion of higher education, probably the fastest educational development in human history.

A situation in which there is an inadequate supply of human capital will not only impede the improvement of the productivity of the Chinese economy as a whole, but also cause employment difficulties for Chinese workers. Despite the widespread labor shortage in recent years, unskilled workers are potentially vulnerable in the labor market. Changes in industrial structures are destroying certain existing jobs while creating new ones, a phenomenon that causes frictional and structural unemployment. For individual workers, whether they can handle the shocks depends on their human capital endowment. Since migrant workers currently make up 35.2 percent of total urban employment and 65.4 percent of the yearly increase in urban employment, what they would face in an urban labor market can be taken as representative of Chinese workers as a whole.

On average, migrant workers only attain an education at the junior high school level, which poses greater risks for them in facing structural unemployment. Without an urban *hukou* identity, which prevents migrant workers from having equal access to social protection in urban areas, they will be extremely vulnerable if they lose their jobs. Presently, when migrant workers encounter shocks in the labor market, they usually go back to their home villages, where they have farm land to work. As the new generation of migrant workers (those defined as 30 years old or younger) increasingly become the dominant majority of migrant workers in urban areas, however, present migration patterns will be changed completely.

As based on CULS data, studies show that the new generation of migrant workers made up over 60 percent of the total migrant workforce in 2010. They have never had agricultural experience and are not willing to work as farmers, since a sizable portion of them grew up in cities with their migrant parents. For example, in 2010, of those migrant workers aged between 16 and 30, 32.8 percent had lived in cities or towns before they turned 16 years old, and 38.4 percent attended primary school in cities or towns. This implies that future migrant workers will no longer reflect the "come-and-go" pattern of migration by following the fluctuations of the urban labor market. As a result, the potential situation in which they lose their jobs and consequently become a vulnerable group without social protections in urban areas will most likely cause social unrest.

9.2 EDUCATION INCENTIVES IN THE LABOR MARKET

The accumulation of human capital requires increasing the educational level of those newly entering the labor market at a much faster pace than the concurrent growth of the economy, so as to enlarge the total human capital endowment of a given society. Therefore, educational development needs to look to the future. Over the past three decades, China has successfully enhanced people's educational attainments through the implementation of universal compulsory education and the expansion of higher education. Thus we can generally consider young people who graduate from one level of schooling and do not enter the next level of schooling as new entrants into the labor market with their given educational attainments in tow.

As is shown in Figure 9.2, since the mid-1980s, of those newly entering laborers, the proportion of primary school graduates to the whole has dropped substantially; the proportion of junior high school graduates has greatly increased (particularly during and after the 1990s), and the proportion of college and university graduates has increased rapidly since the early years of the twenty-first century, accompanied by an increased proportion of senior high school graduates. As a result, whereas the number of new entrants in total has shrunk, the educational endowment of the labor force has been massively amplified.

Meanwhile, the expanded educational attainments of Chinese workers have been transformed into a human capital that is itself a significant driver of the miraculous economic growth of the reform period. In almost all research that employs models of growth accounting or production function, the variable of the number of years of schooling has been incorporated and found to be statistically significant. By choosing different methods of estimation, however, studies may conclude different magnitudes of the contribution of the human capital variable to economic growth in China.

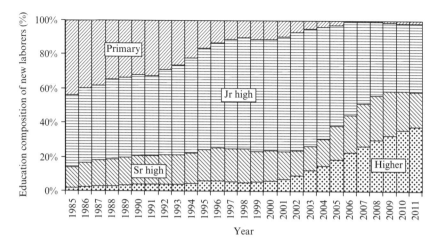

Source: National Bureau of Statistics (2012).

Figure 9.2   The educational composition of new entrant laborers

For example, Kuijs (2010) has estimated China's potential growth rate and its components—namely, TFP, human capital (ratio of human capital to labor), and capital deepening (ratio of capital to labor)—across different periods and concluded that human capital's contribution to the potential growth rate was 5.2 percent in 1979–1994 and 3.2 percent in 1995–2009. While estimating the demographic dividend's contribution to GDP growth, Cai and Zhao (2012) found that, besides capital input, labor input, the dependency ratio, and TFP, human capital accumulation (denoted by years of schooling) contributed 4.3 percent to the economic growth in 1982–2009. Whalley and Zhao's estimate of human capital contribution is much greater. According to their study—which incorporates variables of physical capital stock, labor, human capital stock (years of schooling), and TFP into a neoclassical model of growth accounting—human capital was found to contribute 11.7 percent to GDP growth in 1979–2009. Taking into consideration the different levels of productivity under different levels of education, they estimated a much larger contribution of human capital to growth—that is, 38 percent (Whalley and Zhao, 2010).

Human capital is not an ordinary variable amongst several others, but is instead characterized by increasing returns over the long run. Kuijs (2010), along with Whalley and Zhao (2010), found that human capital has not only contributed to China's overall economic growth but has also offset the adverse effects of unsatisfactory TFP performance.

The significant contributions of aggregated human capital accumulation can benefit individual workers, families, and enterprises that invest in education and training through private returns on skills in the labor market. Such a return on human capital, in turn, serves as an incentive for further investment in workers, families, and human capital in enterprises. Some studies have particularly focused on how further enhancement of the number of years of schooling of workers can bring about benefits to human capital investors.

For example, Wang focuses on how workers can benefit from an increase in the number of years of their schooling by a corresponding increase in their wage rates. The study suggests that, if the number of years of schooling increases from the current levels (9.4 for the average urban laborer and 6.8 for the average rural laborer) to 12 (the level at which students will have completed senior high school), the returns on education will increase by 17.0 percent for urban laborers and 21.1 percent for rural laborers; if the number of years of schooling increases from current levels to 14 years— that is, more people attend higher education before entering the labor market—the return on education will increase by 41.2 percent for urban laborers and 43.3 percent for rural laborers (Wang, 2009).

Another study estimates the effect of enhancing workers' educational attainments on the labor productivity of manufacturing enterprises. According to a simulation by Qu et al., a single additional year of schooling for workers would enhance the labor productivity of manufacturing enterprises by 17 percent. Another way of looking at this effect is that, if all workers can be upgraded from their present status as junior high school graduates or lower to senior high school graduates and junior college graduates (three-year higher education), the labor productivity of enterprises will increase by 24 percent to 66 percent, respectively (Qu et al., 2010).

As the labor market develops, market forces play an increasingly important role in allocating the labor force and motivating human capital investment. That is, private returns on skills serve as a signal directing enterprises and families to invest in human capital. There exists, however, the phenomenon of labor market failure in motivating human capital accumulation, as can be seen in other areas where market forces allocate resources.

The shortage of unskilled workers and the increase in their wages reveal the arrival of the Lewis Turning Point. Correspondingly, a convergence in the wages of skilled and unskilled workers in China's labor market has appeared since 2004. Such a phenomenon is synonymous with a relative decrease in returns on human capital. An estimate on the relative returns on the educational attainments of migrant workers shows that, taking migrant workers who have finished junior high school as a reference group, the additional return on education for workers with above a senior high school education fell from 80.4 percent in 2001 to 75.3 percent in 2005 and

57.1 percent in 2010, and the additional return on education for workers with just a senior high school education fell from 25.9 percent in 2001 to 17.3 percent in 2005 and 16.9 percent in 2010 (Cai and Du, 2011).

Translating these econometric findings into the day-to-day decision making of ordinary households, families have observably shown reluctance to support their children at the higher stages of education. Given the heavy expense families must bear while sending their children to senior high school and university, along with the increased opportunity costs, namely, the potential loss in labor market earnings if their children stay in school, families tend to encourage their children to participate in the labor force right after graduation or even to drop out from the compulsory education stage (junior high school). A survey conducted in poor rural areas found that, in just one year between September 2009 and October 2010, the dropout rate for three grades of junior high school students was as high as 25 percent (Brinton et al., 2012).

For a long time, China's human capital accumulation has been constrained by the insufficiency of educational resources. Still, two extraordinary breakthroughs were made in the reform period. First, the government's push to universalize compulsory education was initiated in 1986, when the Compulsory Education Law was issued. With all the tuition fees for compulsory education gradually eliminated, enrollment rates for the first nine years of compulsory education have eventually reached 100 percent.[1] Second, the expansion of higher education that began in 1999 with the original intention of delaying high school graduates from entering the labor market was implemented so as to ease employment pressure at the time. Consequently, the yearly number of graduates from colleges and universities increased from 850 000 in 1999 to 6.8 million in 2012, and the numbers of enrolled students in colleges and universities per 100 000 increased from 594 to 2335 in the same period.

These two miraculous achievements coordinate with each other almost perfectly in timing. That is, the effect of universal compulsory education on the increase in actual number of years of schooling of the Chinese population began diminishing as enrollment rates reached 100 percent. What's more, the expansion of higher education has not only enhanced the enrollment rate of its own accord, but also increased the enrollment rate of senior high school, thus increasing the number of years of schooling for the new labor force.

While China's education has made great progress from the supply side— that is, allocating far more resources to educational development—adverse incentives rising from the demand side have emerged in recent years. If Chinese decision makers fail to address this turbulence appropriately, the momentum of educational development is very likely to be halted. As a matter of fact, many widely prevalent critiques of the rapid expansion of higher education have emerged based on the reduced quality of university education, employment difficulties facing college graduates, and wage convergence between more educated and less educated workers. What's more, largely as a response to such criticisms, the expansion of higher education has slowed down noticeably since 2008.

9.3　IS THERE OVER-EDUCATION IN CHINA OR ANYWHERE ELSE?

Since the doubts surrounding the expansion of higher education arise partially from employment difficulties faced by college graduates, any convincing response to this doubt requires empirical evidence on whether or not the relative return on higher education has declined in absolute terms. It is not hard to understand that, because there has been a scarcity of college graduates in the labor market, the return on higher education was much higher than the return on basic education in the time before the expansion.

On the other hand, that the rewards of the labor market for college graduates remain higher than those for workers without a college diploma can well justify the necessity of expansion. One study of this kind finds that, since the expansion of higher education started in 1999, the degree to which the wage rate of employees with educational attainments of junior college and above held significant advantages over that of employees without a college diploma increased tremendously. In 2009, for example, the average wage of employees with junior college degree or greater was 1.49 times that of employees without a college diploma (Li, H. et al., 2012).

Still, the gap between labor market rewards to and the urgent demand for higher education exists, especially given the fact that China's sustainability of growth increasingly depends on productivity growth and human capital on the basis of scientific and technological development. When market failures occur, both public opinion and the corresponding policy response are likely to be misled by superficial signals from the labor market. That is, the difficulty of college graduates in finding a job may be considered to be a phenomenon of over-education, and any decision making based on such a fallacious observation may prove to be harmful to the long-term growth of the country. In this regard, the experience of Japan provides a negative example, deserving of serious reflection.

Japanese economist Yoshihisa Godo has collected a significant amount of data on the catching-up of Japanese education with that of the United States, which can help us to draw lessons specific to China. According to the evidence he has provided, during the period 1890 to 1990, Japan's catching-up in educational development was successful if it is measured by the Japan–US gap—namely, the percentage of the average years of schooling of the working-age population in Japan as compared to that of the United States, which increased from 19.7 percent to 84.8 percent. Since the late 1970s, however, while Japan continued to catch up with the US in primary and secondary educations, the Japan–US gap in higher education widened. For example, the percentage of the average years of college of the working-age population in Japan compared to that in the United States declined from 45.3 percent in 1976 to 40.4 percent in 1990, back to the levels seen in 1965 (Godo, 2001).

The stagnation of higher education in Japan can be seen as early as the late 1950s. The cause of such stagnation is quite similar to that of China today—that is, submitting to the increasing concerns and public critiques over the employment difficulties facing college graduates and the decline in educational quality, the Japanese government intentionally checked the rapid expansion of higher education, resulting in far-reaching consequences to the long-term growth of the Japanese economy.

In the early stages of catching up with developed countries, the Japanese economy mainly borrowed and imitated technologies from more advanced economies, with the result that the "great leap forward" development of primary and secondary education for the general population appropriately met the needs of its dual economy development. After the Japanese economy arrived at its Lewis Turning Point around 1960, however, its expected growth should have been increasingly dependent on an increase in labor productivity. In response to this challenge, the Japanese economy accelerated its heavy industrialization after 1960, leading to a substantial increase in the capital–labor ratio of the economy as a whole. At the same time, as a result of lagging relatively far behind the United States and many European countries in terms of technological innovation and the defects in its economic system, TFP growth has stagnated since 1990, which is responsible for the country's "lost decades" (Hayashi and Prescott, 2002) and, to a greater extent, is itself attributable to the country's relatively unsuccessful catching-up in higher education.

While Japan offers object lessons on higher education development, other developed countries can provide lessons on the development of secondary education. Since the United States recovered from its 1991 recession, it has experienced "jobless recovery" following every recession or crisis, which can partially be attributed to a mismatch between workers' skills and the skills required by the job market.

With the development of a knowledge-based economy among developed countries, some semi-skilled workers have been replaced with computers, robot, and other information technologies. In the United States, this creates a trend of labor market polarization—namely, the numbers of both high-skilled workers and low-skilled workers grow quickly, while the numbers of middle-skilled workers grow more slowly (Autor et al., 2006). The global division of labor exacerbates the problem by reallocating semi-skilled jobs among countries—for example, some such jobs relocate from the US to newly emerging economies. At the same time, high-skilled workers and low-skilled workers have not evenly benefited from this economic globalization, with the low-skilled workers being losers as regards the reallocation of jobs (Samuelson, 2004). They turn out to be either unskilled immigrant workers or the products of a "middle school to middle class" model. Since recovery from recession is always accompanied by an adjustment of the industrial structure in accordance with a given country's comparative advantages, further outsourcing and industrial outflows weaken the demand for labor.

This labor market polarization and the resultant income inequality and job market vulnerability are more or less the consequences of educational policies. Although the US has the world's best universities and globally leads in technological innovation, there are also a significant number of young people who neither go to college nor finish senior high school, which has weakened its human capital stock. For example, according to United Nations Development Programme (UNDP) statistics, the mean number of years of schooling for the population aged 25 and older in the US declined from 13.22 in 2000 to 12.45 in 2010, while the ratio of this indicator between the US and the median of the world's other 173 countries decreased during the same period.[2] The resultant low-skilled workers are therefore victimized by economic shocks.

Chinese unskilled and semi-skilled workers now enjoy their "good time" with abundant job opportunities and a rapid increase in wages. This time of economic prosperity will not last long, however, as can be seen from the lessons taught by previous international experiences. If disincentives for human capital accumulation persist—namely, as more jobs are available and rising wages entice young people to participate in the labor force before they complete the necessary education—they will soon encounter severe problems in the labor market as industries upgrade and higher skills are required. In that sense, both economic growth as a whole and the individual laborers will be hurt.

9.4   THE GOVERNMENT'S RESPONSIBILITY TO THE DEVELOPMENT OF EDUCATION

Even though education is not a purely public good, because of its clear distinction between private return and social return, even those economists who strongly advocate for a free market admit the necessity of government involvement in this area. A unique challenge for China, which has just passed through the Lewis Turning Point, is the decline in the relative returns on education in the labor market, a typical market failure. Whereas this phenomenon sends a signal that helps increase labor force participation in response to labor shortages, its consequences will harm the accumulation of future human capital. In cases where market failures occur, the government should move to actively step in.

For a long time, all walks of life in China have called for the expansion of public spending on education as measured by the ratio of fiscal expenditure on education to total GDP. The official goal of 4 percent of such a ratio was first established in *Guidance for Educational Reform and Development in China*, issued in 1993 by the Chinese government. Over 20 years later, and with this goal eventually having being reached in 2012, the question now becomes: (1) is the over 2 trillion *yuan* of GDP equivalent enough for the sustainable development of China's education, and (2) how should the money be allocated in order to use it most efficiently?

While lauding the existing efforts and achievements made by the government, one should be well aware that 4 percent of GDP is not yet a sufficient guarantee of public spending on education by international standards. Indeed, China's share of public spending on education to GDP is still lower than the world average, let alone that of all the developed countries (except Japan). The ratio is as high as 6–7 percent in countries such as Finland, Iceland, New Zealand, Norway, Sweden, and the United Kingdom. Even many developing countries have a higher educational spending ratio than China.

In addition, how much education input is really needed in one country depends on its population age properties. That is, when the country holds a higher proportion of the school-age population to the overall population, it necessarily demands more resources for education development. Therefore, if we normalize education input by the proportion of the school-age population in order to make an international comparison, the result may better reflect the differentials in education input levels among countries. For example, in a previous study—taking as a reference the proportion of the population aged between 6 and 24 over the total population in the United States—we find that, because China has a much higher proportion of this population group than does the US, the normalized ratio of public education spending to GDP in China is reduced by 16.4 percent more than that shown by a simple calculated ratio (Cai et al., 2009).

Even with a significant increase in public input into education, how this input is allocated is as important as the magnitude of the input itself. In fact, the efficient allocation of resources is a more difficult task. Education is an area where human capital investment can bring both private returns through the labor market and social returns embodied in positive externality. In the latter case, investment in education cannot be sufficient if there is no public input. Therefore, not only is a necessary amount of public spending required, but allocating the given amount of public resource in accordance with the degree to which education generates externality is vitally important.

A repeatedly confirmed law is that the social returns on education are the highest at the preschool phase, followed by the basic educational phase (for example, primary school and junior high school), and then the higher levels of general education (for example, senior high and higher education), and the lowest at the phase of vocational education and job-oriented training (Heckman and Carneiro, 2003). Based on these commonly acknowledged facts, we can depict the shortfalls of public spending on education in China.

First, the shortage of public spending is both reflected in and confirmed by the heavy burden placed on households by educational requirements. In 2009, the private share of total educational expenditure was 26.3 percent in China, nearly 12 percentage points higher than the average for most Organisation for Economic Co-operation and Development (OECD) countries.[3] We can also look at the private share of total educational expenditure in China by education type and stage based on the official data, which are categorized as government appropriation for education and private spending (including funds from investors in private schools, donations and fundraising for schools, income from running schools such as tuition and miscellaneous fees, and others) (Table 9.1).

The information in Table 9.1 can be summarized as follows. First, the overall share of private spending on education in China is still too high compared to most developed countries and even to many developing countries. Second, even at the compulsory education phase, which is supposed not to be paid by families, the private share of education expenditure is also high. Third, the private share of education expenditure is excessively high at both the preschool and the senior high school phase, which is not in line with the direction of broadening education given the proven high social return on education at these two phases. Fourth, though it makes some sense that individuals and families should pay relatively more on vocational middle school and higher education than they do in

Table 9.1 Shares of private spending by education type, 2012

Education type	Education as a whole %	Higher education %	Middle vocational %	Occupational senior high %	Ordinary senior high %	Ordinary junior high %	Rural junior high %	Primary school %	Rural primary school %	Preschool %
Shares of private spending	22.13	41.52	23.16	18.05	27.84	6.34	2.50	4.20	1.91	59.19

Source: National Bureau of Statistics official website, http://data.stats.gov.cn/workspace/index?m=hgnd.

other education phases, high costs will still prevent rural and poor families from equally obtaining those types of education.

The excessive proportion of private spending on various types and phases of education will not only divert households' consumptive demands, but also depress their demand for education. That is particularly true for poor rural families, since their household budgets are more constrained and consumption of food and other necessities inelastic. As the endowment of human capital determines the extent to which individual laborers and households participate in the labor market and, therefore, share the outcome of economic development, the inequality of education resulting from an unequal provision of public services will cause not only persistent inequality in participation and sharing within one generation, but also an intergenerational inheritance of human poverty.

What's more, educational resources are unevenly distributed among regions. It has been widely observed that the distribution of educational resources, especially those provided by public sources, are markedly unequal between rural and urban areas, between advanced and lagging regions, and between compulsory education and higher education phases, which adversely impacts the effectiveness of education development. Some researchers argue that such a disparity in education development is in fact much bigger than the existing income inequality (Li, S., 2010).

Although the ratio of fiscal spending on education to GDP reached 4.28 percent in 2012 and some lagging provinces (in terms of social and economic development) marked an even higher ratio necessary in order to catch up with the more advanced regions (Figure 9.3), given the huge difference in GDP size among regions, both the total amount and the per capita level of public spending on education in the central and western provinces are still far lower than in the coastal provinces. Since the local governments are responsible for compulsory education development, the large disparities in public spending on education among regions inevitably lead to persistent shortages of compulsory education resources in less-developed regions.

For example, the ratio of per capita public spending on education based on the resident population in Jiangsu, which is one of the country's richest provinces and holds the lowest ratio of public spending on education to local GDP, is 30.4 percent higher than that in Guizhou, which is one of the poorest provinces, though it holds a relatively higher ratio of public spending on education to local GDP. Additionally, because Jiangsu is one of the major destinations for migrant workers, while calculating per capita public spending on education, the denominator is enlarged by inter-provincial migrant workers, who do not, however, enjoy equal access to public education services. If we use the *hukou* population as the basis for

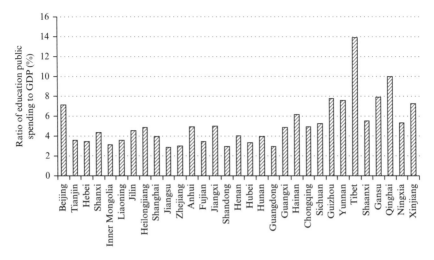

Source: Ministry of Education, National Bureau of Statistics, and Ministry of Finance (2013).

Figure 9.3   Ratio of public spending on education to GDP by province

this comparison, therefore, the gap in per capita public inputs in education between Jiangsu (representing China's developed regions) and Guizhou (representing China's lagging regions) will be much greater.

Finally, in China's transitional period, there are some specific characteristics that result in imperfections of human capital accumulation and pose urgent challenges to its allocation to public education resources. As James Heckman put it, both physical and human capital investment in China are distributed unequally, which is neither equitable nor efficient (Heckman, 2005). The lagging development of education in rural areas resulting from the uneven distribution of resources creates a bottleneck impeding the educational development of the country as a whole. In what follows, we examine the educational status of disadvantaged groups within the population throughout their life cycle.

Rural children lag behind in education from the beginning of their life cycle. A host of researchers have confirmed that preschool education has significant positive impacts on children's future physical development, cognitive ability, and social communication, and thus it brings the highest benefit to society. On the whole, the raw enrollment of kindergarten-age children was 50.9 percent in China in 2009, compared to 83.9 percent across 28 OECD countries and 100 percent in nine of those countries in 2006 (Xu, 2010). For China, it is the status quo of rural areas that keeps preschool from making any overall progress. While compulsory education for rural households and migrant families has noticeably improved since 2004, the difference in preschool education remains significant between rural and urban areas and between urban local and migrant families. For example, despite the fact that the number of rural children is far greater than the number of urban children, the ratio of rural children in kindergarten to urban children in kindergarten was only 83.1 percent as of 2012.

According to a survey aiming to test the impact of preschool education (in which a score of lower than 70 points indicates "not ready for primary school"), the proportion of "not ready" children was 3 percent for urban areas, while the proportion of "not ready" children was as high as 57 percent for rural children (Shi, 2009), a clear indication that rural children are already behind at the starting line due to an unequal provision of preschool educational resources.

The massive labor migration from rural to urban areas has created a large number of rural left-behind children and migrant children. According to a survey conducted by the All-China Women's Federation, in 2010 there were 61.03 million left-behind children, who accounted for 37.7 percent of total rural children aged between 0 and 17 and were clustered in rural areas of major migrant-sending regions, and 28.77 million rural-to-urban migrant children, who accounted for 24.6 percent of urban children aged between 0 and 17 and were concentrated in the cities of major migrant-receiving regions (Liu, 2013).

These left-behind and migrant children, who are just beginning preschool and the phases of compulsory education (the crucial period for human capital formation), tend to retain a severely disadvantaged status. Apart from being ill cared for by parents, having problems with mental and physical health, and bearing the pressure to drop out from school, they suffer persistent obstacles in getting a good education, such as the low quality of compulsory education in rural areas for left-behind children and difficulty in entering public school at the compulsory education level, and then again in gaining admission to education beyond the compulsory phase for migrant children in urban areas.

As a result, after primary school, left-behind and migrant children have a much higher dropout rate than urban children, and their dropout rate tends to get higher at comparatively higher phases of education. For example, in 2005, the proportion of migrant children aged 15–17 remaining in school was only 46.3 percent for boys and 36.6 percent for girls, compared to 82.3 percent and 82.8 percent, respectively, for urban boys and girls (Gao, 2010).

The deficiency of compulsory education and senior high schooling significantly reduces opportunities for left-behind and migrant children to enter universities. According to government regulations, migrant children have to take the university entrance examination in their *hukou*-specified province of origin, where educational quality is significantly lower and the quota for admission is smaller compared with that of urban areas. As a result, the proportion of students originating from rural areas to the total number of university students has fallen from more than 30 percent in the 1980s to 17.7 percent in the 2000s (Li, L., 2009). As a matter of fact, the expansion of higher education has offered opportunities for rural students to enter universities mainly through lowering the standards of student admissions and for conducting new universities and colleges, whereas the total amount and proportion of students from rural areas in highly qualified universities have become even smaller than before.

It is also true that, when looking into the human capital components of those migrant workers who constitute a majority of the labor supply in urban sectors in the present as well as the future, if we divide migrant workers into the "new generation (born after 1980)" and the "older generation (born before 1980)," in 2012, 6.1 percent of the new generation have below a junior high education and 24.7 percent of the older generation, 60.6 percent of the new generation have a junior high education and 61.2 percent of the older generation, 20.5 percent of the new generation have a senior high education and 12.3 percent of the older generation, and 12.8 percent of the new generation have a college or postgraduate education but only 1.8 percent of the older generation (National Bureau of Statistics, 2013).

This has, in fact, generated a vicious cycle within the labor market. Less-educated workers, who face more difficulties in meeting the changing requirements of structural adjustments for upgraded skills, tend to be clustered in the informal sectors and exposed to employment shocks, and, ultimately, become a vulnerable group. The employment informality and insecurity conversely make it harder for training programs to target these specific groups of workers.

9.5   CONCLUSION

According to Professor Aoki, who classifies economic development in East Asia into five distinct, successive phases, an economy will enter the phase of human capital-driven development at the turning point at which the share of the agricultural labor force drops below 20 percent (Aoki, 2012). The experiences of Japan and South Korea show that the key to becoming a high-income country lies in the successful preparation of human capital for the new economic phase, whereas the mistakes made in Japan that have caused the stagnation of higher education may be responsible for the lost decades following the 1990s. As the share of the agricultural labor force in China has already declined to only 20 percent of the total labor force, China is now standing at the turning point at which it will face urgent and severe challenges in the quest to accumulate human capital.

Augmented human capital serves not only as a sustainable driver of economic growth, but also as a solid foundation for social stability by promoting human development and improving income distribution. Therefore, education is one area where externality exists and the government should take more responsibility for its development. That is especially true for China, given that it is currently transitioning between developmental phases. What's more, education should be promoted jointly by society, families, and individuals, as well as motivated by private returns on human capital. All in all, efforts need to be made from both supply side and demand side, which will require a series of policy changes in various areas, including the following matters in which key policy reforms and institution building are most urgently needed.

The first reform we propose is to deepen education by incorporating preschool and senior high school into the period of state-sanctioned compulsory education free of charge while continuing to expand higher education. While the universal expansion of preschool education will eliminate the initial gap in education between rural and urban areas and between poor and rich families, the universalization of senior high school will, on the one hand, broadly augment the number of years of schooling for the labor force, while on the other hand it will help more youth get ready for higher education so that the Chinese economy can be predicated on and built around innovation-led, inclusive growth.

The second proposal is to reform the education system and to improve the quality of higher education. The late Mr. Qian Xuesen, a scientist and likely the most influential activist in public affairs in China, once censured Chinese universities for not being able to foster outstanding talent in a talk with then-premier Wen Jiabao. This so-called "Qian Question" has, in fact, long puzzled many people concerned with China's future. Therefore, continuing to expand higher education by no means undervalues the necessity of fundamental adjustments to the education system, discipline arrangements, curriculum arrangement, and contents of teaching in accordance with the demands of the labor market and socioeconomic development.

Third is to appropriately allocate public educational resources in accordance with the relative values of private and social returns on education in order to maximize the most social benefits with limited resources. One thing that most experts agree upon is that the key to reforming the Chinese education system is to redirect the role of the government from taking control of every aspect of education development to concentrating on mobilizing public resources and equitably allocating them. Specifically, ordinary education, especially in lagging regions, in rural areas, and for poor families, deserves increased constructive support from public resources, whereas vocational education across various levels should rely on labor market incentives that motivate investment in human capital by households and enterprises, given the inherently higher private return on those types of education.

Finally, the human capital stock of the Chinese labor market can be improved through the amplification of on-the-job training. Institutionally, certain barriers systematically prevent such training from functioning effectively, such that there is a deadlock between the insecurity of jobs caused by the *hukou* restriction reducing incentives for enterprises to provide and workers to receive appropriate training, on the one hand, and government-sponsored training programs having extremely limited relevance to the labor market, on the other. To resolve this dilemma, *hukou* reform, labor market institution building, and the development of skills training should be simultaneously carried out so that distorted private returns on training can be corrected and the efficiency of such training can be enhanced through supply-side and demand-side factors.

NOTES

1. In 2013, for example, the gross enrollment rate was 104.4 percent and 104.1 percent for primary school and junior high school, respectively. See National Bureau of Statistics (2014).
2. See the official website of the UNDP: http://www.beta.undp.org/content/undp/en/home. html.
3. See Organisation for Economic Co-operation and Development (OECD) iLibrary, http://www.oecd-ilibrary.org/education/education-resources/indicator-group/english_6932ce5c-en.

REFERENCES

Aoki, Masahiko (2012), "The Five Phases of Economic Development and Institutional Evolution in China, Japan, and Korea," in Masahiko Aoki, Timur Kuran, and Gérard Roland (eds.), *Institutions and Comparative Economic Development*, Basingstoke: Palgrave Macmillan, pp. 13–47.

Autor, David, Lawrence Katz, and Melissa Kearney (2006), *The Polarization of the U.S. Labor Market*, NBER Working Paper No. 11986, Cambridge, MA: National Bureau of Economic Research.

Brinton, Carl, Xinxin Chen, Renfu Luo, Di Mo, Scott Rozelle, Yaojiang Shi, Hongmei Yi, and Linxiu Zhang (2012), "Dropping Out: Why Are Students

Leaving Junior High in China's Poor Rural Areas?," *International Journal of Educational Development*, 32 (4), 555–563.

Cai, Fang, and Yang Du (2011), "Wage Increases, Wage Convergence, and Lewis Turning Point in China," *China Economic Review*, 22 (4), 601–610.

Cai, Fang, and Meiyan Wang (2012), "On the Status Quo of China's Human Capital—How to Explore New Sources of Growth after Demographic Dividends Disappear," *Frontiers*, 6, 56–65.

Cai, Fang, and Wen Zhao (2012), "When Demographic Dividend Disappears: Growth Sustainability of China," in Masahiko Aoki and Jinglian Wu (eds.), *The Chinese Economy: A New Transition*, Basingstoke: Palgrave Macmillan.

Cai, Fang, Yang Du, and Dewen Wang (2009), "A Study on Issues of China's Education Reform and Development Strategy," in Fang Cai (ed.), *Reforming the Education System to Promote Human Capital*, Reports on China's Population and Labor No. 10, Beijing: Social Sciences Academic Press, pp. 1–26.

Chen, Binghua, Jiliang Zhang, and Shuaiqi Zhang (2014), "The Gaps of Value Added Rates in Major Manufacturing Sectors between China and the United States," *China Statistics*, 2, 46.

Gao, Wenshu (2010), "Providing an Education for Left-Behind and Migrant Children," in Fang Cai (ed.), *The China Population and Labor Yearbook*, Vol. 2: *The Sustainability of Economic Growth from the Perspective of Human Resources*, Leiden: Brill, pp. 75–91.

Godo, Yoshihisa (2001), *Estimation of Average Years of Schooling by Levels of Education for Japan and the United States, 1890–1990*, FASID Development Database No. 2000-01, Tokyo: Foundation for Advanced Studies on International Development.

Hayashi, Fumio, and Edward Prescott (2002), "The 1990s in Japan: A Lost Decade," *Review of Economic Dynamics*, 5 (1), 206–235.

Heckman, James (2005), "China's Human Capital Investment," *China Economic Review*, 16 (1), 50–70.

Heckman, James, and Pedro Carneiro (2003), *Human Capital Policy*, NBER Working Paper No. 9495, Cambridge, MA: National Bureau of Economic Research.

Kuijs, Louis (2010), *China through 2020—A Macroeconomic Scenario*, World Bank China Research Working Paper No. 9, Washington, DC: World Bank.

Li, Hongbin, Pak Wai Liu, and Junsen Zhang (2012), "Estimating Returns to Education Using Twins in Urban China," *Journal of Development Economics*, 97 (2), 494–504.

Li, Long (2009), "Why Has the Share of College Students from Rural Areas Been Halved?," *Guangzhou Daily*, January 24.

Li, Shi (2010), "Economic Growth and Income Distribution: An Empirical Analysis on China's Experiences," in Fang Cai (ed.), *Transforming the Chinese Economy, 1978–2008*, Leiden: Brill, pp. 279–315.

Liu, Weitao (2013), "All-China Women's Federation Published Research Report on Status of China's Left-Behind Children," *People's Daily*, May 11.

Ministry of Education, National Bureau of Statistics, and Ministry of Finance (2013), "Statistical Announcement on Educational Funds Conduct in 2012," *China Development Gateway*, http://cn.chinagate.cn/reports/2014-03/10/content_31739829.htm.

National Bureau of Statistics (2012), *China Statistical Yearbook (2012)*, Beijing: China Statistics Press.

National Bureau of Statistics (2013), "China's Monitoring Report of Migrant Workers (2012)," National Bureau of Statistics official website, http://www.stats.gov.cn/was40/gjtjj_detail.jsp?channelid=5705&record=54, May 27.

National Bureau of Statistics (2014), *China Statistical Abstract 2014*, Beijing: China Statistics Press.

Qu, Yue, Fang Cai, and Yang Du (2010), "Population Dividend: Continue or Alter?," in Fang Cai (ed.), *The China Population and Labor Yearbook*, Vol. 2: *The Sustainability of Economic Growth from the Perspective of Human Resources*, Leiden: Brill, pp. 15–27.

Samuelson, Paul (2004), "Where Ricardo and Mill Rebut and Confirm Arguments of Mainstream Economists Supporting Globalization," *Journal of Economic Perspectives*, 18 (3), 135–146.

Shi, Wei (2009), "What Obstacles Are Deterring Rural Students from Entering Universities?," Sannong website, http://www.farmer.com.cn/news/jjsn/200908/t20090826_480926.htm.

Wang, Meiyan (2009), "Universal High School and Mass Higher Education," in Fang Cai (ed.), *Reforming the Education System to Promote Human Capital*, Reports on China's Population and Labor No. 10, Beijing: Social Sciences Academic Press, pp. 163–174.

Whalley, John, and Xiliang Zhao (2010), *The Contribution of Human Capital to China's Economic Growth*, NBER Working Paper No. 16592, Cambridge, MA: National Bureau of Economic Research.

Xu, Zhuoting (2010), "Study and Reflection on Universalizing Preschool Education in China," *Social Science Front*, 11, 278–280.

10. Reducing income inequality

> I have heard that the lord of a state or a family concerns himself not with scarcity but rather with uneven distribution, concerns himself not with poverty but with discontent. (*The Analects of Confucius*)

Since China reached a per capita GDP of 4300 US dollars in 2010, placing it among the upper-middle-income countries, there has been widespread concern about whether the country can avoid the risk of falling into a middle-income trap. One of the phenomena relating to the middle-income trap is income inequality. The relationship between income inequality and the middle-income trap is twofold. First, as a fast-growing economy slows down or stagnates, so too does its income growth. No evidence has ever been found that income distribution can be improved under the circumstances of economic stagnation at the middle-income stage. Second, in such a scenario that income inequality becomes so aggravated that no policy instruments can stop it, social stability and social cohesion risk jeopardization, and inequality would deter the sustainability of economic growth.

As the Chinese economy enters its new stage, the Chinese people have had increasingly high expectations of a significant improvement in income distribution, which poses an urgent challenge to the government. Meanwhile, with the arrival of the Lewis Turning Point being signaled by labor shortages and wage increases for ordinary workers, conditions are ripe for narrowing the income gap formed during the typical dual economy period. One can therefore anticipate a Kuznets Turning Point—that is, the turning point at which income inequality stops increasing and begins to decline. Such a turning point, however, does not come about automatically.

This chapter summarizes new facts related to the theoretical relationship between economic growth and income distribution originally put forward by Kuznets (1955), reviews competing studies on China's income distribution, elaborates upon the current trends of income inequality in China, and concludes with several policy suggestions on creating conditions for bringing about the Kuznets Turning Point.

10.1 NEW KUZNETS FACTS

In his prominent 1955 work "Economic Growth and Income Inequality," Simon Kuznets devoted his analysis to questions of whether income inequality increases or decreases over the course of a country's economic growth, as well as to what factors determine the level and trends of such inequalities. In other words, Kuznets put forward observations, explanations, and empirical tests exploring whether or not a trend exists of income inequality first increasing and then, after a peak, decreasing as a country's economy grows (a reverse U-shaped curve).

Because Kuznets's study was based on incomplete data gathered from a handful of developed countries, follow-up studies by both proponents and opponents have made tremendous progress in addressing his questions, though disagreements remain. Based on the theoretical extension and empirical test of the Kuznets hypothesis, as well as new observations regarding Kuznets-type facts, we can conclude that, while the reverse U-shaped curve hypothesis is a useful tool for thinking about the relationship between growth and distribution, factors impacting income distribution are multifaceted and vary based on a country's economic system, developmental stage, policy orientation, and the dominant forces shaping income distribution.

Although Thomas Piketty convincingly reveals an increase in income inequality by depicting the grand dynamics that drive the accumulation and distribution of capital (Piketty, 2014), which tends to negate the reverse U-shaped change in income distribution, Kuznets's hypothesis can still serve as a starting point and frame of reference for understanding the causes and trends of income distribution in comparing the various competing findings, since an arrival of the Kuznets Turning Point is desirable and worth fighting for.

Several scholars have tried to empirically test the Kuznets curve using China's data, whereas less has been made of the thoughtful ideas, analytical angles, and logic behind the Kuznets hypothesis itself. What we urgently need is to start with a deep understanding of the unique features of China as regards growth and reform in order to thoroughly evaluate the reality and trends of its income distribution and to try to find the conditions under which the Kuznets Turning Point can be reached.

In what follows, we will summarize new facts about the Kuznets phenomena—that is, the research findings that relate to the explanation and testing of a reverse U-shaped curve. It is important to note that, while this chapter is not capable of encompassing, nor intended to encompass, all important studies, we have tried to choose those that are most relevant to the reality of China's income distribution.

One of the first facts regarding the Kuznets hypothesis is the meeting between the Kuznets Turning Point and the Lewis Turning Point. Kuznets surmised that a variety of forces related to a certain phase of urbanization and industrialization might converge to bolster the economic position of lower-income groups within the urban population, for example migrants. Such a phase of urbanization and industrialization is, in fact, the Lewis Turning Point, as manifested by a significant shrinkage of surplus labor along with a constant increase in wages caused by the labor shortage.[1]

Japan can serve as a relevant case study, since it experienced both dual economy development and the Lewis Turning Point. Minami and Ono find that the existence of surplus labor in agriculture can explain the long-term decline of labor's share in national income and the high speed of economic growth (Minami and Ono, 1981), which resulted in a widening of income inequality in Japan. Based on the same economic logic, when the Japanese economy reached its Lewis Turning Point—that is, when the reservoir of agricultural surplus labor significantly shrank—the overall increase in wages and the wage convergence between skilled and unskilled workers were accompanied by a reduction in general income inequality (Minami, 2010). The improvement in income distribution in Japan has been consistent with the changes of developmental stages, especially in regard to the Lewis Turning Point in and around 1960.

A second fact relating to the Kuznets hypothesis is that whether income distribution improves or deteriorates depends largely on how governments intend to tackle the problem of inequality and how institutional policies are thereby implemented. In trying to interpret ways in which the cumulative effect of the concentration of savings could be counteracted, Kuznets pointed to the roles of legislative interference and "political" decisions. A host of new findings show that a sound income distribution does not come naturally, but is influenced by policies and institutions. By reviewing the different policy intentions and practices of income distribution between alternate administrations, Krugman concludes that policies of distribution absolutely matter and that they significantly influence the outcomes of income distribution (Krugman, 2007).

The orientation of government policies is usually embodied in redistribution policies. Since the growth of capital return is faster than the growth of economic volume—and, as a result, inequality inherently tends to expand—as Piketty reveals, a package of redistribution policies including robust taxation of the rich, strengthening public expenditure on social protections, and building labor market institutions is always needed in order to check any increase in inequality (*Economist*, 2015a).

For example, despite conflicting opinions regarding the impact of labor market institutions on labor market flexibility and labor participation incentives, agreement exists as to the role of labor market institutions in reducing income inequality. Empirical studies in both developed and developing countries show that the relative completion of such institutions plays a significant role in reducing income inequality (Freeman, 2008, 2009).

In fact, in many developed countries that are viewed as possessing an equal distribution of household income, the small Gini coefficient is realized only after redistribution. That implies that the arrival of the Kuznets Turning Point can be expected by changes in both labor market forces and government redistribution policies. For example, in 1967, Japan's Gini coefficient was 0.375 in primary distribution. It dropped to 0.328 after secondary distribution, an improvement of 12.6 percent. In 2008, Japan's Gini coefficient was 0.532 in primary distribution, and dropped to 0.376 after secondary distribution, an improvement of 29.3 percent. This experience is representative of most OECD countries (Sun, 2013).

A third fact concerning the Kuznets hypothesis is that income distribution is affected by industrial and technological structures and changes to them. Although Kuznets mentioned that the industrial opportunities resulting from technological progress and the development of the service sector are less obvious factors reducing income inequality, those factors become increasingly influential in income distribution as the world increasingly becomes characterized by the unprecedented speed of technological progress and industrial changes in the context of globalization.

There has been a rich literature providing empirical evidence in this respect. In explaining the widening income gap in the United States, Tyler Cowen, an American economist, points out that, as the rate of technological advancement slows down, cutting-edge technologies tend to be featured as private goods in the country. That is, those innovations use government resources by holding economic and political privileges, lobbying for protections, and do not benefit ordinary people (Cowen, 2011). Similar, too, is the scenario in which income generated by asset holdings does not serve to improve income distribution.

Samuelson demonstrates that free trade globalization does not necessarily always benefit all trade partners and all groups of people within countries. Since workers within a country are not homogeneous, those with low education and skills may become permanent losers in such a globalization schema (Samuelson, 2004). This consequence is directly related to the nature of human capital accumulation. Owing to educational failure, the skills, as well as the ability to obtain new skills, of less-educated workers cannot keep pace with the rapid changes in domestic sectoral restructuring brought about by outsourcing.

For example, the polarization of the US labor market—that is, the expansion of high-wage jobs and low-wage jobs at the expense of middle-wage jobs (Autor et al., 2006)—gives rise to the polarization of human capital. As a result of the outflow of jobs in tradable sectors, a large percentage of US workers without the skills necessary for upgraded industries are unable to find a job and therefore become the victims of the new division of labor, which goes far in explaining the widening income gap in the United States over the past decade or so.

On the other hand, the new technological revolution in the brewing—if it is too early to allege it has already happened—is not necessarily a nightmare for non-skilled and skilled workers, as it has been declared by neo-Ludditism. That is, the marriage of new technologies and new forms of employment does not necessarily make mass workers losers. As many observers point out, for example, the rapid development of the internet, particularly of the mobile internet, has allowed tens of thousands of laborers to become "workers on tap" and thus sharers of technological progress with "zero marginal cost" (see, for example, Rifkin, 2014; *Economist*, 2015b). Consequently, such an application of new technologies can redefine economic development as sharing and inclusive and reduce income inequality.

A fourth fact that helps put together the Kuznets puzzle is that those economic and social policies that focus on income redistribution while overlooking a host of factors that impact economic performance produce much less obvious outcomes in narrowing the income gap than does economic growth per se. In some Latin American countries, as Dornbusch and Edwards (1989) put it, populist economic policies emphasizing growth and redistribution and deemphasizing the risk of inflation, external constraints, and the reactions of economic agents to aggressive non-market policies sometimes led to disastrous consequences for those who were assured of being helped by the policies.

In trying to eliminate the insistent disparity between Northern Italy and Southern Italy (the Mezzogiorno region), the Italian central government implemented policies that overwhelmingly relied on redistributive tools such as income transfers and wage equalization, which strengthened the reliance of the lagging Mezzogiorno region on the central government and the richer North, directed resources towards non-productive (rent-seeking) usages, and depressed private investment. As a consequence, productivities did not converge between the North and South; in fact, the regional disparity actually widened, with the low-income groups not benefiting from the policies at all. After the reunification of Germany, initial experiences in East Germany raised the concern that the country might commit the same mistakes as Italy. Later on, German regional policies became focused on encouraging private investment, institution building aimed at strengthening labor market flexibility, and preventing rent-seeking activities, all of which ultimately helped avoid the Mezzogiorno-type mistakes (Boltho et al., 1997).

10.2 INCOME DISTRIBUTION ALONGSIDE ECONOMIC GROWTH

Various forces have affected China's income distribution during its period of rapid growth. While governmental policies aimed at the alleviation of poverty and income redistribution, together with the expansion of labor force participation, reduce income inequality, there are also certain factors as a result of the process that actually generate income inequality.

The expansion of employment opportunities for rural laborers in non-agricultural sectors has reduced rural poverty and temporarily halted, if not completely eliminated, any further increase in the rural–urban income gap. The Chinese household responsibility system, which is characterized by the even distribution of farmland among households and the equal rights of residual claimants of farm production, guarantees a choice for rural laborers in search of greater pay and a better life. Therefore, even if the wage rate remained unchanged for many years prior to the arrival of the Lewis Turning Point, the expansion of the scale of migration could feasibly increase the farmers' income, a phenomenon which can be observed from three aspects.

The first is to examine the effect migration has on the alleviation of poverty. Except for those without the necessary number of family members able to participate in the labor force, most households experiencing poverty suffer from a lack of employment opportunities. Studies show that, in general, it is easier for those with skills and/or networks to find non-agricultural employment in rural areas, whereas poor households do not have such skills or the networks necessary for grasping employment opportunities in rural areas. Rural-to-urban migration, therefore, is a relatively democratic opportunity for the poor to participate in the labor market and to earn higher income. In a study conducted before the arrival of the Lewis Turning Point, Du et al. (2005) find that poor households gained an 8.5 to 13.1 percent increase in their per capita income by migrating out of rural areas.

Second is to look at the contribution wage income makes to the overall increase in total household income. According to the National Bureau of Statistics (NBS)'s categorization, the net income of rural households consists of wage-based income, households' business income, income from properties, and transferred income. The massive expansion of off-farm employment via labor mobility has significantly enhanced the share wages hold in households' overall income, contributing overwhelmingly to the growth of the income of rural households. Official statistics show that the share of wages to overall rural households' income increased from 20.2 percent in 1990 to 43.5 percent in 2012, while wage income contributed 51.5 percent to the increase of households' income in 2012.

Third is to note that a significant part of migrants' earnings is missing from official statistics. When the NBS separately conducts household surveys in rural and urban areas, migrant households are excluded from the chosen samples of urban households because they usually do not have stable housing in destination cities, and therefore are not considered practical survey samples, while at the same time those households sampled in rural areas cannot fully record their incomes from remittances.

As is explained in the notes on the main statistical indicators of the *China Statistical Yearbook*, first, those households that register with a rural *hukou*, but in which all family members have left their registered places for one year or more, are not considered standard rural households and are thus excluded from the sampling framework. Secondly, those family members who left home for six months or more are not considered to be usual rural residents, unless they maintain close economic relations with their family by sending the majority of their income to the household. While this exception—described as a "close economic relation"—is hard to define practically, those who permanently live and work outside their places of registration are usually not counted as standard rural residents, and their income is omitted from surveys of rural households.

The characteristic of having an unlimited labor supply, however, long prevented migrant workers' wage rates from increasing, at the same time as the *hukou* system put migrants in a vulnerable position in the urban labor market. While the labor market allows wage determination mechanisms to identify human capital and work efforts within the workplace, institutional factors tend to widen the wage gap between local and migrant workers. According to a survey conducted in 2001, migrant workers' average hourly wage was 39.6 percent lower than local workers' and, of the wage difference, 63.9 percent could be attributed to differences in educational attainments and other demographic characteristics, while 36.1 percent could be attributed to discrimination based on *hukou* status (Cai et al., 2011a). Such a distortion of wage determinants comes from both discrimination against migrant workers and protection of local workers. For example, Knight and Song's econometric analysis finds that the ratio of the marginal productivity of labor to wage rate is 3.86 for migrant workers and 0.81 for local workers (Knight and Song, 2005).

As a consequence of market-oriented reforms (which include promoting non-state sectors, capitalizing on natural resources, and privatizing state assets), incomes generated from business operations and properties have gained an increasingly significant share of residents' income. While this helps increase people's income, it also tends to enlarge income inequality. Based on a survey conducted in 2002, the calculated Gini coefficient of residents' properties was 0.550, significantly higher than the Gini coefficient of residents' income (0.454) (Zhao and Ding, 2008). Owing to the lack of transparency and fairness in the marketization process, these resources and assets have been unevenly obtained by a small handful of people who have the privilege of determining distribution.

The government has successfully implemented a host of policies aimed at alleviating poverty, developing poor areas, and narrowing the income gap. Such policies notably include the national poverty alleviation strategy in rural areas and the minimum living standard guarantee program in both urban and rural areas, as well as policies aimed at equalizing access to public services between rural and urban areas. As a result, the number of the population living below the official poverty line has decreased tremendously, and those who remain poor are better covered by the social safety net. Based on consistent criteria, the number of the rural poor decreased from 94.22 million in 2000 to 26.88 million in 2010—that is, the incidence of poverty among the population declined from 10.2 percent to 2.8 percent over these ten years. Meanwhile, the coverage rates of programs such as social pensions, health care insurance, and the minimum living standard guarantee have substantially expanded (Information Office of the State Council of the People's Republic of China, 2012).

On the other hand, one may only want to applaud achievements in the alleviation of absolute poverty, because all indicators show an increasingly widened income gap. For example, the wage differentials across sectors, income disparities between rural and urban areas, and income inequality among households have all increased, drawing great attention from the public.

The widespread labor shortage and substantial wage inflation since 2004 indicate the arrival of the Lewis Turning Point in China. According to Kuznets's speculation, at such a stage of development, a variety of forces may merge in order to reduce income inequality. That is, the Lewis Turning Point can be followed by the Kuznets Turning Point, as is predicted by the current logic regarding economic development.

Not coincidentally, 2004 was also the turning point at which the Chinese central and local governments strengthened their implementation of policies aimed at improving income distribution. First, labor-related legislation and regulations have been accelerated, which helps to construct labor market institutions. Second, the central government has lessened the various burdens shouldered by farmers, initiated various subsidies to farmers and farming, and implemented policies aimed at narrowing the gap in access to basic public services between rural and urban residents, all of which make agriculture more profitable, enhance the opportunity costs of labor migration, and thus help strengthen migrant workers' bargaining power in the labor market.

10.3　THE DEBATE OVER INCOME DISTRIBUTION

Based on the Kuznets hypothesis and the previous experiences of Japan and several other East Asian economies, the arrival of the Lewis Turning Point should feasibly be followed by the Kuznets Turning Point. As to whether the income distribution in China shows any new trend corresponding to the Lewis Turning Point, there are disagreements among researchers using different sets of data and methods. In what follows, we summarize and comment on several relevant studies.

According to Wan's finding, 40 to 60 percent of overall income inequality in China can be attributed to the income gap between rural and urban areas (Wan, 2007), so we can start examining income inequality with an eye towards the rural–urban income gap. Since the existing rural–urban income gap has been formed by institutional barriers deterring labor mobility, in theory, once all such barriers have been eliminated, for example once the *hukou* system is completely abolished, all existing income inequality would disappear (Whalley and Zhang, 2004). Though the reform is far from complete, the institutional barriers to labor mobility have already, to a significant extent, been eliminated, such that a decline in income inequality can feasibly be expected.

Some researchers found the trend towards a narrowing of the rural–urban income gap by digging into and revising incomplete statistics. Trying to avoid the flaw of present household surveys conducted separately between rural and urban areas, Cheng et al. (2011) selected certain households, including NBS samples and others, in Zhejiang, a developed province, and Shaanxi, a relatively underdeveloped province, to observe the degree to which migrant workers' income is being underreported. The study concludes that the existing flaws in the statistical definitions for surveying households' income alone lead to an overestimation of urban residents' income by 13.6 percent and an underestimation of rural households' income by 13.3 percent. That is, the income gap between rural and urban households has been overstated by 31.2 percent.

It is demonstrable in the extent to which the omission of migrant workers' income became larger after the arrival of the Lewis Turning Point. If such an omission can be corrected, statistically speaking, the income gap between rural and urban areas may narrow, which in turn will improve reports of overall income inequality. By using the micro data of a 1 percent population sampling survey in 2005, a study shows that all indicators of income inequality actually improved after incorporating migrant workers' income into either urban income or rural income data-sets, though, owing to the limitation of the data, one cannot confirm the reversal of the trend of an enlarged income gap between rural and urban areas (Cai et al., 2011b).

By employing certain new methods and indicators, particularly those incorporating migrant workers into existing observations, OECD econo-mists have confirmed the positive effects of the easing of restrictions on labor mobility between rural and urban areas and the progressive intro-duction of the minimum subsistence allowance in rural areas and found that the appearance of income inequality has lessened (Herd, 2010). Their estimates show that, after the overall Gini coefficient reached 0.492 in 2002 and climbed to its peak in 2004, it declined to 0.479 in 2007 and 0.464 in 2010.

The Chinese statistical authorities also confirmed the reduction of the Gini coefficient. On several occasions, the National Bureau of Statistics of China provided the official Gini coefficients for the years between 2003 and 2014. Combining this series of figures with the figures estimated by scholars over previous years, we can formulate the changing trend in China's overall Gini coefficient over the 34 years from 1981 to 2014, while finding it consistent with the overall trends in the rural–urban income gap (Figure 10.1).

Researchers have tried to test whether there are any signs of the Kuznets Turning Point in China. For example, by using survey data from rural and urban households and population sampling survey data, Li (2010) con-ducted an empirical test based on both perspectives over time and across sectors, and ultimately denied the reverse U-shaped curve between devel-opment and income inequality. It is not that the author has reason to assert that the test does not support a Kuznets curve hypothesis, but rather that the data did not yet support the appearance of the turning point.

That is not surprising, because according to economics theory we can usually expect that the Kuznets Turning Point is the subsequent outcome of the Lewis Turning Point—that is, in terms of sequencing, the Kuznets Turning Point is more likely to occur after the Lewis Turning Point. Because the data used in Li's study only went up to 2005, it is reasonable for him not to have witnessed the more recent reversal of the country's income inequality. He does find, however, that the status of the income distribution of urban households is closer to the Kuznets Turning Point compared to that of rural households and the national average. That is a

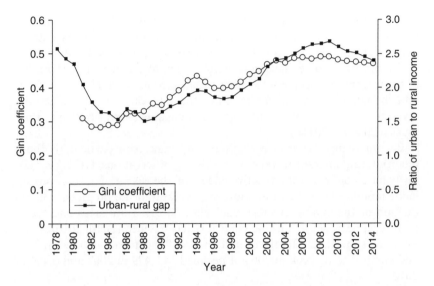

Source: The rural–urban income gap is calculated based on National Bureau of Statistics (various years); Gini coefficients of 1981 to 2002 are cited from Li (2010), those of 2003 to 2012 are cited from National Bureau of Statistics official website, http://www.stats.gov. cn/tjdt/gjtjjdt/t20130118_402867315.htm, and those of 2013 and 2014 are cited from Feng (2015).

Figure 10.1   Gini coefficient and the urban–rural income gap

logical phenomenon, since the major indications characterizing the Lewis Turning Point—notably, labor shortages and an increase in wages—first appeared in the urban sectors.

Some studies seem to indicate that China's Gini coefficient is much higher than the levels shown by official data and shows no significant decline. For example, the results from unique research by a team led by Gan (2012) shows that China's Gini coefficient was as high as 0.61 in 2010. Surveys and estimates by Wang (2013) show that the income of urban residents in China consists of a large amount of hidden income not covered in the regular statistical system, totaling as much as 15.1 trillion *yuan* in 2011. According to his estimates, the real per capita disposable income of urban residents is twice that of the official figures, and more than 70 percent of the hidden income belongs to the wealthiest 20 percent of residents. Three surveys conducted by the author in 2005, 2008, and 2011 show that hidden income is actually still growing. If such huge amounts of hidden income are allocated to different groups in such an extremely unequal way, income inequality will be exacerbated.

In addition, the declining trends of resident and labor income as a percentage of national income have drawn widespread attention. Based on activity recorded in the flow of funded accounts, Bai and Qian (2009) find that, in both primary distribution and redistribution, shares of residential and labor income have seen a declining trend since the mid-1990s, which produces a trajectory of income growth that is unfavorable to ordinary households.

General observations and scholarly research agree that, by international standards, income distribution is highly unequal in China. The intense disagreement regarding this information, however, lies in whether that inequality is being aggravated or being improved, as well as what underlying factors determine the trends of income distribution. It is hard to come to a consensus on income inequality in China. To see the bigger picture, however, requires seeking common ground by synthesizing conflicting arguments, because all serious studies can provide useful angles from which to observe complicated phenomena and complementary evidence. That is, we can use the evidence provided by competing studies in order to form a consistent view on the issue and to draw relevant policy suggestions.

10.4   THE COMMON GROUND OF COMPETING OBSERVATIONS

Income distribution can be examined from different angles (at both the micro and the macro level) and measured by different indicators. Overall income inequality can be comprehensively reflected by those indicators. In current studies being done on income distribution, the evidence and conclusion are often based on different sets of data, and, given the limitation of each dataset and of the different indicators chosen to measure income inequality, studies end up with different focuses and with different—and even conflicting—findings. Since the unequal distribution of households' income is of major concern and contains sufficient information for revealing issues of general income inequality, income inequality will mainly be discussed at the household level.

These conflicting findings—namely, a declining trend of income inequality versus a widening trend of income inequality—are both significant and relevant to understanding both the status quo and the future trend of income distribution in China, as well as in helping to draw relevant policy implications. While the official statistics and those scholarly studies based on official data aim to reveal an overall trend in the changes in income distribution, the uncharacteristic works—e.g. Gan (2012), Wang (2013), and others—are actually trying to find the outliers from the upper echelons of income groupings. Though the latter studies are important because they explore the significant sources of residents' income and the distribution pattern that is unique to a transitioning China, their results are not suitable for cross-country or cross-temporal comparisons, because these observations include more outliers than are generally found in formal statistics.

Statistically, household income is generated from wages, property or assets, and transfers. The relative growth and proportion of these three sources of income to overall residential income determine the level and distribution of household earnings. In the double transitions taking place in China—from a dual economy to neoclassical growth and from a planned economy to a market economy—the ways through which households obtain their income are far more diversified than official statistics are able to reveal. Apart from labor compensation and legal business income, there is a wide range of income whose sources are not necessarily known. As a result, the income of urban residents is also significantly underreported. Since such unreported income is much more unevenly distributed among households than is reported income, the existence of the hidden income can undoubtedly add to and amplify income inequality.

China's transition to a market-oriented system has been accompanied by unequal opportunities and monopolized information in land selling, the restructuring of state assets, bidding of public construction projects, and direct and indirect financing activities. The relation of the income generated from such activities to unfair operations such as tax evasion, rent-seeking activities, and corruption therefore tends to be concealed from official household surveys, and higher-income groups are less willing to report the full extent of their income.

That is, given the official nature of the NBS household survey, income reported by sampling households is that resulting from labor compensation, legally run business income, and transferred income, whereas the estimated hidden income appears outside the statistical system. We assume that the statistics collected and published by the NBS provide accurate and authoritative data on regular income, especially on residents' labor income, but underestimate property income, capital income, and especially hidden income. Thus, we can use the study by Wang (2013) as a data supplement while combining it with official data.

What we intend to do here, in addition to officially published data on per capita disposable income in urban areas denoted by "released" income, is to add the hidden income with a highly uneven distribution among groups estimated by Wang (2013) into official data so as to form another set of data for comparison, which we call the "estimated" income. Based on the two sets of data, we can calculate, respectively, the inter-group ratios to show different trends of changes in their income distribution (for details of data and method, see Cai and Wang, 2014).

The NBS divides urban residents into seven groups according to their per capita household income: the lowest-income group (10 percent, first decile or D1), the low-income group (10 percent, second decile or D2), the lower-middle-income group (20 percent, third to fourth decile or D3–D4), the middle-income group (20 percent, fifth to sixth decile or D5–D6), the upper-middle-income group (20 percent, seventh to eighth decile or D7–D8), the high-income group (10 percent, ninth decile or D9), and the highest-income group (10 percent, tenth decile or D10).

It seems natural to compare the incomes of the highest-income group and the lowest-income group to understand the income gap. Thus we first compare the income ratio of the top 10 percent of the richest households to the bottom 10 percent of the poorest households (D10/D1). Economist José Gabriel Palma finds that, in the era of globalization, the income gap between the rich and the poor is primarily determined by the income of the rich, because the income of the rich impacts that of other groups. For example, it impacts whether the middle-income group is capable of holding on to their income and whether the low-income group suffers more poverty in an unfavorably competitive environment (Palma, 2011). Believing that this pattern in the formation of the income gap can well reflect the reality of China, we then calculate the ratio of the top 10 percent of the richest households to the bottom 40 percent of the poorest households (D10/D1–D4). The calculated income ratios and their trends are plotted in Figure 10.2.

These two scenarios concerning calculated income ratios reveal the following important information about changes in China's income gap. First, the income gap among different groups (as measured by the ratios) has expanded throughout the majority of the years covered in Figure 10.2, which shows a trend consistent with most observations. Second, the momentum of the growing income gap has been more or less suppressed, with a certain degree of income equalization since 2008. This means that the income gap began to narrow after its peak, which is consistent with the changes in the labor market (the trend revealed by the official data) and the efforts that the Chinese governments have made towards redistribution, regulations regarding resources marketization, and anti-corruption campaigns (the trend revealed by the estimated data). Such a change can verify the arrival of the Kuznets Turning Point, if it can last. Third, the income gap increases significantly when hidden income is added to the NBS data, no matter what inter-group ratios are calculated.

It is worth noting that the use of hidden income data surveyed by Wang (2013) is no more than a confirmation of the underestimation of hidden

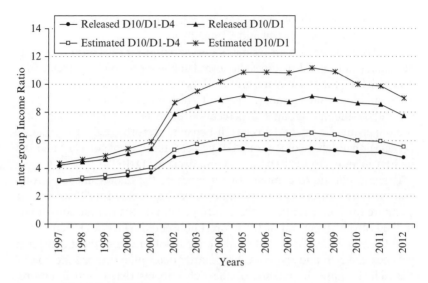

Source: Cai and Wang (2014).

Figure 10.2   Officially released and scholarly estimated income gaps

income (mainly in the form of property income), but it does not mean that we accept the specifics of his estimation. Therefore, the purpose of adding hidden income into the official data is not to determine a real income gap, but to unveil the causes of the existing income inequality—namely, the unfair and unequal distribution of resources—and to make more targeted policy recommendations.

10.5   CONCLUSION

Generally speaking, problems in income distribution are formed in areas of both primary distribution and redistribution; therefore, much can be done in adjusting policies regulating primary distribution and redistribution. In particular, the income gap can be reduced by increasing the income of the low-income group, expanding the size of the middle-income group, and regulating the income of the high-income group.

Several factors of primary distribution have for some time been the cause of an excessive income gap. The country's long-term reservoir of surplus labor has resulted in a biased income distribution tilted towards scarce capital. What's more, in cases where the prices of production factors are distorted, for example, the relative prices of capital may be brought

down artificially, income tends to be distributed in an increasingly inequitable way. Additionally, the unjust, unfair, and nontransparent distribution
of resources and means of production creates opportunities for privileged
groups to take advantage of their special status or use improper means in
order to obtain a larger share of land, the right to explore for minerals and
other natural resources, or the right to use state-owned assets. In order to
solve the problem of income distribution, therefore, China should take the
opportunity to use the arrival of the Lewis Turning Point to carry out in-
depth reforms.

The income gap that forms as a result of primary distribution can be
adjusted in redistribution areas, though redistribution doesn't change the
extant causality of income distribution. In fact, distorted institutional
arrangements and inappropriate policies widen the existing gap instead of
narrowing the income gap in redistribution. For example, if opportunities
for access to social security, social assistance, and other public services are
differentiated by enterprise, region, and *hukou* status or, worse, if certain
groups are excluded from the provision, then such public services, which
are considered redistributive in nature, favor the rich over the poor. In
other words, such redistribution is of a regressive nature and enlarges the
gap in the standard of living between residents.

Therefore, reform of the redistributive system is a necessary prerequisite for adjusting income distribution. In fact, in countries where gaps in
income and public services appear to be small, their relatively harmonious
pattern of welfare distribution is formed only after redistribution. The
present tax regime in China is not conducive to adjusting income distribution in terms of the tax structure. For example, in 2013, direct taxes made
up only 26.2 percent of the total tax revenue, while individual income
tax, which is part of direct tax, accounted for only 5 percent of total tax
revenue, and virtually no property tax was collected from households and
individuals (Gao, 2014). Either adjusting the already-uneven income distribution or regulating the flows of future income, therefore, requires reform
of the tax regime.

The existence of income inequality, an inequitable distribution of
resources causing the income gap, and redistribution policies not conducive to the adjustment of income distribution forming in primary distribution areas are all likely to create vested interests. The existing vested interest
groups, which usually possess bargaining power influencing policy-making
decisions, either intentionally or unintentionally obstruct reform in the
area of income distribution. Breaking the institutional deadlock, therefore,
requires more political courage, greater political wisdom, and increased
efforts to promote reform.

NOTE

1. Many scholars notice that Kuznets's analysis is based on a framework of dual economy development. A related review paper can be referred to in Deutsch and Silber (2001).

REFERENCES

Autor, David, Lawrence Katz, and Melissa Kearney (2006), *The Polarization of the U.S. Labor Market*, NBER Working Paper No. 11986, Cambridge, MA: National Bureau of Economic Research.

Bai, Chong-en, and Zhenjie Qian (2009), "Analysis on China's National Income Distribution Pattern," *Social Sciences in China*, 5, 99–115.

Boltho, Andrea, Wendy Carlin, and Pasquale Scaramozzino (1997), "Will East Germany Become a New Mezzogiorno?," *Journal of Comparative Economics*, 24 (3), 241–264.

Cai, Fang, and Meiyan Wang (2014), "Income Gap and the Risk of Middle-Income Trap Facing China," *China Economist*, 9 (4), 13–19.

Cai, Fang, Yang Du, and Meiyan Wang (2011a), "Labor Market Institutions and Social Protection Mechanism," Background Report for the World Bank.

Cai, Fang, Yang Du, and Meiyan Wang (2011b), *Rural Labor Migration and Poverty Reduction in China*, Working Paper No. 7, Beijing: International Poverty Reduction Center in China.

Cheng, Jie, Wenshu Gao, and Wen Zhao (2011), "The Impact of Rural Labor's Migration on Income Gap Statistics of Rural and Urban Residents," in Fang Cai (ed.), *Challenges during the 12th Five-Year Plan Period: Population, Employment, and Income Distribution*, Reports on China's Population and Labor No. 12, Beijing: Social Sciences Academic Press, pp. 228–242.

Cowen, Tyler (2011), *The Great Stagnation: How America Ate All the Low-Hanging Fruit of Modern History, Got Sick, and Will (Eventually) Feel Better*, New York: Dutton.

Deutsch, Joseph, and Jacques Silber (2001), "The Kuznets Curve and the Impact of Various Income Sources on the Link between Inequality and Development," Working Paper No. 2001-03, Department of Economics, Bar-Ilan University.

Dornbusch, Rudiger, and Sebastian Edwards (1989), *Macroeconomic Populism in Latin America*, NBER Working Paper No. 2986, Cambridge, MA: National Bureau of Economic Research.

Du, Yang, Albert Park, and Sangui Wang (2005), "Migration and Rural Poverty in China," *Journal of Comparative Economics*, 33 (4), 688–709.

Economist (2015a), "Mind the Gap: Anthony Atkinson, the Godfather of Inequality Research, on a Growing Problem," *Economist*, June 6.

Economist (2015b), "Workers on Tap: The Rise of the On-Demand Economy Poses Difficult Questions for Workers, Companies and Politicians," *Economist*, January 3–9.

Feng, Hua (2015), "How Big Is the Income Gap between the Poor and the Rich?," *People's Daily*, January 23.

Freeman, Richard (2008), "Labour Market Institutions around the World," in Paul Blyton, Edmund Heery, Nick Bacon, and Jack Fiorito (eds.), *The Sage Handbook of Industrial Relations*, London: Sage, pp. 640–658.

Freeman, Richard (2009), "Labour Regulations, Unions, and Social Protection in Developing Countries: Market Distortions or Efficient Institutions?," in Dani Rodrik and Mark Rosenzweig (eds.), *Handbook of Development Economics*, Vol. 5, Amsterdam: Elsevier, pp. 4657–4702.

Gan, Li (2012), *Research Report on China Household Finance Survey (2012)*, Chengdu: Southwestern University of Finance and Economics Press.

Gao, Peiyong (2014), "Strategic Perspectives on China's New Round of Tax Reform," *China Economist*, 9 (4), 4–12.

Herd, Richard (2010), *A Pause in the Growth of Inequality in China?*, Economics Department Working Paper No. 748, Paris: Organisation for Economic Co-operation and Development (OECD).

Information Office of the State Council of the People's Republic of China (2012), *White Papers of the Chinese Government 2011*, Beijing: Foreign Languages Press.

Knight, John, and Lina Song (2005), *Towards a Labour Market in China*, Oxford: Oxford University Press.

Krugman, Paul (2007), *The Conscience of a Liberal*, New York: W.W. Norton & Company.

Kuznets, Simon (1955), "Economic Growth and Income Inequality," *American Economic Review*, 45 (1), 1–28.

Li, Shi (2010), "Economic Growth and Income Distribution: An Empirical Analysis on China's Experiences," in Fang Cai (ed.), *Transforming the Chinese Economy, 1978–2008*, Leiden: Brill, pp. 279–315.

Minami, Ryoshin (2010), "Turning Point in the Japanese Economy," paper presented at the Workshop in the Project of "The Discussion on the Changes in East Asia Labor Market Based on Lewisian Turning Point Theory," Institute of Asian Cultures, Tokyo University, Tokyo, July 18–19.

Minami, Ryoshin, and Akira Ono (1981), "Behavior of Income Shares in a Labor Surplus Economy: Japan's Experience," *Economic Development and Cultural Change*, 29 (2), 309–324.

National Bureau of Statistics (various years), *China Statistical Yearbook [year]*, Beijing: China Statistics Press.

Palma, José Gabriel (2011), *Homogeneous Middles vs. Heterogeneous Tails, and the End of the 'Inverted-U': The Share of the Rich Is What It's All About*, Cambridge Working Papers in Economics No. 1111, Cambridge: Faculty of Economics, University of Cambridge.

Piketty, Thomas (2014), *Capital in the Twenty-First Century*, Cambridge, MA: Belknap Press of Harvard University Press.

Rifkin, Jeremy (2014), *The Zero Marginal Cost Society: The Internet of Things, the Collaborative Commons, and the Eclipse of Capitalism*, New York: Palgrave Macmillan.

Samuelson, Paul (2004), "Where Ricardo and Mill Rebut and Confirm Arguments of Mainstream Economists Supporting Globalization," *Journal of Economic Perspectives*, 18 (3), 135–146.

Sun, Zhangwei (2013), "Study on Japan's Gini Coefficient and Redistribution System," *Contemporary Economy of Japan*, 188 (2), 22–34.

Wan, Guanghua (2007), "Understanding Regional Poverty and Inequality Trends in China: Methodological Issues and Empirical Findings," *Review of Income and Wealth*, 53 (1), 25–34.

Wang, Xiaolu (2013), "Grey Income and Income Distribution in China," *Comparative Studies*, 5, 1–51.

Whalley, John, and Shuming Zhang (2004), *Inequality Change in China and (Hukou) Labour Mobility Restrictions*, NBER Working Paper No. 10683, Cambridge, MA: National Bureau of Economic Research.

Zhao, Renwei, and Sai Ding (2008), "Distribution of Residents' Wealth in China," in Shi Li, Terry Sicular, and Björn Gustafsson (eds.), *Research on Income Distribution in China III*, Beijing: Normal University Publishing Group, pp. 255–286.

11. Labor market institutions and social protections

> The Duke of She asked the best way to govern. The Master answered: "it is what satisfies those who are governed and attracts those who are not." (*The Analects of Confucius*)

Alongside China's rapid economic growth, the Chinese government has implemented a nationwide program of poverty alleviation in rural areas, increased labor mobility, strengthened labor market regulations, and established social safety nets for vulnerable people in rural and urban areas. For over three decades, however, the Chinese government's main priority has been to promote economic growth rather than to provide social protections. China's progress in the provision of social protections and public services has lagged behind its economic performance. Additionally, a significant gap still remains between rural and urban residents' access to public services and social protections.

One of the lessons China should draw from the experience of middle-income-trap countries is that the middle-income level of the developmental stage entails many social risks. Both theories and experiences indicate that the inequalities present in the insufficient provision of social protections in developing countries are not just due to constraints on governments' financial capacity, but also caused by a lack of incentive for the government to devote adequate resources to provision in social areas. Since both capacity and incentives alter as the stages of development change, it will be useful to explore how the Chinese government's social protection policies change as the national economy enters its new stage.

This chapter depicts the effects of the Lewis Turning Point on the labor market, explores the increasing demand of workers for labor market institutions, narrates the progress of the building of labor market institutions and strengthening of social protections, discusses the incentive mechanisms necessary for this transformation, and offers suggestions about the most important areas of policy reform.

11.1 TRANSFORMATION OF THE LABOR MARKET

As the Chinese economy passed through the Lewis Turning Point, the country's labor market began its profound transformation from a dual economy scenario to a neoclassical one. Though there is a wide spectrum between these two scenarios of the labor market, we can summarize the contrasting differences in terms of wage determination, mechanisms for realizing labor market equilibrium, major employment problems, and government responsibilities in promoting employment so that we gain a better understanding of this transformation.

Under a dual economy system (under which China has been operating for a long time), farmers receive a subsistence-level income based on their average product—as opposed to a marginal product—in agriculture and, based on this, wages in the non-agricultural sectors are determined institutionally. That is, the existence of institutional barriers deterring labor mobility causes a persistent labor surplus in agriculture and prevents wages in the non-agricultural sectors from rising to that level identical to workers' marginal product. As a result of this and underemployment or hidden unemployment in both rural and urban areas due to the lack of employment opportunities, the government's responsibility is to promote employment and eliminate institutional obstacles in the labor market.

With the transformation of the stages of its economic development, the Chinese labor market will become more and more neoclassical, which is characterized as follows. First, wages overall are based on the marginal productivity of labor and formed by combining market forces and institutions of the labor market. Second, the labor market can correct its own disequilibrium in the supply of and demand for labor over the long run. Third, there are three basic types of unemployment—namely, cyclical, frictional, and structural—all of which need to be addressed with macroeconomic and labor market policies.

By examining changes in employment status, we may empirically illuminate the transformation of the Chinese labor market from a dual economy scenario to a neoclassical scenario. At any given time, an insufficiency of employment can result from hidden unemployment, structural and frictional (namely natural) unemployment, and cyclical unemployment (Figure 11.1).

In the typical dual economy period of China, not only are 30–40 percent of agricultural laborers considered surplus (Taylor, 1993), but a similar proportion of workers in the urban sectors are considered redundant as well (Zhang, 2008). Such an excessive supply of labor causes underemployment or hidden unemployment, which has long characterized the Chinese labor market. In previous chapters, we have narrated the significant

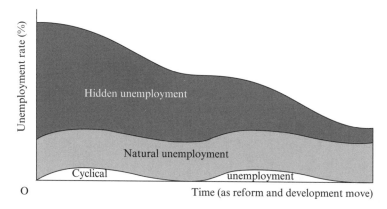

Figure 11.1   Changes in characteristics of the Chinese labor market

reduction of hidden unemployment brought about by the Lewis Turning Point, which takes the labor market towards a neoclassical scenario.

In western countries where a dual economy does not exist, scholars in macroeconomics and labor economics mainly focus on two types of unemployment: cyclical unemployment and natural unemployment (which includes frictional and structural unemployment). In a neoclassical labor market and under normal conditions, macroeconomic fluctuations are associated with temporary changes in the relationship between labor demand and supply. When a macroeconomy is in decline, cyclical unemployment occurs as an aberration of full employment (with only natural unemployment).

By contrast, natural unemployment, in the form either of frictional unemployment or of structural unemployment, is mainly related to the mismatch between job seekers and employers. More specifically, such a mismatch exists all the time and reflects either the time cost of the job search or changes in skill requirements, respectively. Let us begin picturing the past and present employment situation by demystifying several unemployment indicators provided by China's official statistics and scholarly research.

The first indicator is the registered unemployment rate, which applies only to the labor force with urban *hukou*. Over more than a decade, it has remained unchanged, fluctuating roughly around 4.1 percent (Figure 11.2). Most critics believe that this labor market indicator is not particularly useful in reflecting the existing employment situation, as it excludes migrant workers, who do not have urban *hukou* but make up 35 percent of urban total employment.

A second indication of unemployment can be found in the surveyed unemployment rates as defined and recommended by the International Labour

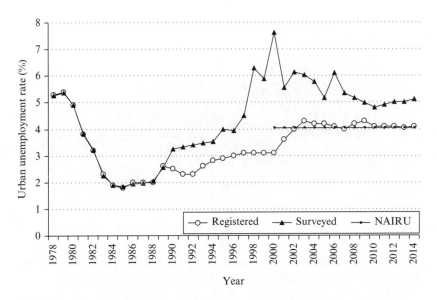

Note: NAIRU—non-accelerating inflation rate of unemployment.

Source: Data of registered unemployment rate are from National Bureau of Statistics (various years); surveyed unemployment rates were assumed to be identical to registered unemployment rate before 1989, and were calculated based on National Bureau of Statistics (various years) and Department of Population and Employment, National Bureau of Statistics (various years) for 1990–2004, 2006, and 2007, estimated based on macro data of 2005 1% population sampling survey for 2005 and on 2010 Population Census, and were reckoned according to Li (2013) and Cai (2015); NAIRU (natural unemployment) is cited from Du and Lu (2011).

Figure 11.2   Unemployment indicators with Chinese characteristics

Organization (ILO). The NBS has conducted a labor survey since the mid-1990s, though these unemployment rates have not been publicized. By using available data from this survey and making some reasonable assumptions about them, we can estimate the economically active population and the employed population (their difference is the unemployed population) and therefore calculate the surveyed unemployment rate (the ratio of the unemployed population to the economically active population) in urban areas.[1] As can be seen in Figure 11.2, after it peaked at the turn of the century, the surveyed unemployment rate decreased steadily and has remained relatively stable in recent years. In his opening speech at the Annual Meeting of the New Champions 2014, also known as the Summer Davos Forum, Chinese premier Li Keqiang announced that the surveyed unemployment rate was around 5 percent during the first eight months of the year.

Third is the natural unemployment rate—or, as macroeconomists put it, the non-accelerating inflation rate of unemployment, or NAIRU. According to this definition, statistically, the natural unemployment rate can be obtained by eliminating a cyclical part of the surveyed unemployment rate that is associated with macroeconomic fluctuation. According to Du and Lu's estimation, this rate is about 4.0 to 4.1 percent (Du and Lu, 2011). It is no coincidence—and thus no surprise—that the estimated natural unemployment rate has been almost identical to the registered unemployment rate in recent years. Since only urban residents are entitled to register unemployment, the identical rate of registered unemployment and of natural unemployment implies that urban laborers suffer from natural unemployment but not cyclical unemployment. That is to say, in present-day China, migrant workers alone bear the consequences of labor market shocks caused by the cyclical downturn of the macroeconomy in the form of entering and quitting the urban labor force from time to time.

11.2 THE GROWING DEMAND FOR LABOR MARKET INSTITUTIONS

As hidden unemployment, or the labor surplus, declines, the labor shortage situation gradually improves the bargaining power of ordinary workers in the labor market. The changed relationship between the supply of and demand for labor, however, has not eliminated the vulnerability faced by specific groups in the labor market.

The first and foremost of these is that, being informally employed (and therefore lacking social protections), migrant workers are subject to cyclical unemployment, though their unemployment is often not covered by official unemployment statistics. That a large proportion of migrant workers employed in the urban sectors do not have formal labor contracts with their employers puts them in the position of having job insecurity, lack of access to social security programs, and weak bargaining power in regard to equal pay and working conditions. Figure 11.3 shows significantly lower coverage by basic social insurance programs for migrant workers as compared to urban employees, who are by and large workers with urban *hukou*.

Second, graduates from various levels of education, particularly university graduates, encounter mismatch problems that cause structural unemployment. For example, based on CULS data, the surveyed unemployment rate was 4.8 percent for the average urban labor force, whereas the surveyed unemployment rate was 9.6 percent for those aged 21.

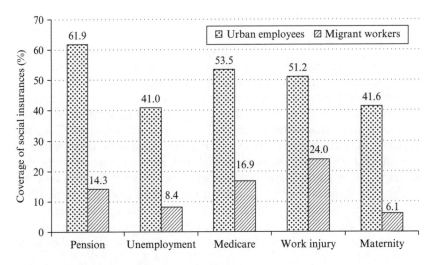

Source: National Bureau of Statistics (2013).

Figure 11.3 *Coverage by social insurance of urban employees and migrant workers*

The reason behind the employment difficulties facing graduates is twofold: (1) the current position of China's manufacturing at the bottom of the value chain reduces the demand for workers with higher education; and (2) what is taught at the university level is divorced from the requirements of employers, which leads to a mismatch in the labor market.

Third, the human capital deficiency of urban local workers is typically associated with older age, less formal education, poorer health, and outdated skills. The urban labor market has been experiencing painful adjustments since the late 1990s, with a total of 40 million workers laid off in the years leading up to 2002. As the economy continues to grow and the labor market to evolve, those who had been laid off and officially registered as unemployed have either found new jobs or retired. It seems therefore that, while these kinds of adjustments help eliminate hidden unemployment in urban areas, older workers are still vulnerable to frictional and structural unemployment.

According to calculations done by Wang, G. and Niu (2009), 33 years old is the age of demarcation separating those workers who have attained nine years of education (which is required for all Chinese citizens) or longer, and those who have attended school for fewer than nine years. That is, urban workers who are older than 33 are markedly at a disadvantage in terms of human capital.

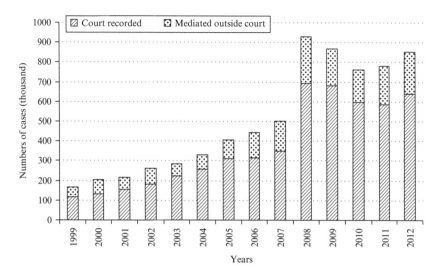

Source: National Bureau of Statistics and Ministry of Human Resources and Social Security (various years).

Figure 11.4 Increases in the incidence of labor disputes

Both the awakened rights of workers in general and the existing or potential risks facing vulnerable groups in particular have raised the demand for labor market institutions in China. This can be seen from the increased cases of labor disputes regarding compensation, working conditions, labor contracts, and provisions surrounding social security. In recent years (particularly after 2008, the year in which several labor-related laws were passed or updated, heightening workers' awareness of their rights and entitlements), the incidence of labor disputes in China has increased sharply. According to official records, the total number of labor disputes in 2012 was triple what it was in 2003 (Figure 11.4). Moreover, the number of incidents of severe unrest triggered by conflicts in labor relations has also grown.

This increase in labor disputes, however, is not necessarily a sign of the worsening of labor relations, but may be more indicative of a stronger demand for labor market institutions. In his seminal work, Hirschman points out three mechanisms—namely, exiting, voice, and loyalty—by which citizens, consumers, and workers can express their dissatisfaction with conditions in the market (Hirschman, 1970). Here, we borrow these expressions to describe the changed labor relations in China after the arrival of the Lewis Turning Point.

In the course of a dual economy development characterized by an oversupply of labor or job scarcity, workers with a job usually choose not to use their rights of exit owing to the difficulties faced in finding other jobs, and they also choose not to use their voice to demand improvement for fear of losing their present job. As laborers in general and migrant workers in particular begin to enjoy more employment opportunities in urban China as a result of the Lewis Turning Point, there appears to be greater room for them to exercise their rights by "voting with their feet," that is, by choosing to exit, and therefore to exercise their right to voice their dissatisfaction.

How individual workers use their power of choice depends on the degree to which they cherish their present jobs. For example, workers who are dissatisfied with their jobs in small enterprises with poor growth prospects may simply quit, since the odds are fairly good that they can find a better job elsewhere. But, for those workers dissatisfied with but reluctant to leave their jobs in large companies with some degree of industry recognition and growth potential, their efforts to seek higher pay and better working conditions may take the form of overt actions such as vocal complaints, collective bargaining, and, in more extreme cases, strikes, all of which are different forms of voice.

Based on both aggregated statistics and survey data, Cai and Wang find that the incident rate of labor disputes tends to be significantly higher in more developed regions, formal sectors, and larger-sized enterprises, despite the fact that they usually pay higher wages, do better in providing forms of social insurance, and offer more favorable working conditions to their employees than their counterparts in less-developed regions, informal sectors, and small enterprises (Cai and Wang, 2012). This evidence convincingly suggests that the surge of labor disputes after the arrival of the Lewis Turning Point is not a reflection of the deterioration of labor relations, but an indication of workers' awareness of their rights and an increased demand for labor market institutions, which includes the enforcement of labor-related laws, a minimum wage system, and collective bargaining for wages and working conditions.

In addition, as technological progress accelerates and industrial upgrading intensifies, migrant workers, new graduates, and older workers with urban *hukou*—who together make up the majority of non-agricultural employment—will inevitably encounter labor market shocks. Therefore, broadly defined social protections, which include labor market institutions, social insurance programs, and various forms of social assistance such as minimum living standard guarantee programs in rural and urban areas that cover all Chinese workers, are urgently needed.

11.3 THE TRANSFORMATION OF THE GOVERNMENTS' ROLES

Labor market development has taken China's rapid economic growth and transformed it into an expansion of employment, enabling Chinese workers and households to increase their income. By contrast, building labor market institutions and social protection mechanisms to mitigate the risks facing ordinary households in employment depends primarily on the governments' efforts. The active role of the central and local Chinese governments in promoting economic growth has been widely recognized and roundly analyzed by scholars as developmental states, state corporatism, competitive government, and the like.[2]

For example, a host of studies find that the Chinese governments—local governments in particular—have been deeply involved in the process of economic development as entrepreneurs motivated by fiscal incentives. Through fiscal decentralization, Chinese local governments have had strong incentives to spur local economic development. This ensures that local governments function efficiently and compete with neighboring localities. If China is to achieve its goal of building a wealthy and harmonious society, it will need to show the same enthusiasm in providing social protection to its citizens.

The Chinese governments' role in spurring economic development, however, cannot be understood solely from the point of view of fiscal incentives. Throughout the entire process of reform—from the decision to initiate reform in the first place, to the process of reform itself—the Chinese leadership has always taken the improvement of the people's standard of living as the key indication of the legitimacy of reform. At the early stages of development, however, national income represented by GDP and resultant government revenue has become the material basis of increasing per capita income and the welfare of the Chinese people. For this purpose, the country's central leadership has designed a system across various levels of government which effectively evaluates, supervises, and stimulates economic development. Such developmental motivation has been translated into an overwhelming pursuit of local economic growth, while social development has been neglected.

In the country's planning period, before reform, all welfare services enjoyed by workers were provided by enterprises or work units (单位, *danwei*), excluding those workers not engaged in urban employment. The division of functions between the government and work units contrasts totally with that of market economies: in China's planning period, the government made the production decisions and the work units provided social protections (Lindbeck, 2008). Social protection measures ranged

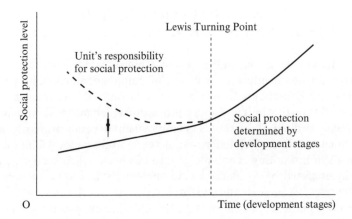

Figure 11.5   Social protection and the stages of reform and development

from lifetime employment (the "iron rice bowl" [铁饭碗, *tie fanwan*]) to work units committed to medical care, support for the elderly, housing, children's nursing, and even compulsory education, which replaced socially pooled programs of insurance and socially run public services.

In the course of economic reform, a distinction had to be made between SOEs losing money through mismanagement, on the one hand, and through policy-imposed burdens, on the other. This distinction aimed to enliven SOEs, and as a result social responsibilities have been gradually detached from SOEs' functions. Such a detachment did not, however, mean that the government was able to fully take over those social responsibilities. As a matter of fact, SOE reforms left a huge, unfilled gap in social protection, owing to both the imperfection of the institutions and incomplete development, as shown in Figure 11.5.

Since work units have ceased to provide social welfare services, the government has had to bear huge legacy costs. These costs are unaffordable because of the lack of accumulated funds and adequate mechanisms for running these social services in the planning period. To address these problems, the Chinese central and local governments have committed themselves to developing national and regional economies while leaving some responsibility for social protection to enterprises; such a strategy is logical in terms of the political economy and China's particular stage of development.

Since the beginning of the reform period, the Chinese leadership has used economic development—which leads to an improvement in the standard of living of the Chinese people—to legitimize overall reform. In addition, political stability has been considered key to attracting widespread support for further reform.[3] Therefore, the central and local governments have paid equal attention to liberalization and regulation in the process of labor market development, while the SOEs were required to take partial responsibility for providing workers with social protection. These provisions include official trade unions for assisting vulnerable employees when they fall into poverty, persuasion by the government of firms not to fire workers even when they encounter operational difficulties, and, finally, enterprises providing old workers with institutional wages, thus shielding them from competition in the labor market.

The most typical example of this type of schema took place in the late 1990s, when Chinese workers were hit by employment shock. At the time, a large number of urban workers were laid off by their employers and, as a result, for a few years the urban unemployment rate rose. At this time, there was no unemployment insurance system available to provide security to the laid-off workers. To avoid possible social shock, a unique form of unemployment insurance was arranged. This unemployment insurance scheme was established at the level of enterprises, providing those laid off from work with a basic living allowance and providing them with a social security premium. Together, enterprises in their role as former employers, governments at the central and local levels, and unemployment insurance funds share the expenses paid for the basic living allowance of the laid-off.

Figure 11.5 also shows how, after the Lewis Turning Point, the level of social protection is expected to increase, not only because of the strengthening of fiscal capabilities, but also because of increased incentives for the two levels of governments to provide better public services. In studying the emergence of labor shortages along with rapid economic growth in Europe after World War II, Lewis noted that institutional labor market arrangements such as collective bargaining were no longer restricted, because issues such as overpopulation were no longer a main point of concern (Lewis, 1979).

Given that the Chinese local and central governments work together as a unified developmental state while individual local governments compete against one another, the transformation of their roles since the Lewis Turning Point can be understood by employing a Tiebout-type model. Using a "vote with their feet" model, Tiebout explained the local governments' provision of public services as trying to find a "market-type" solution for public goods (Tiebout, 1956).[4] This hypothesis implies that, given the particular needs and preferences for relevant public services, potential migrants choose their destinations based on the information about public services provided by local governments. Similarly, by adjusting the manner in which public goods are provided and thus creating externalities, local governments try to attract or reject potential migrants in accordance with their own demands and preferences for the number and composition of local inhabitants.

Before the arrival of the Lewis Turning Point, local governments (even of a developmental type) did not intervene in economic development through labor markets; rather, they focused on attracting physical capital inflows and constructing public infrastructure like roads, bridges, and airports, which also created employment opportunities. At the same time, the reform of the revenue-sharing system in 1994 gave the central government (and to a lesser extent provincial governments) the necessary fiscal capacity to undertake basic social protections. In tackling the employment shock of the late 1990s, in particular, the central government implemented a pro-active employment policy and established a basic social security system, which—in principle at least—enabled urban residents to be covered by social safety nets. Since then, spurred by the concept of equalizing public services among residents regardless of their *hukou* status, social protection-related schemes have rapidly been extended to rural residents and migrant workers.

As governments recognize that the Lewis Turning Point has actually arrived and labor has become a constraint on economic growth, they have consciously shifted their policy orientation from being business-centered to being human resources-centered, from focusing on employment opportunities to concentrating on job quality, and from protecting only locals to including migrants in their social protection schemes. Whereas the longstanding dual social structure brought about by the dual economy can hardly be broken overnight, Chinese local governments are increasingly motivated by Tiebout-type incentives in order to attract human resources by enriching and equalizing public services.

11.4 THE DEVELOPMENT OF SOCIAL PROTECTIONS

China's central and local governments have responded to the arrival of the Lewis Turning Point by enacting legislation and enforcing laws, strengthening the role of labor market institutions, building an inclusive social security system, and accelerating the reform of the *hukou* system. Despite the marked progress in the institution building, buttressing social protections in those specific areas, there are still persistent institutional barriers preventing sufficient and equal provision of social protection from being applied to all citizens.

The first Chinese Labor Law was issued in 1994. At the time, China had an unlimited supply of labor along with a sense of urgency to transfer labor from the agricultural to the non-agricultural sectors, and as a result the law was not enforced properly. Enterprises, especially joint venture enterprises, did not witness the losses expected to arise from enactment of the law. While some developing countries considered China to be a role model in successfully lowering labor costs and gaining comparative advantages in labor-intensive goods,[5] the Lewis Turning Point arrived in China. Since then, the government has actively advanced legislation and law enforcement in order to regulate the labor market and strengthen social protections.

In 2008 alone, three labor-related laws were implemented. The Employment Contract Law emphasized employment security and protections for migrant workers and vulnerable urban workers. The Employment Promotion Law claimed that governments are responsible for promoting employment and eliminating various kinds of discrimination within the labor market. Finally, the Labor Disputes Mediation and Arbitration Law was intended to provide a legal framework for improving labor relations. The central government allowed local governments to ease into the implementation of these three laws, particularly the Employment Contract Law during the financial crisis of 2008–2009, yet the legal obligations imposed by these laws still significantly regulate the hiring activities of enterprises and have escalated labor market institutionalization.

The literature of labor economics shows that labor market institutions play different roles at different stages of development (Freeman, 2008). As developing countries reach the Lewis Turning Point, wage rates, working conditions, and labor relations become increasingly determined by institutions rather than by market forces. One of the representative indicators of this trend toward institutionalized labor relations is the increase in the frequency and scale of minimum wage adjustments. In the 1990s—the early years of this program—minimum wage standards were low, rarely increased, and hardly applied to migrant workers. As labor shortages became widespread after 2004, the central government required local governments to adjust the minimum wage levels every other year and to apply the program to migrant workers. Pressured by labor shortages, municipal authorities have since increased the frequency of adjustments along with the locally determined level of the minimum wage.

Between the late 1990s and the early 2000s, the development of China's social security system focused on incorporating urban residents into social protection safety nets that included a minimum living standard guarantee program, the basic pension system, basic medical care insurance programs for both urban workers and residents, and an unemployment insurance program. Since about 2004, such institution building has been extended to rural areas by introducing the rural minimum living standard guarantee program, the new rural cooperative medical care system, and the new rural pension system.

While the central government assumes the major responsibility for designing and pooling the social security system, local governments have been more impressive in their implementation of related programs.

First of all, the magnitude and proportion of expenditures on social security by local governments have increased quickly. The World Bank shows that, between 2003 and 2007, the ratio of subsidies on pension expenditures to GDP borne by the central government remained stable, while the ratio borne by local governments increased significantly (World Bank, 2010).

Secondly, in those areas where the local economy suffered most acutely from labor shortages, governments have made overtures towards enhancing the participation of migrant workers in social security programs. When governments were tackling the financial crisis of 2008–2009, the central government introduced a series of employment support policies that allowed eligible enterprises to postpone their social security contributions and reduce workers' contributions to social security funds. Taking advantage of this temporary flexibility, some regional governments—especially those in areas where labor shortages had been strongly felt even before the onset of the financial crisis—increased the social security coverage of migrant workers by decreasing contribution rates.

Thirdly, migrant children's access to compulsory education has been significantly expanded. Although the central government introduced regulations for the equal inclusion of migrant children in compulsory education schemes in urban areas, the problem has remained unaddressed for a long time because expenditures on compulsory education are borne exclusively by local governments. Only when the local governments of those regions receiving a significant migrant workforce are willing to provide this public service can education coverage be measurably widened.

Lastly, local governments have made unprecedented efforts to help migrant workers claim wages in arrears, arbitrate labor disputes, and push for the equal treatment of urban local and migrant workers (Wang, M., 2006). In fact, while arbitrating labor disputes, local governments tend to skew towards partiality towards employees because of increased concerns over social stability and labor shortage.

Institution building and reform are far from being complete, and the existence of institutional barriers still prevents equal provision of social protection to all groups within the population. The cause is threefold: (1) overall fiscal capacity restrains the level of social protection provisions, which has to do with the developmental stage of the country as a whole; (2) local governments do not have adequate revenue to finance social protection programs locally; and (3) as the result of such a scarcity, both the central and local governments do not have sufficient incentives for fully implementing social protection programs. That brings to the forefront the urgency of accelerating reforms in relevant areas, particularly the *hukou* system, that enable and encompass all three causes mentioned above.

For quite some time, under the constraints of an unlimited supply of labor and the scarcity of public service resources, the competition in employment opportunities and welfare provisions between migrant and local workers in urban areas has prevented reforms from being accomplished, urbanization from being complete, and the floating population from becoming a stable supply of labor and regular consumers. According to the official definition, migrant workers who have lived in a particular city for six months or longer are counted as urban residents, though they do not have urban *hukou* and thus continue to lack equal access to social protections in urban areas.

This can clearly be seen in the difference between statistical and actual urbanization—that is, while the proportion of the population living in cities was 53 percent in 2012, the proportion of the population possessing an urban *hukou* was only 36 percent (Figure 11.6). Rural-to-urban

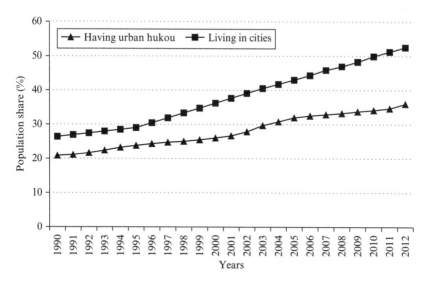

Source: Department of Population and Employment, National Bureau of Statistics (various years).

Figure 11.6   Statistical and actual urbanization

migrants contribute greatly to the 17 percentage point difference between the two statistics.

As the Lewis Turning Point arrived in China, seeking a new engine for economic growth, the country's central and local governments set their sights on deepening urbanization by settling migrant workers. That has, to some extent, created incentives for governments implementing *hukou* reform and has strengthened the incentive compatibility between central and local governments and between migrant workers and urban native residents. As a result, *hukou* reform has been pushed forward in both depth and width.

In different regions, governments have their own motives for starting *hukou* reform. For example, it's done in the interest of attracting and keeping human resources in the coastal areas, of tapping demand for infrastructure investment in the central and western regions, and of breaking the land bottleneck in the economic development of those regions in the process of catching up. These different motives have led to dissimilar designs of institutions as well as ways of implementing them, forming a diversification of reform. This diversity is not only the natural approach taken towards such reform characterized by decentralization, but also where the advantage of reform lies. Allowing diversity thus assures the reformists incentives, impetus, and a chance of success.

The ongoing reform has its limitations, which involve the consensus between central and local governments. To initiate *hukou* reform, local governments need not only incentives, but also legitimacy, which grants them the central government's support and approval. As can be seen in the experiences of pioneering provinces in *hukou* reform,[6] some shortcomings need to be overcome in this regard.

Firstly, the point of intersection between the top concerns of the central government and the legitimacy of the local governments in accelerating urbanization is to retain the designated amount of arable land. Owing to the extreme scarcity of arable land in China compared to many other countries in per capita terms, neither industrialization nor urbanization can proceed at the expense of transforming land from agricultural to non-agricultural use. The pilot reform in Chongqing, a relatively agrarian municipality in southwestern China, is a typical example of a city trying to obtain the necessary land for urban expansion, which conflicts with the red line of farmland area required by the central government.

The land voucher program, an innovative institution in Chongqing, is intended to unify land usage and development on a region-wide basis. Namely, the municipal administration issues vouchers for the increase of land area generated by reclaiming the house plots and collective construction sites vacated by out-migration from villages and trading them in a government-run land exchange. Those who buy the vouchers get the quota of land use for non-agricultural development within the municipality. Such a program has to assure that all plots of vacated land are reclaimed for cultivation in order to be approved by the central government.

Secondly, both the central government and the governments of those cities to which migrants flock are concerned about the construction of labor market institutions and of a social protection mechanism that helps avert urban diseases in the course of urbanization. As the result of the advent of the Lewis Turning Point, migrant workers have become an indispensable source of labor for the urban sectors—in other words, non-agricultural sectors' demand for migrant workers has become unvarying, or rigid, on the one hand, while agriculture has rapidly mechanized so that it no longer serves as a reservoir of surplus labor, on the other. While migrant workers as a whole can no longer go back to agricultural production, individual migrant workers face the risks of becoming the urban poor. So *hukou* reform has to be comprehensive in tackling these risks, from inclusive social protection policies in urban areas to the flexible relocation policy of arable land.

Thirdly, the coordination between policy measures conducted by local governments and the holistic vision of the country under *hukou* reform impacts the overall effect of the reform. Policies put forward in the reform of Chongqing and Guangdong are set for migrant workers to officially reside in cities yet benefit only the residents of those provinces or municipalities. In 2014, of China's 168 million migrant workers, 46.8 percent migrated across provincial boundaries. That the inter-provincial migrants can hardly benefit from the *hukou* reform currently being undertaken in many provinces implies that nearly half of these migrants, whose ancestral homes are mostly in the poorer central and western areas, are still excluded from the complete urbanization process.

Hukou reform has so far motivated local governments' initiatives by breaking through the constraints of local development. In regard to public policy reform, *hukou* reform requires "top design" (which we will discuss further in Chapter 12) and nationwide coordination. That is, in addition to encouraging various reform initiatives by the local governments, the central government, based on domestic and international experiences and lessons, should also put forward a general guideline regarding the contents and coverage of social security programs, ways of managing the plots of vacated land, sharing of the costs and dividends of reform, and the nexus between practical policies and the overall objectives of reform.

11.5 CONCLUSION

Although the arrival of the Lewis Turning Point grants both the central and local Chinese governments much stronger incentives to strengthen their social protections and to build labor market institutions, being confined to the revenue-sharing system, the responsibilities for providing such public services have often been divided inequitably between the central and local governments. That is, while the central government possesses the lion's share of fiscal revenue, local governments have to take increasingly greater responsibility for the provision of public services. This has put the local governments in a tight fiscal position if they are to be willing to meet the demand for building properly functioning labor market institutions and for strengthening social protections.

Fiscal constraints on the local governments have not only delayed necessary reforms, but also impeded the long-proposed transformation of growth patterns in China. For example, local governments have found that most of the expenses associated with social protection programs need to be raised from local revenues, which can only come from GDP growth. That is, unless the problems of asymmetry between governments' financial capacities and their responsibilities can be solved, economic growth still has a higher priority than does social development.

In the meantime, the powerful ministries of the central government, which are currently responsible for providing social protections, hold on to as many resources as they can by proposing various implementable programs. Such centralization of resources and decision-making powers tends to fragment the governmental social protection programs, thus reducing the efficiency of resource utilization. For example, an increasingly large number of transfer payment programs operated by the central government have been granted to programs with specified purposes in the name of helping developments in poorer regions, which gives more power to the ministries but leads to an insufficiency of resources for financing those social protection programs that are both necessary and critically imperative.

Thus, an increase in the share of the revenue of local governments, which will come about through the reform of the fiscal and revenue systems, is a necessary condition for strengthening social protections and is in line with potentially advantageous government reforms. First, the social protection programs currently being implemented by the central government have laid a foundation for integrating new programs that are expected to be initiated by local governments. Second, wider coverage and the more targeted allocation of social protections to disadvantaged areas will have to build upon the initiative and abilities of local governments.

As the old Chinese saying goes, "The empire, long divided, must unite; long united, must divide." Financial centralization and decentralization, both of which aim to redistribute the fiscal revenues between central and local governments in accordance with the division of tasks between them, have been implemented during the reform period, and also over the entire course of economic development under the People's Republic. One question that arises, then, from the proposed fiscal decentralization and implementation of a locally biased fiscal redistribution is: will it start another unsolved circle, or can this effort avoid becoming a Sisyphean undertaking?

The argument here is that those Tiebout-type incentives that provide appropriate social protections can help local governments move from the direct promotion of economic growth to providing public services, which is the essential role of government. If local Chinese governments' enthusiasm for positive transformation is, indeed, in earnest, the decentralization of fiscal revenues is likely to come about in order for the economy as a whole to avoid falling into the middle-income trap.

NOTES

1. For a detailed explanation regarding this estimation, see Cai and Wang (2004).
2. See, for example, Walder (1995), Oi (1999), and Herrmann-Pillath and Feng (2004).
3. Öniş pointed out that the distinction between the developmental strong state and the despotic state is that there was wide social interaction and dialogue in the former (Öniş, 1991). By following the principle set up by the Party—representing the fundamental interests of the overwhelming majority of the Chinese people—the Chinese government has oriented its policy-making agenda to conform to the people's demand for institutions. Thus, the government can be conceptualized as a developmental state with Chinese characteristics.
4. Chan uses this concept to explain the motivation spurring Chinese farmers to migrate to cities. See Lague (2003).
5. For examples, see Government of India (2006).
6. For details of those pilot reforms, see Cai (2013).

REFERENCES

Cai, Fang (2013), "The *Hukou* Reform and Unification of Rural–Urban Social Welfare," in David Kennedy and Joseph Stiglitz (eds.), *Law and Economics with Chinese Characteristics: Institutions for Promoting Development in the Twenty-First Century*, Oxford: Oxford University Press, pp. 441–454.

Cai, Fang (2015), "Finally Comes the Surveyed Unemployment Rate," in Fang Cai (ed.), *Policy Changes for the Goals of 2020*, Reports on China's Population and Labor No. 15, Beijing: Social Sciences Academic Press.

Cai, Fang, and Meiyan Wang (2004), "Changing Labour Force Participation in Urban China and Its Implications," *Social Sciences in China*, 4, 68–79.

Cai, Fang, and Meiyan Wang (2012), "Labour Market Changes, Labour Disputes and Social Cohesion in China," OECD Development Centre Working Paper No. 307, Paris: OECD Development Centre.

Department of Population and Employment, National Bureau of Statistics (various years), *China Population Statistical Yearbook [year]*, Beijing: China Statistics Press.

Du, Yang and Yang Lu (2011), "The Natural Rate of Unemployment in China and Its Implications," *Journal of World Economy*, 34 (4), 3–21.

Freeman, Richard (2008), "Labour Market Institutions around the World," in Paul Blyton, Edmund Heery, Nick Bacon, and Jack Fiorito (eds.), *The Sage Handbook of Industrial Relations*, London: Sage, pp. 640–658.

Government of India (2006), *Economic Survey, 2005–06*, New Delhi: Ministry of Finance.

Herrmann-Pillath, Carsten, and Xingyuan Feng (2004), "Competitive Governments, Fiscal Arrangements, and the Provision of Local Public Infrastructure in China: A Theory-Driven Study of Gujiao Municipality," *China Information*, 18 (3), 373–428.

Hirschman, Albert (1970), *Exit, Voice, and Loyalty: Responses to Decline in Firms, Organizations, and States*, Cambridge, MA: Harvard University Press.

Lague, David (2003), "The Human Tide Sweeps into Cities," *Far Eastern Economic Review*, 166 (1), 24–28.

Lewis, Arthur (1979), "The Dual Economy Revisited," *Manchester School of Economic and Social Studies*, 47 (3), 211–229.

Li, Keqiang (2013), "China Will Stay the Course on Sustainable Growth," *Financial Times*, September 9.

Lindbeck, Assar (2008), "Economic–Social Interaction in China," *Economics of Transition*, 16 (1), 113–139.

National Bureau of Statistics (various years), *China Statistical Yearbook [year]*, Beijing: China Statistics Press.

National Bureau of Statistics (2013), *China Statistical Yearbook (2013)*, Beijing: China Statistics Press.

National Bureau of Statistics and Ministry of Human Resources and Social Security (various years), *China Labor Statistical Yearbook [year]*, Beijing: China Statistics Press.

Oi, Jean (1999), "Local State Corporatism," in Jean Oi (ed.), *Rural China Takes Off: Institutional Foundations of Economic Reform*, Berkeley: University of California Press, pp. 95–138.

Öniş, Ziya (1991), "The Logic of the Developmental State," *Comparative Politics*, 24 (1), 109–126.

Taylor, Jeffrey (1993), "Rural Employment Trends and the Legacy of Surplus Labor, 1978–1989," in Yak-yeow Kueh and Robert Ash (eds.), *Economic Trends in Chinese Agriculture: The Impact of Post-Mao Reforms*, New York: Oxford University Press, pp. 273–310.

Tiebout, Charles (1956), "A Pure Theory of Local Expenditures," *Journal of Political Economy*, 64 (5), 416–424.

Walder, Andrew (1995), "Local Governments as Industrial Firms: An Organizational Analysis of China's Transitional Economy," *American Journal of Sociology*, 101 (2), 263–301.

Wang, Guangzhou, and Jianlin Niu (2009), "Composition and Development of the Chinese Education System," in Fang Cai (ed.), *Reforming the Education*

System to Promote Human Capital, Reports on China's Population and Labor No. 10, Beijing: Social Sciences Academic Press, pp. 104–123.

Wang, Meiyan (2006), "Wage Arrears of Migrants: An Empirical Analysis Using China's Urban Labor Survey Data," *China Rural Survey*, 6, 23–30.

World Bank (2010), *China: A Vision for Pension Policy Reform*, Washington, DC: World Bank.

Zhang, Xiaojian (ed.) (2008), *The Reforms and Developments of the Chinese Employment*, Beijing: China Labor and Social Security Press.

12. Reaping China's reform dividends

> But this complement may be much inferior to what, with other laws and institutions, the nature of its soil, climate, and situation might admit of.
> (Adam Smith)

Before China completes the full transition to a market economy, its economic system still faces numerous institutional barriers constraining the labor supply, investment efficiency, and the improvement of TFP. Eliminating these barriers through economic reform can, therefore, immediately increase the potential growth rate and reap reform dividends. Lessons drawn from countries long stuck at the middle-income stage suggest that many middle-income countries cannot escape economic stagnation, because they fail to remove institutional obstacles hindering economic growth. For China, the only way to avoid the middle-income trap is to advance reform and establish a market economic system.

The prevailing belief is that, in order to implement the proposed reforms, China must somehow sacrifice speedy growth—that is, any reform must be of an anti-growth type. Even a serious study conducted by the International Monetary Fund (2014) suggests that reform will fuel long-term growth, but that there must initially be a short-term trade-off between reform and growth. Those views, however, are misleading for two reasons. First of all, a growth speed stimulated by policy instruments at the expense of the sustainability and healthiness of the economy is not only worthless, but harmful. Therefore, one should not view an economic slowdown caused by abandoning an inefficient growth pattern as an (opportunity) cost. Second, reforms in certain areas will generate not only a net positive but an immediate effect on growth—or, put another way, it will result in a reform dividend.

Recognizing this reform dividend is of not inconsiderable importance, because it aids in reaching a consensus on reform, choosing an appropriate approach to push reform forward, and forming incentive compatibility when carrying out reforms. This chapter discusses the objectives of the new round of reforms drawn up by the current Chinese leadership, demonstrates empirical estimates on reform dividends, and reveals the political economy logic that guarantees the success of the reform.

12.1 HAS CHINA'S REFORM BEEN AT A STANDSTILL?

Many researchers and observers suggest that, after the bold and dramatic reforms carried out during the 1980s and 1990s, reform in China has been at a standstill since the beginning of the new century. For example, Sun Liping, a sociologist, asserts that the transitional pattern of China's system—formed at the halfway point of reform—has become fixed and unchangeable, which serves the purpose of protecting vested interests. He describes such a phenomenon as a "transition trap" (Sun, 2012). We can judge such an assertion by examining the current stage of Chinese reform and whether the process of implementing reforms conforms to its own internally consistent logic.

In China, the word "reform" means to revise the constituents of the system and to adjust their interrelationships when both the constituents and the interrelationships impede economic development. That is, reform is an institutional change in which agents in economic activities—including the governments, production units, and individuals—seek to eliminate the defects of the system. According to the logic of a political economy, institutional change occurs when the benefit exceeds the cost in carrying out such an institutional change. During the early period of reform in China, flaws in the traditional economic system were apparent, which provided numerous chances for all agents to gain net benefits from reform. Reforms, therefore, began popping up in various areas of the system, with several significant characteristics.

First, the early reforms were carried out predominantly in a bottom-up fashion. Once they had discovered the opportunities for enhancing efficiency through improving incentives and removing institutional obstacles, production units and individuals tended to spontaneously abandon certain elements of the system, while also seeking legitimate approval or acquiescence from higher authorities. In many cases, as long as such reform experiments were proven to be economically effective and politically harmless, the government gave them official recognition and allowed them to be implemented in wider areas. In the end, the practices were officially written into the formal documents of the central government and/or of the Party.

The introduction of a household responsibility system in rural areas is a classic example of this kind. At the very beginning, a handful of production teams in several poor rural areas secretly tried to contract farmland to households to cultivate with local cadres' acquiescence. Such a practice was then approved by higher-level officials when it was proven to be effective in improving incentives and thus increasing agricultural output. It was gradually admitted by the official documents of the Party from time to time, until it was eventually accepted as a basic operational system of agriculture by the Chinese constitution.

Second, the early reforms were characterized by the "Pareto improvement"—that is, they benefited some groups while generating no harm to other groups. That does not mean that there were no vested interests at the early period of reform and therefore no political risks for pushing them forward, just that, among multitudinous reform options at the time, those reforms that had minimum political costs and maximum political benefits were most likely to be introduced and widely spread.

In addition, in the early period of reforms, a significant number of so-called vested interest groups were actually low-income residents. Those affected by commodity price deregulation were low-wage earners and would have had difficulty in maintaining their standard of living with a radical liberalization of prices. Therefore, introducing a double-track system of pricing—namely, allowing for the coexistence of planned prices and market-determined prices—coincided to combine the overall goal of liberalizing commodity pricing with the objective of using reforms to raise people's living standards.

The economics law of diminishing returns can be applied to the process of institutional change. As the transition from a planned economy to a market economy progresses, some of the institutional factors that suppressed economic incentives have been gradually eliminated, and opportunities that may improve economic efficiency can be seized whenever they appear under a decentralized system. As the low-hanging fruits have already been dealt with, the chances for Pareto improvement become fewer and fewer, and further reform will have to disturb vested interests, which are either legacies of the traditional planned system or a result of reforms up to this point.

Still, reform has to show that it helps to improve people's living standard from time to time if it is to move forward. As the old Chinese saying goes, the principle of Kings Wen and Wu was to alternate tension with relaxation, which adequately characterizes the approach to and rhythm of reform with Chinese characteristics. That is to say, by and large, the Chinese reform tends to be of the Pareto improvement type, benefiting the Chinese people either instantly or by stages in the reform process. In that sense, the period of the first decade of the twenty-first century—which some observers consider to be a period of reform stagnation—is necessarily complementary to the reforms that took place in the late 1990s.

While the radical reform of state-owned enterprises (SOEs) in the late 1990s hardened the soft-budget constraints of the SOEs, broke the "iron rice bowl" employment system, nursed the development of the labor market, and thus revitalized the SOEs, in the end it also caused turmoil in Chinese society as manifested by the massive layoff of urban workers. After that round of reform, therefore, the needs of society and thereby the priority of further reform have shifted from radically abolishing the old system to building a social safety net so as to translate the achievements of the reform into tangible benefits for the masses.

Professor Sun is not the only critic of the Chinese reform. Many observers—who are mostly outsiders to the Chinese reform process—tend to judge the progress of reform in China based on external criteria, for example the Washington Consensus. For instance, Lindbeck, a Swedish economist, sums up the major and most important dimensions of the economic system as: (1) enterprise ownership; (2) asset ownership; (3) economic decision-making methods; (4) operational processes of the economy; (5) enterprise incentive mechanisms; (6) individual incentive mechanisms; (7) degree of competition facing enterprises; (8) degree of competition facing individuals; and (9) degree of opening to the outside world (Lindbeck, 2008).

Although such criteria cover some important dimensions of the economic system, they fall short by misjudging the progress of Chinese reforms and missing some key angles of the reform's purpose.

First, according to such criteria, the widely used phrase "the state sector advances, the private sector retreats" is used to characterize the present situation of the SOEs' monopoly and non-state enterprises' lack of a level playing field. After the initiation of the SOEs' reform, characterized by "grasping the large, letting go of the small," namely, that large SOEs are concentrated in natural monopolistic sectors while small and medium-sized enterprises are privatized, the share of SOEs has declined and their size has substantially grown.

As shown in Figure 12.1, the declining trend in the shares of SOEs in terms of output value, fixed assets, and employment in total industry has continued through the first decade of the twenty-first century. Correspondingly, the relative importance of the non-state sectors has increased over time. The conclusion, therefore, is that there is no such thing as "the state sector advances, the private sector retreats" at all if one looks into the structure of ownership, decentralization of autonomy, power of decision making, degree of openness, and, to some extent, competition of the economy as a whole.

On the other hand, restructured SOEs dominate in those sectors characterized by natural monopolies, significantly sapping competition and reducing the efficiency of resource allocation in the economy as a whole. Taking into consideration the fact that these giant SOEs get an enormous amount of both subsidies and monopolistic power to gain profitability, and that they transform these profits into high income for managers and

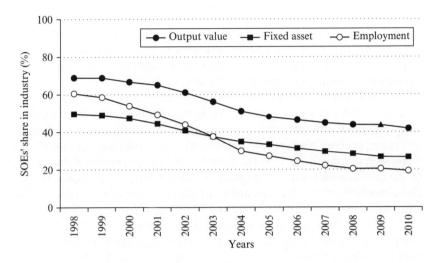

Source:　National Bureau of Statistics (2011).

Figure 12.1　Industrial shares of state-owned and state-controlled companies

workers, as well as investment in real estate and other profitable sectors, instead of submitting them to the state, the phrase "the state sector advances, the private sector retreats" does, in fact, make some sense in context.

A study conducted by the Unirule Institute of Economics (2013) shows that, in 2011, the monopoly of the crude oil and petroleum industries caused an enormous welfare loss to Chinese society through the monopolistic supply and pricing of products, government subsidies, and the underpayment of rent for land and resources, which is consistent with studies that compare the efficiency of SOEs with that of non-publicly owned enterprises, as cited in Chapter 7.

Second, one of the weaknesses of Lindbeck's (2008) classification is that it is merely a one-dimensional framework used for descriptive analysis of an economic system. While alluding to the inherent relationships among those aspects of an economic system, Lindbeck fails to clearly reveal their hierarchical and logical relationships. The economic system of any given country is a unified whole made up of different but interconnected institutional components, within which the superior institutions govern and determine lower-level institutions.

As Lin and Wang put it, the development strategy that is chosen endogenously determines almost all components of an economic system

(Lin and Wang, 2010). For China, in the early 1950s, the adoption of a heavy-industry-oriented strategy successively induced (1) an environment of macro policy focused on artificially depressing the prices of capital and other factors of production, (2) a central planning system for allocating resources and commodities, and (3) a micro-management system based on state-owned industry and collectively owned agriculture. While talking about the traditional economic system, then, it actually means the integration and interaction of these components.

In contrast to the ways in which the traditional economic system was logically formed in China, economic reform began at the micro level by allowing grassroots industrial and agricultural production units to directly tackle problems of incentives and efficiency. This paved the way for reform to advance by following a path from a micro-management system to resource allocation system, macro policy environment, and development strategy, successively (Lin et al., 2003).

During the course of the country's early economic reforms, since there was no lack of motivations or incentive for reform—that is, parties involved with such reform could immediately profit from institutional changes—reforms continued until all apparent defects of the system were eliminated. In that case, one did not need to worry about the stagnation of the reform process, and, what's more, there was no necessity for the "top design" of such reform. As these reforms have proceeded up to this point, however, when superior institutions become restraints on further reform, or when there emerges an incompatibility among the incentives for different parties in carrying out reform, a top design for reform that combines an approach both from the bottom up and the top down is urgently needed in order to power further reforms. In conclusion, as the low-hanging fruits of reform have already been grasped, a new round of reforms will necessarily have totally different characteristics and thus require that new ways of pushing it forward are found.

Third, while the Lindbeck (2008) framework comprehensively covers the aspects of a system that impacts economic efficiency, it neglects those social angles that are also able to indicate the goals of reform, assess the achievements of reform, and measure how the gains of reform are distributed among social groups. Though Professor Lindbeck himself cares about the social consequences of Chinese economic reform, he did not include these aspects in this particular framework.

During the period from 2002 to 2012 (the two terms of leadership under Hu Jintao, then general secretary of the Communist Party of China (CPC)'s Central Committee, and Wen Jiabao, then premier of the State Council), China became the world's second-largest economy, with its per capita GDP measured by RMB in real terms increasing 1.56 times, lifting

China into the upper-middle-income group as classified by the World Bank. At the same time, both the central leadership and local governments recognized that enterprises had been exposed to market competition and that some individuals had acquired a vulnerable status during the course of reforms centered on efficiency improvement, alongside the reduction of the opportunities of the Pareto improvements.

With the enhanced national strength and strengthened fiscal capacity of the central government, therefore, China has implemented a host of programs and strategies aimed at promoting inclusive growth during this period. They include, for example, implementing regional strategies aimed at balancing socioeconomic developments among the eastern, central, and western provinces, establishing basic social insurance programs and minimum living standard guarantee programs in rural and urban areas, raising levels and widening the coverage rate of minimum wages, completely abolishing agricultural taxation, and expanding education at various levels, along with on-the-job training for employees. Most importantly, all these programs have been conducted through policy adjustments and institution building. In that sense, reforms during this period were, in fact, impressive, particularly in areas of social development.

12.2   CHARACTERISTICS OF THE NEW ROUND OF REFORMS

The Chinese leadership set certain goals for the years leading up to 2020, which were predicated upon building a holistically well-rounded society and accomplishing reform tasks in key areas. Unlike the reforms of previous periods, the proposed reforms will not benefit all involved parties at the same time; instead, they will not stint on breaking certain vested interests in order to maintain enduring political stability, social cohesion, and economic sustainability. Corresponding to China's new stage of development and position in international affairs, the success of this new round of reforms will depend tremendously on "top design" and comprehensive coordination. In what follows, we summarize some key characteristics of the new round of reforms.

First, there is a need for transformation from partial reform to comprehensive reform. The 3rd Plenum of the 18th Central Committee of the CPC laid out a blueprint for deepening comprehensive reforms in the areas of economic, political, cultural, social, and ecological systems and the Party system (Central Committee of the Communist Party of China, 2013). Such all-around reforms with increasing levels of complexity and risk are bound to face various degrees of interference from extremists on both the left and the right. The reforms will proceed smoothly only by following the "top design" put forward by the Chinese leadership, while also allowing for comprehensive coordination between reform initiatives and measures as well as among the different parties involved.

The phrase "top design"—proposed by the country's leadership to guide the present round of reforms—does not contradict a reform approach characterized as "crossing the river by feeling the stones," a particular approach to reform proposed by former senior leader Deng Xiaoping, which is opposite to that described by Vaclav Havel, the former Czech leader, of "it is impossible to cross a chasm in two leaps" (World Bank, 1996). The experiences under Chinese reform have so far proven that it is the gradual approach, rather than the radical approach, that is better suited to China's national conditions in regard to the introduction of reform initiatives.

That is, there was no guiding blueprint for the initial introduction of reforms in China; the purpose or aim of the leadership in initiating such reform was not to reach a specific, ideological target, but to raise the people's standard of living and boost national strength. Proceeding from this purpose, China has gradually explored and blazed a trail of reform with unique Chinese characteristics in order to realize the transition from a planned to a market economy. Marketization itself was not adopted as a goal for reform from the beginning, but was instead sometimes chosen as a means to an end when necessary, with the end being improving people's livelihood and boosting national strength. Chinese philosophy and the purpose of reform have prevented this reform from falling into any type of *a priori* dogma.

Take SOE reform as an example. After decades of reform in this area, incentives for workers and managers are no longer a critical problem. The central issue for SOEs is that their monopolistic position excludes competition and thereby impedes technological innovation in the long run. Given that SOEs, as beneficiaries of such monopolies, seek to maintain their vested interests, with some even using national security or ideology as an excuse for keeping their privileged status, only "top design" can push forward reforms capable of breaking SOEs' monopolies.

Second, an appropriate approach to reform is not only to overcome the obstruction of vested interest groups, but also to create incentive compatibility for the reform. As China becomes an increasingly diverse society, various groups within the population have distinct expectations for the reform, and disagreements over concrete reform matters remain enormous. As the result of decentralized decision making, designers and executors themselves are often the vested interest groups; therefore reforms initiated by such groups tend to strengthen their powers and interests instead of weakening them. For that reason, there is a need for the central leadership to act as designer and coordinator of any significant reforms.

Despite the obvious net benefits gained from reforms, there may not necessarily be any correspondence between those who shoulder the costs of a reform and those who receive the benefits of the reform. In other words, in many cases, the groups who assume the costs are not necessarily the exclusive beneficiaries of that same reform, or may even not benefit at all. Therefore, in order to reach a consensus regarding incentive compatibility among parties involving reforms, higher-up decision makers have to coordinate a symmetric sharing of both the costs and the benefits of reform and, if necessary, compensate those who pay without benefiting, an approach to reform that can be called "the Kaldor improvement."[1]

We can take *hukou* reform as an example in this regard. The central task of *hukou* reform is to transform migrant workers and their families into legitimate urban residents with full access to public services such as social insurance programs, minimum living standard guarantee programs, compulsory education, and so on. At present, a large number of public service programs are financed and provided by local governments, particularly at the provincial and municipal levels. Despite the fact that more people enjoying these services implies an increase in both fiscal expenditure and tax revenue (and that, eventually, local economies will benefit from such reform), the tangible and immediate increase in public expenses will pose a burden on local governments. In addition, the social benefits of such a reform will spill over beyond localities nationwide. Therefore, to carry out the reform as a Kaldor improvement requires a top design for a mechanism of sharing costs and benefits symmetrically.

Third, major reforms must be made on the basis of laws and legislation. Throughout the early period of reform, the Chinese legal system was neither complete nor perfect, which led to two consequences: (1) in many cases, there was no law for the reform procedure to follow; (2) very often, reforms meant breaking the bonds of conventional laws and regulations. After more than three decades, in 2011, the National People's Congress of China announced that a legal system containing all levels of laws with Chinese characteristics had come into being. As a result, the political and legal environment for economic reform has been fundamentally altered. As a companion to the 3rd Plenum, the 4th Plenum of the 18th Central Committee of the CPC held in the autumn of 2014 took rule of law as the theme and called for coordinating legislation and reform decision making. Implementing reform in accordance with the existing laws—and necessarily revising or abolishing some laws—will guarantee that reform is undertaken in the correct direction and that it is both irreversible and legitimate.

Take rural land reform as an example. The groundbreaking proposals for the reform of rural land issued by the 3rd Plenum allow for three major sections of rural land to be capitalized on through the land market. First, contracted arable land, which is collectively owned by villages and individually utilized by households, can be transferred between households within rural communities and between rural households and agribusiness and other agricultural producers. By law, such a transfer must not be conducted between agricultural and non-agricultural usages, which safeguards the bottom line of arable land necessary for food security. Second, rural homestead and rural collective construction land can generate property income for farmers by trading it among users. The trade of this form of land between rural and urban residents, however, conflicts with the current laws and regulations, which require necessary revisions. Third, contracted arable land and rural homesteads can be used as mortgages and guarantees so that farmers can capitalize their usufruct on two such forms of land. That also requires the necessary revision of laws and regulations in order to put it into practice.[2]

12.3   WHERE ARE THE REFORM DIVIDENDS?

While the comprehensive reforms drawn up by the Chinese leadership look forward to long-term economic and social developments and political stability, reforms in certain areas that focus on enhancing the supply of production factors and productivity will bring immediate benefits to medium-term growth. These reforms should be prioritized as key areas because of their three most prominent features, which are all concerned with significant reform dividends.

First, they have received the maximum consensus from both the grass-roots and the intermediate levels necessary to push them forward to the top, and are therefore capable of gaining strong political support. In authoritative documents issued by the Chinese leadership, for example, the lists of reform areas have generally been chosen by identifying their significance in enhancing political stability, social coherence, and people's livelihoods, and announced reforms have been widely discussed within and among all parties involved.

Second, they can be implemented in a Kaldor (if not a Pareto) manner, because a significant benefit of such reforms is that they can be used to reasonably compensate the participants who are supposed to bear the costs of reform. The gradual implementation of Chinese reforms has been proven to be successful over the past 30 years. That is, the harm to any parties involved in the reform process should be minimized. When certain vested interests ought to be broken in order to bring about a broader public good, necessary compensation is needed so as to make the reform dividends more equally shared.

Third, following the breakthrough in these areas, economic effects can ripple out to other areas of reform following the logic of the economic system. Assuming all participants in the reforms are rational about playing a role in the process, one can expect economic reformation to deeply penetrate social and economic structures only if benefits have been and can be seen as a result of the previous, present, and future reforms.

The theory of institutional change, which says that change occurs only at the point at which the benefits from reform outweigh the costs, refers only to the political benefits and costs that are considered by decision makers—that is, whether the political support (benefits) brought about by reform exceeds its opposition (costs). But, in general, when the gains surpass the losses in economic terms, there is sufficient reason to convince policy makers to implement reform. China's economic reforms that are proposed by its leadership mainly aim to improve the efficiency of resource allocation, to reduce income inequality, and to enhance the equalization of the level of basic public services across different groups of people, all of which are consistent with the government's goals of achieving a more equitable society.

Therefore, in implementing these reforms, China can benefit from both direct and indirect reform dividends. One would need to identify the causes of economic slowdown in order to implement the relevant reforms that can have a direct effect on improving the potential growth rate, as well as other indirect effects that are conducive to social equity while positively impacting economic growth in the long run.

According to an estimation by Lu and Cai (2014), *hukou* system reform, improvements in education and training, SOE reform, and the relaxation of China's population policy will bring about a significant increase in the potential growth rate of the Chinese economy through increasing the labor force participation rate, expanding human capital stock, improving the TFP, and raising the TFR. The simulated results of different combinations of these reform effects are shown in Figure 12.2 and explained in the following paragraphs.

First of all, the baseline scenario assumes that TFR can be kept at the level of 1.60, an assumption upon which we forecast China's potential growth rate. Thirty-four years after the implementation of China's one-child policy, which led to a fairly low TFR of 1.40, in 2014, the population policy began to relax to allow couples either of whom is an only child to have a second child. It is a reasonable (though optimistic) assumption that such a policy change will increase TFR to 1.60 for at least some time.

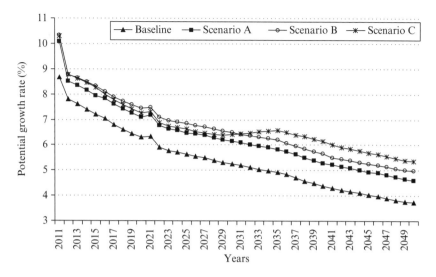

Source: Lu and Cai (2014).

Figure 12.2   Potential growth rates under different reform scenarios

Without any significant reform effects, the trend of the potential growth rate would reflect exactly the baseline scenario shown in Figure 12.2.

Second, scenario A demonstrates the trends in China's potential growth rate on the basis of a TFR of 1.60, by assuming that the labor force participation rate can be increased by 1 percentage point each year, the TFP growth rate by 0.5 percentage points, and the graduation rates of junior high school and senior high school by a total of 3 percentage points and 5 percentage points, respectively, through the year 2050. This scenario suggests a significant increase in China's potential growth rate as compared to the baseline scenario.

Third, scenario B also forecasts the trends of China's potential growth rate on the basis of TFR remaining at 1.60, by assuming that the labor force participation rate can be increased by 1 percentage point annually, and TFP growth by 0.5 percentage points, and that the government will adopt certain policy measures improving job training instead of increasing the graduation rate in order to expand the human capital stock. That shows an even more significant gain in the potential growth rate as compared to scenario A.

Finally, on the basis of simulation B, scenario C shows the trends in China's potential growth rate by assuming that China's TFR could be raised from 1.60 to 1.94 in the future. In the short term, this increases the population dependency ratio, decreasing the capital formation rate of GDP as well as capital stock and thus producing a negative impact on China's potential growth rate. In the long term, however, newborns will grow to enter the labor market, increasing the supply of labor and then producing a positive impact on the potential growth rate. Therefore, the short-term effect is negative and minor, while the long-term effect is positive and significant.

In the same study, Lu and Cai also found that, although the effect of the increase in the labor force participation rate on the growth rate is significant, it tends to diminish over time; on the other hand, TFP promises to be a long-lasting, driving force behind the potential growth rate. That can actually be reasonably well expected from the theory of growth and extant experiences in global economic development. That is, when referring to those developed countries characterized by neoclassical growth—where economic growth is almost entirely powered by TFP growth—long-term growth in China will increasingly rely on the improvement in TFP as the Chinese economy moves into its neoclassical stage.

It is worth noting that reforms and adjustments from the demand side, particularly those that expand private consumption demand and thus help to balance the macroeconomy, should not be undervalued. Given that the factors constraining economic growth are not of the demand side but of the supply side, however, reforms relating to demand-side factors and the rebalancing of the demand structure should be aimed at increasing the share of consumption in total demand overall while avoiding employing measures that stimulate investment demand.

Although reforms that are aimed at balancing the demand structure do not seem to have the immediate effects as do supply-side reforms in terms of increasing the potential growth rate, they have an even more profound significance in maintaining social cohesion and political stability. For example, reforms that can enhance the share of consumption in total demand through reducing income inequality and the building of a social safety net will serve both to promote social justice and fairness and to sustain economic growth. In fact, reforms in some areas can generate positive effects from both the supply and demand sides, thus bringing about a reform dividend.

The *hukou* system reform that centers on transforming migrant workers and their families into legitimate urban residents is one such type, because one can express its effect as "killing three birds with one stone." That is, *hukou* reform can significantly expand the labor force participation rate, sustain the reallocative efficiency of resources, and increase migrants' consumption altogether, since it is quite clear that supply-side factors help to increase the potential growth rate and demand-side factors help to balance the macroeconomy, and thus sustain long-term growth in both theory and modeling. In what follows, we examine the possibility that *hukou* reform can muster further labor mobility from the agricultural to the non-agricultural sectors by comparing China with Japan and South Korea.

Let's begin by examining the differentials in the transfer of labor from the agricultural to the non-agricultural sectors between China and Japan and South Korea. Until the early 1980s, when economic reform was initiated, China's industrialization had not been accompanied by a corresponding decline in the share of agricultural labor because of the institutional barriers deterring labor mobility across sectors and regions. Taking the late 1950s as the starting point of industrialization and the early 1980s as the starting point of measurable labor transfer, we can see that the latter lagged behind the former for more than 20 years. What's more, throughout the reform period following the early 1980s, the institutional barriers deterring labor mobility were not eliminated with one blow, as can be seen from the continued existence of the *hukou* system, which has delayed labor transformation by at least another ten years.

By looking at the shares of agricultural labor across comparable periods—namely, the respective Lewis Turning Point in China, Japan, and South Korea—one can see two features that are unique to China (Figure 12.3). First, mainly owing to the delayed transfer of labor, the share of agricultural labor in China was significantly higher than that of Japan in corresponding periods. For example, when Japan arrived at its Lewis Turning Point in 1960 (Minami, 1968), its share of agricultural labor was 30.2 percent, whereas that same share was 46.9 percent in China according to official data and 35.2 percent according to scholarly estimation, respectively, in 2004. Second, because China has gone through a much more rapid demographic transition than South Korea, the share of agricultural labor in China in 2004 was significantly lower than the share of agricultural labor of 50.5 percent in South Korea in 1972 when it arrived at its own Lewis Turning Point (Bai, 1982).

Experiences in Japan and South Korea, however, show that agricultural laborers continued to shift to urban sectors after the arrival of the Lewis Turning Point. Agricultural labor made up 7.2 percent of the total in South Korea in 2008 and 4.0 percent in Japan in 2010. Considering that agricultural labor was still as high as 22.7 percent in China (according to scholars' estimation), there's still room for China to transfer its labor force from the agricultural to the urban sectors, giving *hukou* reform the great ability to generate reform dividends, from both the supply side and the demand side.

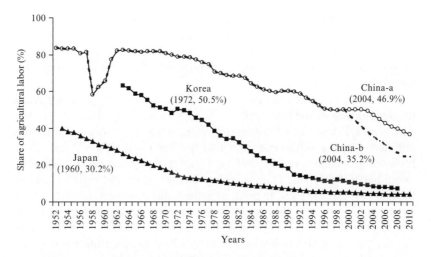

Note: China-a—official data; China-b—scholarly estimation.

Source: Data for China are from National Bureau of Statistics (2005, 2011); data for Japan are from Minami (1968) and the official website of the Statistics Bureau of Japan, http://www.stat.go.jp/; data for South Korea are from the database of the National Statistical Office of South Korea's official website, http://kosis.kr/eng/database.

Figure 12.3   Shares of agricultural labor in China, Japan, and South Korea

12.4   CONCLUSION

Unlike in the early industrialized countries of Europe and North America, where economic growth and the increase in per capita income were slow because every progressive step had to rely on the improvement of productivity at the technological frontier, those economies in the process of catching up can enjoy the so-called "advantages of backwardness" (Gerschenkron, 1962), which come from the gaps between them and their more advanced counterparts and which enable them to grow at a much more rapid rate. Based on historical data compiled by Maddison (2007), we can look back at the growth rates of per capita GDP for the United Kingdom, the United States, and Japan respectively in their "fast-growing" periods.

During the United Kingdom's period of rapid growth from 1880 to 1930, the annual growth rate of per capita GDP was only 0.9 percent. Based on the average life expectancy at the time of 50 years, an average British person born in 1880 could expect to see only a 56 percent increase in his/her standard of living over his/her entire life. Still, that achievement was the foremost revolutionary breakthrough in human history after thousands of years of stagnation in a Malthusian poverty trap.

The United States was the first country to become an economic superpower outside of Europe. In the course of its catching-up with the UK during the period 1920–1975, the per capita GDP of the US grew at an annual rate of 2.0 percent. Based on an average life expectancy of 55 years, an American born in 1920 could expect his/her standard of living to nearly double in his/her lifetime. What makes this particularly outstanding is that the US has sustained a similar growth rate in its per capita GDP even after it became the number one economy in terms of economic size, and its overall national strength and standard of living have remained superior to those of the rest of the world.

Japan was the first country in Asia to be counted among the richest countries in the world, and was the second-largest economy after the US for many years. During the period of time between 1950 and 2010, the annual growth rate of per capita GDP in Japan was 4.0 percent. On the basis of an average life expectancy of 60 years, a Japanese citizen could witness a tenfold improvement in his/her standard of living over his/her lifetime. The economic performance and improvement in the standard of living in Japan since 1990, however, have been stagnating.

Since the early 1980s, policies of reform and opening-up have set the Chinese economy on track for rapid growth. According to official data, in the period from 1981 to 2011, per capita GDP in China grew at an annual rate of nearly 9.0 percent, an improvement equivalent to 15 times the standard of living during this time. Based on an average life expectancy of 68 years, a Chinese citizen born in 1981 can expect to live at least to 2049. If the growth rate of per capita GDP can be sustained, that person will experience an improvement more than 300 times his/her current standard of living when the People's Republic of China celebrates its 100th anniversary.

It is a fact that the speed of improvement in the Chinese people's standard of living over more than three decades is unprecedented, whether compared with China's past or with other countries during the same period. Maintaining a similar speed over the next few decades, however, is an unrealistic assumption. Although a diminishing or even negative growth of the population will help to increase per capita GDP over the next few decades owing to a reduction in the denominator, the same demographic factors will have a negative effect on GDP growth as well. That is, the place that the Chinese economy has reached to date can be considered both a remarkable achievement that draws worldwide attention and an unprecedented challenge that has to be seriously addressed.

Going forward, the Chinese economy will have to continually address both reform and growth as the marginal effects of both diminish. While the gaps in science and technologies, management abilities, market sophistication, and industrial structures between China and more developed economies remain large, they have been substantially narrowed compared to the past, implying a less significant advantage of backwardness for China. Such a change has important implications.

Economic growth in China will have to rely more heavily on technological and institutional innovations, industrial upgrading and structural changes, and the improvement of TFP, all of which require a fundamental transformation of growth patterns. Gerschenkron, the inventor of the "advantage of backwardness" concept, asserted that the process of the backward countries' catching-up tends to introduce a host of policies that are characterized by further government interventions, the biased development of large enterprises, and an imbalanced industrial structure, all of which are accompanied by a corresponding economic system (Gerschenkron, 1962). Therefore, as the advantage of backwardness weakens, a country must face head on the tough tasks of transforming its growth pattern and institutional reforms.

The process of innovation is replete with the risk of failure; structural changes cannot guarantee that industrial upgrading will proceed at an equal pace among enterprises. On the contrary, the rapid changes in technology and industrial structure inevitably give rise to creative destruction—that is, those investors and enterprises that fail to address such changes are bound to be driven out of business. Since such consequences are unavoidable at the current stage of China's development, the government has to build a social safety net to protect workers and families impacted by ruthless competition, on one hand, yet at the same time the government should not protect backward economic behaviors in order to avoid jeopardizing the creative destruction mechanism.

The existence of the fierceness of outside competition and the enormous risk of failure may motivate previously privileged enterprises and sectors to seek policy protection, or even to try to hinder reforms. Any concession to those vested interest groups not only will delay economic reform but may also cause further economic slowdown or even stagnation. In order to sustain economic growth and accomplish the goal of modernization, therefore, China ought to break through obstructions from implicit and explicit vested interest groups, push forward reforms in key areas, and accomplish the transformation from the demographic dividend to the reform dividend.

NOTES

1. A Kaldor improvement is a change in which the total gains outweigh the total losses so that it is possible for the government, on behalf of the beneficiaries, to compensate the non-beneficiaries for the losses they suffer. See Kaldor (1939).
2. For a related discussion, see Tao (2014).

REFERENCES

Bai, Moo-ki (1982), "The Turning Point in the Korean Economy," *Developing Economies*, 2, 117–140.

Central Committee of the Communist Party of China (2013), *Decision of the Central Committee of the Communist Party of China on Some Major Issues Concerning Comprehensively Deepening the Reform*, Beijing: People's Publishing House.

Gerschenkron, Alexander (1962), *Economic Backwardness in Historical Perspective: A Book of Essays*, Cambridge, MA: Belknap Press of Harvard University Press.

International Monetary Fund (2014), *People's Republic of China: 2014 Article IV Consultation—Staff Report*, IMF Country Report No. 14/235, Washington, DC: International Monetary Fund.

Kaldor, Nicholas (1939), "Welfare Propositions of Economics and Interpersonal Compensations of Utility," *Economic Journal*, 49, 549–551.

Lin, Justin Yifu, and Yan Wang (2010), "China's Integration with the World: Development as a Process of Learning and Industrial Upgrading," in Fang Cai (ed.), *Transforming the Chinese Economy, 1978–2008*, Leiden: Brill, pp. 201–239.

Lin, Justin Yifu, Fang Cai, and Zhou Li (2003), *The China Miracle: Development Strategy and Economic Reform*, rev. edn., Hong Kong: Chinese University Press of Hong Kong.

Lindbeck, Assar (2008), "Economic–Social Interaction in China," *Economics of Transition*, 16 (1), 113–139.

Lu, Yang, and Fang Cai (2014), "China's Shift from the Demographic Dividend to the Reform Dividend," in Ligang Song, Ross Garnaut, and Fang Cai (eds.), *Deepening Reform for China's Long-Term Growth and Development*, Canberra: Australian National University E Press, pp. 27–50.

Maddison, Angus (2007), *Contours of the World Economy, 1–2030 AD: Essays in Macro-economic History*, Oxford: Oxford University Press.

Minami, Ryoshin (1968), "The Turning Point in the Japanese Economy," *Quarterly Journal of Economics*, 82 (3), 380–402.

National Bureau of Statistics (2005), *China Compendium of Statistics 1949–2004*, Beijing: China Statistics Press.

National Bureau of Statistics (2011), *China Statistical Yearbook (2011)*, Beijing: China Statistics Press.

Sun, Liping (2012), "Middle Income Trap or Transition Trap?," *Open Times*, 3, 125–145.

Tao, Ran (2014), "The Issue of Land in China's Urbanisation and Growth Model," in Ligang Song, Ross Garnaut, and Fang Cai (eds.), *Deepening Reform for China's Long-Term Growth and Development*, Canberra: Australian National University E Press, pp. 335–377.

Unirule Institute of Economics (2013), "A Theoretical Research and Reforming Solution on Opening the Markets of Crude Oil and of Petroleum Products," http://www.unirule.org.cn/index.php?c=article&id=112.

World Bank (1996), *World Development Report 1996: From Plan to Market*, Oxford: Oxford University Press.

Index